A COUCH NAMED MARILYN

DIANA MARTIN

A COUCH NAMED MARILYN

MY BIG FAT MESS CALLED PTSD

Diana Martin

BellaVista Publishing House
164 N. Main St.
Natick, MA 01760

www.acouchnamedmarilyn.com

ISBN: 978-0-9961103-0-3 (trade paperback)
ISBN: 978-0-9961103-1-0 (e-book)

LCCN: 2015911772

Cover design by Pete Garceau
Book interior by Morgana Gallaway

This edition was prepared for printing by The Editorial Department
7650 E. Broadway, #308, Tucson, Arizona 85710
www.editorialdepartment.com

This is a work of creative nonfiction. The events are portrayed to the best of the author's memory. While the events portrayed in this book are true, some names and identifying details have been changed to protect the privacy of the people involved.

Excerpt from *The Future of Ice: A Journey Into the Cold* by Gretel Erhlich used with permission of Penguin Random House LLC

To Ruthie and Stella Mae

Because of CTR and SMR

INTRODUCTION

I LOVE DOGS, SO I HAVE TWO CATS. LIFE POKES FUN AT ME IN SNEAKY WAYS. When I owned dogs, I trained them, and they taught me about loyalty. Life with cats is more about trying to outsmart them, and they show me the meaning of anarchy. I did not set out to be a cat owner this time around. On separate yet equally vulnerable days, a cat selected me, announcing his arrival in a "this was destined" tone of voice. Both times, I fell for flirtation. I am a pushover for these two.

I assure you this is not 336 pages of boring stories about two pampered cats. Stay with me here. This next story is relevant.

Pierre is firm, muscular, and lean—the Ferrari of felines. Spartacus is a sprawling acre of cat and weighs twice as much as Pierre. Though unrelated, they share identical markings—wonky islands of charcoal in an ivory sea, Holstein cattle with claws, or the spots on a Gateway computer box. The markings have a clownish effect.

These two cats only invest their time in the finer things of life—the clink of crunchies in a bowl and finding the freshest blankets for naps, followed by showy, screech-filled wrestling matches. When I leave for work in the morning, I tend to question the assumption that we humans enjoy a higher level of evolution. Cats appear to be the ones who have it made.

A few days ago, I opened the front door as Spartacus exploded into the living room, bestowing a fat, flailing mouse upon me. A momentary unclenching of his proud jaws dropped the mouse to the floor. After my predictable and involuntary "eek," I wiggled my hands into an old pair of purple rubber gloves.

Once on, the gloves made me fumble with a broom and dustpan, on a mission to save the mouse or find and remove the—you know—less fortunate one. Spartacus was thrilled to have an attentive audience. Twenty-three pounds of spoiled housecat lumbered, leaped, and batted the mouse in glee. Sensing my intense involvement, he found the tortured rodent even more interesting, homing further in on his prey. I swallowed the urge—a lump in my throat the size of a pecan—to yell at him to stop.

I fought this urge because I knew that telling Spartacus to stop acting like a cat would be akin to my best friend yelling at me to quit being a jumpy white girl who is hard-wired to squirm in the presence of a struggling mouse. Spartacus is programmed to catch mice, whether I like it or not.

Bursting with the chemistry of fight or flight, the mouse easily escaped my flimsy dustpan clutches. Spartacus took another swat at the furry creature. I stepped back in awe as the mouse retreated and reared up on its hind legs. He beat at the air, boxing, fighting tough, and roaring in a squeal. He stood his ground against Spartacus. That was one impressive mouse.

I managed to scoop and toss the weightless warrior outside before Spartacus could dash out the door. I checked several minutes later; the mouse was gone. After that, a nagging image of the brave boxing mouse revolved through my memory, in a bleak photograph of the predicament of natural forces. The mouse fought back against a supersized, unsympathetic, smug, and clueless housecat. As the saying goes, against all odds.

I love a good underdog story. So did my Alaskan mother-in-law. We used to exchange books. I dumped my husband but kept my mother-in-law. That has a good ring to it, though in truth, he is the one who dumped me. After the divorce his mother, Stella, told me she was no longer my mother-in-law; she wanted to be my mother-in-love. What is not to melt about that?

In May 2013, an Alaska Airlines jet flying south from Anchorage to Portland landed at the Seattle airport to extract an unruly passenger who, at thirty thousand feet, had attempted to open one of the emergency exits. I giggled the first time I listened to the news report but not because of the perilous situation. It was the way the reporter emphasized the fact that men *and women* in the aircraft tackled and subdued the unsuccessful escapee. That is an Alaskan woman for you—she does not hold back and wait for someone else to repair the heater, build the cabin, kill the food, or in that case, use force to take a troublemaker down.

Stella was an Alaskan woman through and through. Alaska is a daunting place, with numbing cold and logistical challenges at every turn. Many people who move north turn tail quickly, exhibiting what I perceive as a high level of intelligence. The rest of us, those who decide to stay, learn that you cannot wait for someone else to do something if you want to avoid death and starvation. Alaskan women are a strong, independent, and resourceful bunch.

Most Alaskan women do not look as rough and burly as you may think. Stella was petite and wore a lot of Coldwater Creek sportswear. She did not look anything like a lumberjack.

I once phoned Stella from a hotel in Seattle. Overnighting in Seattle is a normal, sometimes rigorous part of Alaska living. When I called, two maintenance men were working on her commode. I overheard the diagnosis, delivered with manly authority: a part was broken, and they needed to fetch a replacement. A husky voice assured Stella, "Little lady, don't worry—everything will be okay." They left to get the replacement parts.

No sooner had the door closed than I heard Stella lift the toilet tank lid, followed by a digging-through-her-purse rustle until she whipped out one of her Leatherman tools. I say "one of" because her ex-husband gave each of us at least two different sizes of Leatherman tools, three Christmases in a row.

I listened to her fiddle with the plumbing as we discussed Chase— her grandson, thus, my teenage stepson. Stella and I devised a theory we could both live with, convincing ourselves that sweet Chase had escaped to a rare and faraway planet, leaving a silent, brooding alien on Earth as his decoy.

A few minutes later, I heard a loud, satisfying flush of the toilet. Our conversation continued for about an hour, and I never heard the maintenance men knock on her door.

You can always relax if there is an Alaskan woman on your flight.

My friend Russell is appreciative of, and amused by, the self-sufficiency of even the most manicured and high-heeled Alaskan women. Russell teases me that even my rubber boots have high heels. He says he loves Alaskan women because when they call for directions, they have a map in front of them.

The point being, I come from hardy stock and a long line of strong, can-do men and women. I thought I could handle anything until one October day when life brought me to my knees.

PART ONE

The Autorotation

CHAPTER ONE

I MOVED TO ALASKA IN 1977, WHEN I WAS TWENTY-TWO YEARS OLD. Twenty-four years later, on September 11, 2001, I lived in a small town called Juneau, far away from Manhattan. Knowing it is impossible to quantify sorrow, my grief was deep, yet meager compared to those who lost their loves and lives that day.

In the weeks that followed, I grieved for the aggrieved and for the wicked violence of it all. I invented what became referred to as the "bath towel cry." Sitting in a rocker, facing the gray rain of our hillside, I gave up on tissues and wept into my full-sized towel. The chair rocked on a bumpy tile floor as I watched the national news. Periodically, I pressed the "mute" button and unfolded the Dear Jane letter my husband (Stella's son) had handed me two days prior, on September 9.

A month after inventing the bath towel cry, I watched another dark winter approach. In an impetuous blast, I decided to move south, some-where closer to the sun. I developed a sound rationale: we all have to deal with grief no matter where we live, so why not work on overcoming these uncomfortable emotions in the sunlight?

The decision to flee came about on one October day. A dense Juneau fog hunkered down in a heavy mist that we knew would last for at least a week. The fog was a break from a four-day siege of wind and horizontal rain. My office window faced straight across the harbor, with a clear view of my very-recent ex-husband's new house. I checked the time on the computer. It was 8:13; I had logged on at 8:04. Nine minutes into the workday, and all I could think about was sunscreen and margaritas.

I am nothing if not determined. I packed up, sold out, and eventually landed under the great red sun of Austin, Texas. It took me about three days to adjust—I instantly felt at home there, and I have no way to account for that. Some places simply feel like home. Some afternoons I lay low, hiding small secrets, missing Alaska's broad shoulders and challenging ways. However, those were rare minutes. I was happy to be in Texas. One man there asked me if I liked big states. I think he had a point. The people in Texas are as big as they are in Alaska, just in a different way.

Alaska is tough love. It is not an easy place to be, but the living itself is raw, real, colorful, and wild. In those tender winks of longing, I realized that I missed Alaska *nostalgically* versus *actually*. I preferred living in the sun, wearing sandals, and hiking without a full set of rain gear. I savored the contrast from heavy coats and mittens.

By 2007, I loved my work in Austin. That in itself was new. I like to work, but "being employed" is not my forte. I have always envied people who knew they wanted to be a dentist or a mother or a teacher. I never found the career groove. For unknown and illogical reasons, I enjoy occupations that involve virtually no money-making potential. Joy comes to me through being a visual artist, writing sarcastic poems, or carving perfect arcs through powder snow on telemark skis. Therefore, I have worked numerous and often unusual jobs to support these passions. Finally, in Austin, I was getting up every day and going to work with zest, instead of showing up for a job.

After completing what some might consider a useless degree in fine arts, I learned that being an artist has gobs more to do with perseverance than actual talent. This was not a problem; I do not give in easily. Well-meaning college professors warned us: we art students were signing up for a lifetime of rejection and poverty. After graduation, I decided the best way around this sticky issue was to work two jobs and to focus my energy on large-scale projects rather than creating silver rings or water-color paintings.

There is nothing wrong with that kind of artwork. I just decided to do art on a bigger scale. I had already renovated a few houses, so I set out to build art into homes. For thirty years, I flipped houses before "flipping" was a term. I held on to each property for two or more years while completing the renovations. That involved living in the downside of the equation: dust, stepladders, and chaos. However, the formula worked well for decades. One by one, I remodeled or renovated houses, including a few cabins, a boat, and a lavender farm in Oregon.

Until 2006, working on houses continued as a side business to whatever day job I held, being cautious about the market and guarded with my money. In 2006, I made the grand leap, trusting the imploring words of career gurus: do what you love. I gave up the day jobs, studied regional markets, moved to Austin, and started my own renovation business.

I bought small houses in grave need of TLC and transformed them into unpretentious, compact, and efficient dwellings, in contrast to the bloated McMansions of the time. Converting old structures felt like cleaning up the world one house at a time. I was on to something, and people liked the concept. Thus, my company was born: *Martini Homes, LLC—Classy Dwellings with a Twist.*

Besides using an obvious reference to my last name, I designed each "Martini Home" after its namesake: simple, clear, elegant, expensive, and unquestionably efficient. When a bartender mixes a martini just right, it is worth the hefty price. My realtor said her clients' faces transformed when they entered my houses; people smiled and slowed down. I loved that. A musician I hired to move furniture nicknamed me the "Queen of Cozy," because he said he felt comfortable and relaxed in my abbreviated houses. That was exactly what I was getting at.

In addition to my love affair with dilapidated houses and the sun, I love to meditate. Wait! Allow me to rephrase that: I hold dear what I have learned from the practice of meditation. The actual act of meditation is difficult, time consuming, tedious, boring, antagonizing, agonizing, uncomfortable, and inconvenient.

Within these discomforts, I sometimes discover subtle slices of calm, when thoughts decelerate, dropping a sense of fire, impatience, or *wanting* something. These unintelligible openings do not mirror other meditators' descriptions of long, transcendental experiences devoid of thought— blissful states melting into the ultimate manifestation of nirvana. I do not profess to be a guru or disciple. I simply try to sit still long enough to refrain from jumping to a conclusion or taking an action I might regret later. Learning to be still in this busy world is not as easy as it sounds.

By mentioning my meditation practice, I risk painting the picture of a strict, puritanical goody-goody, one who might legally change her name to Deva Tara within the course of this story. You may get the impression that I have a religiously correct, serious, incense-filled lifestyle. Perhaps you will envision a bald Buddhist in maroon robes or an angelic being wearing diaphanous shawls and rhinestone slippers—a deeply spiritual, devout, perfect person.

In truth, I drink Coke after acupuncture treatments. I drive a Suburban. Sometimes I use plastic grocery bags, watch *The Bachelor* and *The Bachelorette*, execute embarrassing faux pas, and grapple with moments (okay, hours) of negative thinking.

My best friend, Christie, gave me a refrigerator magnet depicting an adorable, blond *Rebecca of Sunnybrook Farm* character, pretty much what I looked like at five years old. The little darling's hands are sweetly folded in prayer. The bubble above her head says, "So where's my fucking Pony?" That sums up my less-than-enlightened personality.

I drink chilled vodka martinis and devour rib eyes on the rare side. Being me is not all light, love, and success by American standards. I am a misfit, perhaps. I hold no ambitions to be a high-powered executive or a movie star. Eschewing the benefits of Botox (not for moral reasons—it terrifies me), age has etched my fair face with a few wrinkles and slightly yellowed, imperfect teeth. I would be out of place in L.A.

I generally tell people what I think, which does not always go over super-well. I sometimes ignore voice mails (rude in this electronic age), and catch myself yelling at the evening news. I want to assure you: meditation has not transformed me into a spiritually perfect being, radiant with bliss and beauty.

Sometimes I cry rather than yell at the news. It is not easy to be sensitive. I have come to a point of radical acceptance: I am far from perfect, with no plans to change or improve, which feels perfect. I do not meditate to become something better or more. I meditate to make friends with myself, just as I am.

After years of soul-searching and careful study of several religious traditions, it finally sank in that I am not a human being in search of spiritual experiences. Sometimes I am a spiritual being having human experiences. Other times I am a human being, being human, which often ends up feeling like a spiritual experience. It all depends on how you look at it.

CHAPTER TWO

I REMEMBER THE DAY CLEARLY: SEPTEMBER 6, 2007. MY FATHER HAD passed away years earlier, but September 6 was his birthday. Thinking of him, I smiled. Everything felt relaxed after my half-hour of meditation and a nice cup of coffee. Life seemed perfect. My escape from Alaska led me to a warm, creative, happy life in Austin. Driving to the current building project, I waved to a regular panhandler at I-35 and Riverside. The transmission in my faded Ford Ranger skipped a beat. Slot-machine dollar signs flashed and rolled in my mental QuickBooks tabulation. I did not need another bill.

I digested the inevitable future expense, telling myself, "The price of doing business. Just a hiccup in the pickup, right?" I had more pressing issues as I mentally prepared for another angry, fruitless argument with my obstinate building contractors. I was dealing with a band of slow-drawling, fast-talking Texans, whom I unfortunately liked.

As the enabler, I was embroiled in an attempt to teach grown men to finish the job they started. I tried a reasoning approach: "Let's just complete the last to-do list, so we can enjoy the rest of our lives without each other." Then I tried threats, bribes, and jokes, to the point of exasperation.

The contractors had no idea how panicked I was. I had to get that house on the market. A change was coming. There were headlines followed by more in-depth stories about the subprime market. I watched in alarm, as the 2006 blastoff of the Austin housing market seemed to be plummeting to the ground.

My realtor whispered, "Buyers are scared. They've stopped calling. No one even wants to look." Everyone was anxious. I had three mortgages. I had named the houses attached to those three mortgages "The Three Martinis."

I lived in the First Martini on Alta Vista Avenue in Travis Heights. The Second Martini was on the east side, about five miles from where I lived. I rented out that house and used a large shop in the backyard to store building materials. The Third Martini (which, let's face it, is never a good idea) was about a mile away from the second one, also on the east side of I-35.

I parked in front of the Third Martini and listened to the roosters in the yard behind me. I had bought the house four months earlier, with a plan to renovate the original six hundred square feet and add another seven hundred square feet. This project was rapidly draining me of life force, cash, precious time, and patience with the contractors.

I got out of the truck to clean up debris in the front yard as I waited for the contractors. The neighborhood roosters continued their wake-up calls that began at two a.m. Some solar-flare space-time continuum problem for the birds, I guessed, having no idea how much I would resent those roosters later on. I remember wearing paint-stained khaki pants, beat-up clogs, and a ratty (hopefully witty) T-shirt. I felt healthy, fit, and optimistic, despite fretting over the real estate market.

Inside, the new floors buckled and wheezed, rippling in the daylight. I was losing sleep over that floor. In hindsight, that was the least of my problems. At the time, it was a true and symbolic compromise in quality. As the floor crumpled, my money ran out. The installing contractor was in the same financial position. His apathetic and dismissive argument—"There is nothing we can do"—left me feeling betrayed, angry, and frustrated. I fumed at the estrangement.

Fortunately for that guy, I had gone through the change and had muddled through enough home-improvement projects to understand that only a lucky few still spoke to each other by the project's end. Collaborating with interesting, multitalented people is rewarding and creative, when things go well. The reality is that many post-construction relationships are tenuous and frustrating for a while, if not forever.

My internal seething added plenty of heat to the morning sun. I picked through construction waste and contemplated an appropriate avenue for discussing the floor. Before eight a.m., my friend Mansel die-seled up in his truck and poured himself out of the dusty red rig. Mansel and his crew completed three projects for me. Over time, we grew to be sure friends. So there you go—respectful post-construction relationships can happen.

I watched him hobble, a result of a wild Texas youth, details unknown to me. I didn't know his age—none of my business—still it was easy to see that his bones suffered, worn by the years. He bobbed on every stride, compensating with an agile mixture of grace and grimace. My joints used to ache just watching him, yet I never heard the tough, weathered Texan utter a word of complaint. He loved to talk, but he never whined.

Mansel knew me well enough to see that my usual cheery manner was not holding up to the pressure. I tossed nails into a rusty Folgers Coffee can as he patiently listened to me rant, "I am *never* going to get this house on the market at this rate!"

Finally, I stopped talking. Everything quieted, even the roosters. I looked up and noticed that a palm tree across the street sorely needed a trim. From there, my eyes migrated to Mansel's creased face, wearing an expression I'd never seen before.

He leaned in close with a breath of urgency, whispering, "Listen, girl, I am really worried for you. You have a ton of money in this house right now. I see a storm and, darlin', it is not looking good. You gotta get rid of this place. Something is about to happen that is going to eat people alive."

My arm hair stood up. Mansel examined my face to see if I was truly listening. I remember a pause. I stopped breathing—no thought, just shock. Another pause as I gulped air, recording Mansel's words in high definition, forming permanent grooves in my mind.

CHAPTER THREE

M ANSEL HITCHED UP AND INTO HIS TRUCK IN ONE FULL ARC, turning the key as he fixed his eyes across the hood and down to the crumbling road ahead.

Crap.

I looked straight at the sun, reviewing Mansel's words. I wanted to think of him as a naysayer, a cynic, a conspiracy theory type, or "the man who cried wolf." I found no inaccuracies in his logic—just a flat, distinct knowing that he was right. He was a true friend for saying what he'd said.

Crap.

I had already missed full nights of sleep, my muscles taut, wondering why the real estate market—or more precisely, our entire economy—mysteriously flipped a switch. I would lay awake remembering my parents, all of their hard work, their focus on education, saving, and bargain hunting. My parents worked damn hard to leave each of us an inheritance. Every stock and cent we received came from their prudence. I had risked my modest inheritance without considering the possibility of losing it all. I was ensnared in an imperceptible, yet real, financial trap.

Everything I earned from working in Alaska was on the line too. I had spent years working as a cook, living in tents out in the bush. I packed salmon eggs on cannery rows and worked the oil fields at sixty below zero degrees, all so I could build a nest egg of investments. Losing that time and hard work terrified me. And I was ashamed to think of wasting my parent's disciplined investments.

I heard the flooring contractor's truck rumbling down the street. I gazed up at the sun and the untrimmed palm, and I vowed to my parents that I would do whatever it took to protect our hard-earned assets. I needed to devise a new business plan, a new paradigm, right away.

Over the next two weeks, I continued the grueling process of nagging large men to roll rocks uphill and finish their work. I stayed up late, painting walls, cleaning up the final mess, or sitting at my desk, opening bills and trying to figure out how to pay them.

Finally, all of the contractors left. My realtor, nicknamed BB, which is short for Busy Bee, is also very short. She leapt into motion with paperwork, a contract, cleaning rags, and a bleach bottle. We polished, photographed, and listed that house in record time. The Third Martini had an apathetic audience. BB held open houses every weekend, and people said they loved the house but would never consider buying it, admitting they were curious and looking for something to do on a Saturday.

Those of us with mortgages and construction loans still faced the first of each month, whether there were buyers or not. An eerie hush overtook the neighborhoods, lumberyards, and real estate offices. Elliot, my mortgage broker, worked every angle he could to help me refinance. I was locked into a construction loan that was about to jump to a 17 percent interest rate. I schemed, worried, and strategized twenty-four hours a day.

Weeks of restless sleep and anxious working hours dragged on. My property values evaporated in a few months. Curious lookers stopped looking. I had meager amounts of cash to spare, and I was in a dangerous, overextended position in the market.

I want to say a few words about personal responsibility. Before that fateful conversation with Mansel in September 2007, I consciously placed myself in the monopoly game of real estate and financial services. I am fully accountable for the square on which I stood the day Mansel delivered those prophetic words to my front door. That being said, there are many facets of the financial crime called the Great Recession for which I cannot and will not take personal responsibility.

However, I did heavily invest in a market that appeared healthy and growing. I placed all of my eggs in one basket. I hocked my life savings and inheritance to start a business. Armed with education, experience, assets, a creative eye, a business plan, and a dream, I leaped into the unknown.

As the reality of my position became even scarier, I meditated and prayed yet never expected God to step in and solve my financial problems. I *wanted* to have a God to accept the burden and reassure me it would turn out well. However, I doubt that rescuing me from a gritty financial position is part of God's job. Then again, I have no concept of what God's job is, so my credibility is questionable.

I had no idea how many elements of our financial system were unraveling all at once. Most of us did not. I noticed that some people, the ones who had savings accounts, wanted to deny the sudden economic paralysis. I remembered my initial urge to shut out Mansel's words. I understood why people did not want to hear.

Based on rough figures on a cocktail napkin, *Martini Homes* might have stayed afloat, if I had a dollar for every person who offered sage and unsolicited advice.

"Have you ever thought of renting one of the houses?"

"It takes time to sell real estate. Just wait, be patient—the house will sell!"

"Keep working!" "Do all you can—make new flyers, advertise online. Stay busy and it will all work out!" Or "Just put the house on eBay!"

Ultimately, those conversations would circle around to the person saying, "Have you read *The Secret?*"

For those of you who do not know about that book, I encourage you to read it or watch the DVD, to arrive at your own conclusions. The author makes a compelling and reassuring argument that God and The Universe are standing by, waiting to accommodate my personal, selfish, egotistical needs, especially for things. If I can just *think*, I mean, *truly imagine* owning a house on the beach, God is waiting to take my order and make it so.

Believers in *The Secret* do an excellent job of urging me to feel much worse about any situation. On top of my problems—which God apparently dumped on me because I did not think correctly in the first place—I am also not thinking the right thoughts now. If I cannot visualize God building me that beach house, *of course* it is not going to happen.

I am not denying the thread of wisdom these teachings offer. We do attract much of what we focus on. I also grew up under the impression that I was around to do something in the name of God and for others, not pray for what God can give to me.

I stopped going out and refrained from talking to people about *Martini Homes* or *The Secret.* As an alternative, I stayed home and paced the First Martini's old yellow floors. I spoke to every banker and broker I knew. I wanted a way out of the Third Martini's construction loan, especially if the house would not sell. Elliott dedicated a lot of time to find alternative financing for me. We agreed the market shift seemed fishy. Every time Elliott approached a bank, the underwriters simply said "no." The game rules had changed overnight.

Each lending institution created a successive list of reasons as to why they would not approve a mortgage for the Third Martini. The same banks who had courted me a few months prior treated my loan applications with haughty scorn. I had excellent credit scores and valuable assets. But the lenders hedged, consistently finding the rules to avoid a loan approval. What they did was corrupt and unfair, and spot-on. I held a great deal of debt in a paralyzed market. Even if someone did want to buy my house, a buyer would have a difficult time qualifying for a loan or selling their home before buying mine. The banks knew more than I did about all of that. They knew I was a walking time bomb of risk. And they knew how strapped they were.

In early November, two months after Mansel's proclamation, I paced the old oak floors, and I gave up on the notion of *Martini Homes* staying whole. Moving on to other projects was impossible, yet I would do everything I could to keep the Three Martinis. To do that, I needed a paycheck.

The first step sounded simple although finding any type of employment proved challenging. Those of us in the construction, real estate, and mortgage industries suddenly found ourselves without income. We all competed for work that did not exist. Little did we know, that was only the beginning.

CHAPTER FOUR

I SEARCHED FOR WORK AND EXPLORED ALL THE ANGLES TO SAVE *Martini Homes*. I still had good renters in the Second Martini on Willow Street. I found a renter who signed a nine-month lease for the First Martini. Even though the rent check did not cover taxes or insurance, it was still a big relief. I moved into the Third Martini, hoping that some furniture and an artistic touch would help it sell.

It was sad to leave the First Martini. Living there felt like floating in a quaint tree house. It was a tiny cottage perched on a long, narrow hillside, away from the street. I thought of it as a solitary pearl within the sea of old, palatial homes in Travis Heights. I adored that cottage, and I was willing to move wherever to hang onto the Three Martinis until the economy turned around.

I found a position as an independent contractor for a floor installation company that worked exclusively for one of the major home-building chains. I accepted the position, despite a cloud of doubts. That acceptance was a life decision I will continue to question. I wonder: Should I have held out longer for a better job? Or was that the best I could do? A man named Steve started work the same day I did. We had sat next to each other while waiting for our interviews. He called me two days later to say he quit. I wonder what happened to Steve. And what would have happened if I too had made that decision?

I stayed with the company and received just enough training to understand the process and to be dangerous to myself. My role was to drive to customers' homes, measure their floors, and write up estimates for a flooring installation. The dangerous part was a dirty little thing called "the chargeback." I knew the basics about installing floors, and even less about the company's particular way of doing it, so it took eight full months to learn how to work smart as an estimator. I asked a thousand questions, turned in hundreds of estimates, and began to learn the trade.

In the meantime, the pesky little "chargeback" showed up on my paycheck as a negative number. Say I ordered three five-gallon cans of Bostik glue for a floor installation, fifty miles out of town. If the installers needed a fourth gallon of Bostik, the company charged me for the additional can of glue and the mileage to go get it. Every paycheck was a wonder.

But I was an art major, not a quitter, so I drove and drew. I enjoyed trips through gorgeous hill country one day, and sat in hot, tense San Antonio traffic the next day. Gas prices were high. I owned a fuel-efficient car, and still, my costs expanded as the paychecks shrunk.

Over time, I earned enough money to keep my head above water, as long as I worked seven days a week, at least eighteen hours a day. Paid by the project, I drove between one and two hundred miles per day. I pulled into the driveway around five or six at night, in time to make calls to schedule the next day's appointments. I would gulp down leftovers, if I was that prepared, and spend the following eight hours drawing up floor plans and calculating estimates. I would sleep for a few hours and then caffeinate for the same routine the next morning.

Living in the Third Martini was an unexpected joy. I had designed it thinking that I would not be the one living there. With three bedrooms and two and a half baths, it was bigger than anything I wanted to fill. The cats roared up and down the long hallway, enthusiastic, extensive runs on slick, albeit lumpy, new wood floors. I left most of my furniture at the First Martini, so the new house was a luxurious mix of open space and color, touched with minimal furniture—old made new and fun. I complemented the colors of fresh flowers to blend with carefully chosen tones on the walls. Just like a martini, it was clear, efficient, and elegant, squeaky clean. The formula had always worked.

I knew how to quickly sell a house at top price. Could I sell this one fast, for a not-so-top price? I thought about getting a conventional loan and living there, selling one of the other places. And often thought about selling them all and getting out.

Elliott continued to work every angle on a refinance for the Third Martini. My income was barely paying the bills. If I could get out from under the financial strangulation of a construction loan, I might be able to keep up with my payments. The situation would almost be sustainable. I told myself that I was not a quitter—I could pull it off. How could I know the banks were working to write the new rules that would prevent that from happening?

CHAPTER FIVE

I PERSEVERED WITH ESTIMATES FOR SIX OR SEVEN MONTHS. I NO LONGer fumbled with the measuring tape, as I did on the first nervous weeks of what Christie refers to as "The Bloody Carpet Job." By then, I could visually scan a room and easily sketch it, coming close to the measurements before even using the tape measure. The chargebacks still popped up now and then. Like a dreaded case of shingles, you knew that probably was not the last red bump.

BB and I were not prone to pessimism. She has five grown kids, a husband, two dramatic sisters, and an aging father; she sells real estate and once owned a restaurant. A person could not pull that off without optimism. BB claims she is around five feet tall. I have my doubts, measuring her up to about four feet eleven inches. When we walk next to each other, I feel like the Incredible Hulk, and I am only five feet six inches, one hundred and twenty pounds. She wears cute leopard-print dresses and sandals with rhinestones. Her hair is always stylish and her nails perfectly polished in deep metallic red. How in the world does anyone have time to keep up with all of that?

I think it is because she is a detail person, with a flair for wit. Either a person has an eye for details, or they don't. BB started out as my realtor; soon after, we became friends. I coveted her as my agent because she can hang onto a million different threads. I knew the calendar dates on contracts were correct, and the inspections would happen on time.

The same could be said for a sense of humor—either you understand each other's funny side, or you don't. BB and I were tired of feeling gloomy about real estate. We started joking about the market being limp. The last word opened the opportunity to mimic something shriveling. Our creativity in that area never waned. We sent each other late-night emails with funny thoughts and quotations. At Christmastime, while eating barbecue downtown, she leaned over and whispered, "Not a creature was stirring, not even a house." There is always room for levity.

Neighborhoods stood still; bank lobbies held a quiet, tactile tone. BB's income had halved over the past twelve months. By May, I gave up on the illusion of refinancing. The lending institutions were still implementing novel and more protective underwriting policies. One of the new requirements stated that any house taken off the market had to stay off for at least three months before a bank would consider refinancing it.

Unaware of the future rule, I took the Third Martini off the market for six weeks in late 2007. There were no buyers, especially around the holidays, and I needed time to make some big decisions, revise my plan. Although I listed the house again in early January, the rule prevented me from applying for a loan until late spring.

Any reasonable consumer would say, "Why is that?" or "May I see that in writing?" When my mortgage broker asked those questions, he got, "These are the rules." Period. By May, after the three-month wait, I still could not get a loan. My credit remained clean, but I was low on cash, owed credit card companies for construction materials, and had three mortgage payments. Of course I couldn't find a bank to lend me money.

On my work route, I talked with builders, investors, and homeowners every day. We all looked into each other's "deer in the headlight" eyes as we realized the economy had stalled in midair. In defeated tones, some of the men told me they were getting ready to "hand the keys back to the bank." I wondered how you did that. Others played a harder pitch, confident in their abilities to sell fast. I watched the market closely. A few closings; nothing moved fast.

Many people began talking about sudden loss, yet no one could put their finger on precisely what had changed. We agreed there was something ominous in the housing industry, and most of us were running out of money. As I drove between estimate appointments, I listened to interviews on NPR, like the story of a man in the heating-oil business who described the day he had to lay off some of his long-time employees. As many businesses do, he relied on a credit line to keep payroll going through the lean months. Overnight, the banks decided not to extend credit to the likes of him; it required too much risk.

The lenders simply turned off the faucet on thousands of businesses. At the time, most of us did not know about their magnificent bonuses. As I listened to that discouraged and heartbroken businessman on NPR, tears rose to a puddle between the lids of my tired eyes.

The local bank offered to extend my construction loan on the Third Martini, as they did for many builders in similar positions. I was grateful for the alternative to foreclosure, knowing the gesture would not have come from one of the big banks. I owed the local bank a fat payment every month, and they knew I was a risk, but they were stuck with me.

The bank did not want to end up holding all of their builders' houses in such a weak market. Although there was temporary relief with the loan extension, it locked me into the high monthly interest I had tried to escape.

Late at night, after hitting the send button for the day's estimates, I crossed my feet on top of the desk and admired my office, located in what is patronizingly called "the master suite." I set my office up in that room because of its high ceilings, peaked windows, and warm, peachy walls. There was ample space for a cluster of large potted plants, which thrived in the soft northern light. An icy can of Tecate beer in my hand, I gazed up and grinned at the twenty-foot wall to the left, where Christie suggested that I paint "*Martini Homes LLC,* World Headquarters" in big letters. Below that, she wanted to hang a portrait of my portly cat Spartacus, with the inscription "Director of Communications, *Martini Homes.*"

After a satisfying sip of beer, I considered all my options for the umpteenth time. There I was, one person living in a three-bedroom, two-and-a-half-bathroom house. I abhor that level of waste. I knew how to feel at home in a tent or a small cabin, but there I found myself living in a home I could not afford. The Third Martini's kitchen sported hip, 1950s-style, pastel yellow appliances—purchase price equal to six current house payments. I bought that mod stove and round-shouldered refrigerator for someone else, not me. It was not that I disliked the appliances; I picked them, after all. I loved them as design decisions, but that did not mean I wanted to own them.

By the end of May, I knew it would be impossible to keep up with the bills. The for-sale sign outside the Third Martini seemed invisible, like a token effort. The idea of roommates came up on a thousand different days. I reviewed different options, arriving at the same conclusions: If I rented out rooms to people, it would bring in revenue, but it could be harder to show the house. Who wants strangers examining their bedroom when they aren't even there? How would I know if roommates would keep the house neat? Further, why would someone agree to rent a place that is for sale? There is scant stability in that arrangement.

The tipping point seemed to hinge on the same question: Who on this good green earth wants roommates at age fifty-something? Particularly when your stress meter is operating at warp factor ten of ten? The thought of choosing a roommate from Craigslist set fire to my last healthy nerve. I did not feel comfortable with strangers staying in my home, even if it was too big for me alone.

Music bounced through the unfurnished rooms on those nervous nights. I would walk, waiting for solutions to arise. Every step involved examination. It had come down to avoiding foreclosure, or maybe even bankruptcy. It was a shock to get there so quickly, especially when I was working so hard. I was not the kind of person to stop paying my debts. I held multiple mortgages over thirty years and never missed payments or paid late fees. I was the Girl Scout of good credit.

When I lived at the First Martini, I developed a pacing pathway, which I called "the circle of my worry." That was a set, oval route: from the living room, take a right through the kitchen, an immediate right through the bedroom, and another right through the bathroom, which leads back to the living room—a perfect O.

At the Third Martini, it took a short time to develop a new worry path, in the shape of a wiggly figure eight. The hallway in the middle formed a long, straight stick between two oval paths on each end. I followed a similar route as the cats, only they skied down the hall as I walked barefoot, wrenching my hands and creasing my brow. I carved paths through each bedroom along the way. It was a twisted pretzel route, compared to Alta Vista's compact O.

Christie mailed me a pair of K. Bell socks with the dancing Goddess

Lakshmi woven into the ankles. Lakshmi is the Hindu Goddess of Prosperity. We agreed that anything was worth a try. Wearing a special pair of socks as I coursed my trail of worry was nothing more than magical thinking, and I was all for it. I hand-washed those socks every night, and superstitiously put them on under my black boots every morning. I emulated the Energizer Bunny, marching in time, urging myself along, forcing myself to keep up the momentum.

As long as language has existed, opinions follow in the tracks of words. Pundits said we were too big and powerful to fail. Economists called it a burp in the bubble. I was unconvinced. Some things did not add up, but how could we know what we did not know?

The unsustainable position was wearing me down. The paychecks and rental revenue helped, yet my income still did not equal the outflow. Mathematically, it was simple and clear; how to deal with the reality of the math was sheer mystery. I was losing ground fast, unsure of the next move. Nothing worked on paper and nothing worked in real life. Money evaporated while the problems and debts remained. It is much easier to solve problems when you have money.

A skilled helicopter pilot can navigate a mechanically failed machine to the ground in a controlled crash, a slick maneuver called an autorotation. I was in financial autorotation, which is *not* a slick maneuver. When a helicopter autorotates, sphincter-tight minutes pass before you know whether or not the landing worked. I knew my financial autorotation was not a matter of minutes, hours, or days. This desperate feeling could last far longer.

Tension and her posse were there for the long haul, bringing months or maybe years of implied doom. In my case, there was no eject button, no parachute, no escape from the effects of the slowly turning rotor blades, fussy and unstable.

When I was not writing estimates, I continued to mow lawns and attend to plumbing disasters, all the small joys of home ownership, in triplicate. I plodded on, squeezing out the payments. I got up every day and did my best to put a smile on a worried face as I walked out the door for the next round of estimates. Arriving at the client's door was usually entertaining. Often the man of the house greeted me with a mixture of "Huh, this might be fun. She's kinda cute. I wonder if she has a clue what she is doing. How could she know anything about construction?" This kind of guy will always assume he knows more, on account of his genitalia, I guess. On the other side of the pancake, just as many men treated me with respect and courtesy.

In all fairness, I do see why some people underestimated me. My petite, girly frame does not instill confidence in the casual construction observer. I am not burly, despite my Alaskan roots. I have wild, curly hair, and I wear makeup and nail polish. I am a girly girl. Most people did not guess what I did for a living.

People who know and love me enjoy a good jabbing—telling me dumb-blonde jokes, feigning misogyny, or displaying "pat the cute girlie on the head" behavior. They do that because they love the absurd as much as I do. Despite the well-known saying, most of us do judge the book by the cover. I am used to getting teased about this and must agree that the disparity between what I look like and what I do is complicated.

I am fortunate to know and love an aggregate of male characters. Each man uplifts me with his own brand of laughter, Q&As, auto repair, philosophical musings, and treasured friendships, as well as intimacies. Wise men play fair and know better than to poke Mama Bear. They know it is foolish to underestimate a woman's power, even if she looks blond and fluffy.

In contrast, for appointments when a woman opened the door, she usually expressed surprise and delight to invite a female into her home. I often detected a softening, an almost a visceral relief in their bodies. Many women commented, "I am so glad you are not a man. I feel creeped out sometimes when men come into the house."

". . . And most of them make me feel so *stupid*."

CHAPTER SIX

ONDAY THROUGH FRIDAY, I WOKE UP ANGRY. IT HAD NOTHing to do with work or the economy. On those particular mornings, at six o'clock sharp, four hours after the roosters got started, I awakened with a start. Two houses down, an early-shift worker apparently carpooled. Instead of doing anything civilized, the driver pulled up to the house and honked his horn until the drowsy rider emerged through the front door.

Meditation teachers say that irritation and chaos is the "good news" because it awakens my awareness to strong feelings such as anger and irritation. The horn worked every time.

October 2008: it had been over a year since Mansel lumbered out of his truck and delivered his prophetic proclamation. Once again, I stood in Third Martini's front yard. The palm tree across the street still needed a haircut. I was in the process of moving again.

The nine-month lease on the First Martini expired, and the renter declined to renew. I ran a few ads, but Alta Vista was in the high rent district, and people were looking for deals. Without that rental income, I could not pay the mortgage on the First Martini. No matter where I moved, or how many estimates I finished, it was the same old story. I was still not making enough money.

So I rented out the Third Martini and moved back to the First Martini. BB quickly listed the First Martini for sale on the MLS (Multiple Listing System), placing her sign and flyers near the street. It was worth a try to sell the First Martini. As long as the estimates kept coming, I could hold on to the two other Martinis.

It freaked me out to see how quickly I needed to sell, or I would be "handing the keys back to the bank," whatever that meant. It sounded too simplistic, suspiciously cut and dried with no mention of lawsuits or paperwork. Returning to the original "circle of worry," I admired Alta Vista's simple beauty, specifically the quality of her natural light. I was selling a friend and a dream: the first *Martini Home*. I would stay there until it sold or the bank took it back, whichever came first.

A few generous people loaned me cash. Borrowing money from friends and family is something that would be against my religion, if I had a religion. A friend owed me money, enough to pull me out of the immediate crisis; however she was a realtor, herself struggling, and unable to come up with the sum. I felt I had to borrow the money, somehow.

The act felt desperate, a new low. In 2008 we were still early in the game. Even the thought of foreclosure conjured images of shame, failure, and giving up. I was on the tip of the foreclosure tsunami. The banks were ready to jump on a delinquent mortgage. Only later would a dearth of empty houses make the banks feel overloaded and burdened.

There were many reasons that handing the house back to the bank felt like a defeat. The default on my mortgage, the ding on my credit score was tough, yet the biggest thorn in my skin was how much I loved that particular home. Of all the houses I had groomed and pampered, the First Martini on Alta Vista felt most like home. In Spanish Alta Vista means "high view." I admired how the cottage sat up straight, reserved, private, almost meditative. Inside, I looked through large windows at oaks' underbellies and felt blessed.

Travis Heights is a long-established, quirky, special neighborhood, with beautiful old homes and giant trees. In 2007, the First Martini would have sold quickly, with its inexpensive price tag compared to its larger neighbors. A year later, the occasional car drifted in, and the arm of a curious window-shopper would pull a flyer from the box, then float on by. Pedestrians strolled and craned their necks, casually reading flyers. That was it. Only a few people actually walked up to the house to see it.

I used to be a realtor; when I started *Martini Homes*, I decided to focus on building and development. I needed an agent working for my interests, while I herded contractors. Luckily, I found BB, who knows how to look out for someone else.

That fall, as BB and I watched the cars slow by the curb without reaching a full stop, we joked about luring people in to see the house. She teased me about my approach with the most recent renter at Alta Vista.

There had been a for-sale sign out front a year prior, exactly where we stabbed the ground on that day. We laughed that staking the for-sale sign felt like déjà vu. The last time, a man had come to the door. He was there to meet his agent to view the house. I had not received any calls for the appointment, but I instantly put on my realtor hat and decided I had better not let that one get away. He checked his phone and realized the intended house was actually three doors down, to the left. I smiled and said, "Well, this is a really, seriously, beautiful house. So if you don't like the other one, come back to check mine out." He laughed. Twenty minutes later he returned and signed a lease.

BB grinned and wanted to know what kind of trick I had come up with this year. It needed to be a doozy.

CHAPTER SEVEN

Saturday, October 11, 2008, was a glorious autumn day. I remember the touch of toasted air on my arms, noting a rich musk from fallen leaves, and an echo of music from South Congress Street. At the First Martini, my office sat in the front of the house, a narrow glassed-in porch, like a sunroom, deep enough for my desk and a chair. From that vantage point, I looked beyond the deck and downhill to the quiet street below.

As usual, a pile of estimates lay in wait on my glass desk, stimulating guilt and avoidance. I called a client to set an appointment for Monday. Out of habit, I scribbled the date and time on the customer information sheet, using my favorite green Sharpie: 10-11-2008 12:54 p.m. I looked up from the green ink in time to see a man walking up the driveway, carrying one of BB's flyers. I had watched him grab a flyer before my phone call and thought nothing of it because those days, people just moved on.

He knocked three times, and I opened the front door to greet him. He commented on the sign advertising an open house the next day, asking if he could see the house right away. Of course, I showed it to him, recalling the recent conversation with BB about the random luck of drop-in customers. As he walked in the door, I examined him carefully. I did that as a matter of course. You learn a great deal about a person before they ever speak. I imagine all salespeople take an initial assessment. Most realtors do.

I studied his five o'clock-shadowed face and determined he was about forty-five years old. The arm of his clean, gray polo shirt almost brushed me as he passed. I decided he was almost handsome, and I smelled a whiff of arrogance. No cologne or alcohol (I check that too). The man looked as though he lived down the street, fit the neighborhood profile of wealthy-casual. I suddenly missed the east-side funkiness of the Second and Third Martinis.

In addition to the flyer, he held a classified section of the *Austin American-Statesman*, folded loosely in quarters. I asked him if he was looking to buy or rent. He said, "Which one is this?" which struck me as odd. I responded by saying something like, "As the two signs say, the house is for sale or lease." In that case, he was looking to buy, he said.

As a realtor and a seller, I have shown hundreds of houses to people. It fascinates me to see what is uniquely important to an individual: what each wants, what to examine first, what one considers tacky or attractive, what draws one's attention. He walked straight through the living room for the back door, striding with purpose into the backyard. I peeked out the door. In realtor speak, I pointed out the laundry room/ storage space and fully fenced yard. Ignoring the laundry room, he did a thorough poke around the backyard and then returned to inspect the inside of the house.

I thought: I bet he wants a backyard for a big dog. Everyone has his or her own priorities. If his wife were there, I bet she would have been opening the kitchen cabinets. He came back inside, and I showed him around. The house was so small the tour took only a few minutes.

The house hunter seemed like a curious window-shopper, not a serious buyer. In the last room, a small front den, I noticed his eyes shift from me to the door. I had an odd feeling, so immediately turned to walk into the kitchen to fill an old plastic milk jug with water. I decided to go out to the front deck to water plants while he looked around. Standing by the kitchen sink, I felt a tiny nudge against my head, behind my ear. I remember thinking, Yuck, a bug.

No, not a bug . . .

Then I felt the same nudge again and experienced a swirl of confusion, thinking, Is this guy *touching* me?

I turned my head a few degrees to the left, toward the pressure on my skull. He was not exactly touching me. He was holding a handgun against my head.

His voice hissed, "Just do what I say."

CHAPTER EIGHT

———————————————

I STOOD STILL.

Looking straight ahead, I strained to digest all of the information. Three images flashed in my mind: a crosshatched design on the gun handle, the cold, steady face of a stranger, and his straight arms, poised to shoot a bullet into my skull.

I thought I heard the raspy voice of my meditation teacher whispering in my right ear. "Head and shoulders."

Pause.

"Prepare to die."

Pause.

I knew precisely what "head and shoulders" meant. I'd repeated those words in my mind many times. It is a simple reminder to hold my body erect, with the confidence of a queen, and then just breathe in, breathe out, focusing on the present moment.

I corrected my posture.

The "prepare to die" part sounded about right. It looked like this was my time to go. Sensing no other choice, I stood tall, straight, and proud, waiting for the bullet. A second later, I was still standing. No bullet yet.

I recalled listening to a television program about self-defense. The expert said to find a way to disrupt the situation and make a lot of noise to attract attention, in order to get help. I kept my eyes toward the front window, to see if my neighbors on the left were home. I knew that if anyone could hear me, they would be the only ones. The driveway sat empty, glaring in the hot afternoon sun. No one was home.

Years ago, hiking alone, I inadvertently stepped on the mouth of a badger's den. I jumped at the sound and mist of her urgent hiss. Up close, a badger is impressive—black, squinty eyes, wild, sharp teeth, striped fur standing at attention, and jagged, filthy claws. I smelled rage. That badger scared me so much, my lip hairs stood on end.

I turned away from the window, toward the gunman. I *became* that badger. I jumped that man with the instincts of a rabid beast. I shouted for help, swinging my fists in wild circles, inept pounding, and wrathful motion.

I decided to jump on him again. Midair, on my way to striking his shoulders, a few thoughts occurred to me: Ah, hello? One slight problem here. You are acting like one of Charlie's Angels, but you are not a Charlie's Angel. You have no technical training in self-defense. You are not a badger. You have absolutely no clue how to fight.

It was too late for that.

I continued to flail about, as tidbits of advice flew to my mind. My friend Anne in Portland told me that trying to hit a guy with your arms is a waste of time—use your legs. I kicked his hairy shins; his tennis shoes' rubber soles squealed on the old oak floor.

Craig the Crazy Cowboy once told me that if I ever punched someone, I should keep my thumb out from under the thrusting knuckles. Or, did he say to keep the thumb inside to protect it? I couldn't remember.

I covered all the bases by tucking the left thumb inside, and my right thumb outside, and continued to pound on any body part I could reach. I screamed again for help and aimed my fingernails for his eyes.

I remembered Anne's advice, rethinking that plan, knowing my arms were too short. I launched my right leg up toward the family jewels. That got his attention. I watched my raised leg and sandaled foot head straight for his khaki crotch.

Do you remember with old movies, how a splice of damaged film resulted in an abrupt blackout, followed by a bright flick of light, another jump to black, and then, with a snap, the film carried on smoothly? I watched my foot go for his shorts, and the seconds after that kick have disappeared. The moments were spliced out of my continuum, much like a worn-out film's burned, split frames.

When the movie frame slammed back into place, I was on my hands and knees staring down at the yellow planks of the kitchen floor. I was close to the cats' glass food bowls, and made a mental note regarding the floor's lack of cleanliness. The yellow floor turned red. My head rocked to my chest and then bounced back up. I realized The Guy was beating me on the head with his gun.

I felt my front teeth chipping and cracking from the blunt force. Blood dripped through my eyes before landing in splats on the floor. I thought of my dentist in Portland, who rebuilt my back teeth. It felt like those were holding up.

The whacking stopped. Bright blood pooled in the floor's dips and nicks. My head was ringing; the kitchen was spinning in a clockwise direction. I was still on my hands and knees. I was sure this was a nightmare or an Alfred Hitchcock movie.

That was my moment of horror—when I fully realized that it was not a movie or a dream.

CHAPTER NINE

FURROWED MY BROWS IN AN EFFORT TO THINK AS THE ROOM CON-
tinued to spin. I kept my hands on the floor for balance. I could see
his white shoes and hairy legs a few feet away. His breathing sounded
labored, a rhythm of gasps. I lowered my head and took a few gulps of
air. I did not know what was happening, or remember how to take a deep
breath. Breathe in, breathe out, breathe in, breathe out. I prayed for a
steady heart and talked to myself.

Do not panic. (Yeah, right.) Do not lose consciousness. Do not lose
consciousness.

I pulled one more good breath before he spoke:

"Jesus *Christ*! You *fucking* bitch!"

I heard it all when I worked in the oilfields of Alaska, every nasty,
condescending, snide word in the dictionary. Nothing can shock me, and
I have a retort for every occasion. I wanted to fire back, "Really? *I'm* the
fucking bitch?"

I did not say anything. It is generally a mistake to read into someone else's thoughts or feelings. You just never know. This freak seemed used to getting his way. He was cocky, which is easy if you are the one with the gun. Still, I was willing to bet that he had no experience tangling with an Alaskan woman. He struck me as one of those guys who thinks he can get away with poking a stick at Mama Bear.

Except so far, his approach was working. He got me to stop screaming, and I was on the floor. He gripped the gun handle and held it about eight inches from my face. He glanced back and forth, probably trying to figure out what to do. He addressed me again, spitting out words like snake venom, "You *fucking* bitch. What the hell were you thinking?"

What was *I* thinking? I cleared the liquid from my eyes, pulled in another bloody breath, and steadied myself on one knee. He stood above me in what I call a tennis-ready position. His knees were bent, legs parted, arms stretched out strong and straight with the barrel pointed at, just barely touching, my forehead.

I studied his face, promising myself that if I got away from this monster, I would hunt him down, until the end of time. He weighed about one hundred and eighty pounds, and I estimated his height at six feet. His full head of brown hair appeared to be recently trimmed. He looked like a menswear model in a JCPenney catalog. Christie would find him smarmy. My Aunt Jean would have called him ruggedly handsome.

I figured mid-forties on age. He looked athletic. I noticed his gray polo shirt had a name embroidered in royal blue on the left side, David Something. The pockets of his cargo shorts bulged in odd shapes. I looked for a wedding ring or a watch. Nothing.

That all transpired in a few seconds. I was on one knee, watching him look back and forth, unconsciously swaying the gun as he moved his head. Suddenly, he stopped moving and stared at me. I felt a wave of panic—he'd caught me studying his face.

His even, dead serious eyes looked down the gun barrel to my eyes. I needed to think of something. I thought of the television show. They'd said to negotiate with an attacker, try to start a conversation. I made solid eye contact and heard my voice say, "What do you want? Just tell me what you want."

"I want your money, you fucking bitch. Just give me your money."

Whoa, he wanted money from me? Get in line, buddy.

Instead of saying something stupid like that, I pointed a shaking finger toward my office. "My purse is over there, by the door on that small table. Take it! I have cash and credit cards."

"Where? What does it look like?"

His voice was feverish, jumpy.

He took a few steps backward, toward the door. His shoes again squeaked across the old oak, the sound of a basketball game in a gymnasium. I felt hopeful. Maybe he would take my wallet and run. He kept the metal aimed at my face. I watched him stop, reconsider, and then walk back to me. The wallet was not enough.

"Fucking *bitch*, stay on your knees, move . . . get in there." He pointed the gun to a spot behind me, to the bedroom. His legs were close to my face. I tried to smell him, so I sniffed hard. No cologne or soap, just the breath of my blood and fear. I slowed every gesture, buying time to strategize as I crawled to the side of the bed.

I was dizzy. I remember talking to myself: I have to stay awake. I must stay alive. I need to think. I wiped away more warm blood, to clear my vision as I inched toward the bed. My peripheral vision caught the gun sliding into one of his bulky pockets, as a pair of mirrored sunglasses and some zip ties emerged from another.

I thought: he knows I have memorized him, and now he wants to hide behind a pair of sunglasses. I felt a spike of rage. I thought of all the women in the world who had suffered at the hands of a dick like this. And I was going to be one of them.

CHAPTER TEN

On the outside I remained cool, faking indifference, acting slow and disoriented, buying seconds, trying to figure out what to do. He pulled the gun out of his pocket, set it down on the nightstand.

He said, "Give me your hands."

Using thick white zip ties, he strapped my wrists together in front of me. Pre-cut duct tape strips materialized from another pocket. He smoothed the tape across my mouth.

As he touched my face, I could see that his hands were shaking. In a measured drop of my eyes, I looked at my own hands. To my amazement, they looked rather calm. Maybe all of those uncomfortable hours of meditation had paid off. I managed to slow my heart rate and clear my mind.

I saw more zip ties, thick strong ones. I assumed they were for my legs. Time stretched. I needed a plan. He was the one who was shaking; I was not. I knew I had to take advantage of that. After securing my arms, he went back into his tennis-ready stance at the end of the bed and hissed, "Get up on the bed, and lie on your stomach."

I thought about his shaking hands. I had to make a move. Feigning injury, acting dazed and slow, I rose from the floor to sit on the edge of my mattress.

I considered jumping through the den window, involving a six-foot drop to the driveway and some broken glass, which sounded reasonable. However, I knew the window was paned and glazed and had an outside screen. I ditched that idea and assessed the bedroom's other windows. That option was worse: tempered glass.

He told me again to get up on the bed and turn over onto my stomach. Slowly, deliberately, I rose for the bed, my gestures weak, vague, and tentative. I sat on the side of the bed and groaned, as if I were in pain. Then I made my move.

I lay straight out on the bed and spun myself like a rolling pin across the bed to the other side. It was as if someone had flipped me out of a hot taco.

I finished the spin and landed on my feet, my back to the bathroom door. A deep, urgent voice whispered fiercely in my left ear, just behind my shoulder.

"Now run like hell!"

So that is what I did. All of those tedious years of running and hiking paid off right then. Pumped, twitching muscle fibers and adrenalin jolts launched me through the bathroom toward the living room. I felt another adrenalin blast gush up my calves to my thighs. I knew the feeling from the days when I skied all the time. I felt *strong*.

I noticed my hand smear blood on the bathroom door as I faced a decision. If I went left, I would be outside in four to five paces. If I turned right, there were more strides, probably a dozen. I decided the gravel in the back would slow me, plus the fence would hide us from the neighbors.

I shot to the right, toward the front door, wasting no motion and gaining momentum. I ran in a dead heat, breathing loud. I could hear the man's footsteps behind me, and I could tell he was moving fast. Briefly, I thought about films where damsels in distress run in high heels, looking back over their shoulders and crying, "Oh! Oh!" That thought pissed me off. Who in their right mind would take the time to look back and coo like a dove? Women obviously did not direct those movies.

I remembered an important tree-skiing rule: when skiing through the woods, never, ever look at the trees. Only look at the white. As I ran I focused straight ahead, only looking at the front door. I could hear his breathing close in behind me. I was wearing sandals with heels, disappointing footwear for the occasion.

When I made it to the door and reached for the knob, I realized my hands were tied in front of me. I could reach for the doorknob. A jolt of amazement fired through me—why did he do that? How could I be that far ahead of him? I yanked the door open with exaggerated force, still fueled by adrenalin.

Have you ever walked in front of a grocery cart driven by a child? The entire time you have this nagging feeling that by the blessed moment the shopping trip is over, someone is going to have bloody heels, and that someone will be you. I felt a similar flavor of foreboding when the door opened—a realization that the next cart shove was coming.

His foot stopped the door.

He pulled me back, tearing my SEEKING ENLIGHTENMENT T-shirt off at the shoulder. Pressing the gun between my two chicken wings, he hissed, "You *fucking* bitch, you go out that door, I'll kill you."

There was no thinking going on. Pure reptilian rage and fear sent my hands back to the doorknob. I decided it was better to be outside, where someone might find me. I yanked the door until there was barely enough room to shimmy through the opening. I made it outside to the deck. My ankles twisted above those loose, silly sandals as I ran across wooden planks to the stairs. I tore the duct tape off my mouth and screamed for help.

My voice, shrill and desperate, shook me. The experience felt exactly like a nightmare in which you scream over and over again for help, but no one comes to the rescue. Other than the sound of my unfamiliar voice, it was quiet. I did not hear footsteps behind me. I jumped off the deck and continued down the driveway, thinking, cripes, I wish I were wearing running shoes.

My ankles were twisting around like ball bearings on grease. My legs pumped. They were fueled, primed pistons gaining speed on the down-hill slope. I jammed every decibel into a cry for help.

The streets lay still and quiet. It was a soft, tepid day and everyone seemed to be outside, albeit outside somewhere else. Familiar neighbors' cars were gone, not one person was walking to the pool, and no one was riding by on a bike. It was a sinister silence behind the sound of my sandals slapping, slapping, and that strange, desperate voice shouting for help.

I spotted a car in the driveway across the street, at Jackie's house. I did not know her well, enjoying occasional conversations and frequent waves as one of us swept the drive or started our cars. Still anticipating his footsteps, or a bullet in my back, I ran toward Jackie's front door. I refused to look behind me.

I stumbled to the front step and saw Jackie coming around the side of her house. She wore loose, dark-blue workout clothes and gardening gloves. I will not ever forget the sight of her: smart square glasses, a for-ward, assertive posture. I still imagine her with wings—a bespectacled angel wearing sweatpants.

I crouched for a moment, half sitting on her cool concrete step, gaining breath. For the first time, I looked back toward my house. Was he still after me? I did not see him. Between gasps of sweet air, I pleaded with Jackie, "Please, please, please help me. This guy is trying to kill me."

I then realized she had no idea who I was. Looking down, I saw brick red paint spattered on my shirt and remembered wet pools of blood on the kitchen floor. I said, "Jackie, it's Diana. I live across the street. Please, this guy is trying to kill me." She looked up at my house, did an about-face, put a finger to her lips in the language of shhh, and waved for me to follow. I couldn't help but notice that the angel in sweatpants wore tall rubber boots.

I followed her through a sun-bleached, wooden gate and into her backyard. I glanced to see if there was a lock on the gate. No. Thick tree trunks arched high, throwing shade across her private yard. I remember crisp, browned leaves on the ground, a rough rocky patio, and several rustic terraces.

Jackie motioned to one of the stone walls and said, "Heather, go hide over there—behind that wall." I was more than willing to be called Heather or anybody else at that point. I headed toward the stone wall as she ran inside the house, presumably to call the police. It was just a matter of time before the stranger would follow us there. I crawled over a low limestone wall and lay on the ground, out of view from the gate.

I sunk into dead leaves, swollen and fragrant with autumn. Instinctively, I wrapped my arms tight around my torso. I was fighting to contain my bucking heart. I thought the force would lift me off the ground. My body flopped up in an arc then buckled and slammed to the ground, much like a hooked fish flopping on a riverbank. The action seemed like a pure reptilian, muscular, neurological duty. My body had given over to uncontrolled flips and jolts. Everything—hands, teeth, bones—rattled and quivered.

I recalled a book called *Waking the Tiger: Healing Trauma*. The author noted a common behavior in wild animals: they shake violently after a narrow escape. The duck will walk away from a fight and flap his wings; a tiger will shake and strut. That is how they release stress from their bodies, after a crisis.

Often, humans attempt to bypass that step and go into "Hey, dude, it's cool" mode. I decided to let my body go wild, to see if I could shake it off. I sensed that I was lying still as the ground rippled and heaved under me. It was like sitting on a jet as it backs out of the gate, that momentary illusion where the carts and people on the ramp look like the ones moving, and the jet is standing still.

The leaves smelled moist, though they felt and sounded dry. I wondered if the stranger with the gun was on his way through the gate, and if I would remain locked out of Jackie's house. Then I heard a sliding patio door open, and on an updraft of my trembling, I glimpsed Jackie.

She was standing outside, phone in hand, and waving her arms. "Come in. Come in," she whispered in an urgent tone. In an electric jerk, I levitated over the rock wall and fled for the door before The Guy came around the corner.

CHAPTER ELEVEN

T HE 911 DISPATCHER STAYED ON THE PHONE WITH JACKIE AS I practically dove through her open sliding glass door. Jackie ran to lock the entry behind me. I remember sitting on her dining room floor. The ground was still rotating clockwise.

The dining and living rooms were in the midst of a remodel. Walls were naked, down to studs. The concrete floor felt cool and safe. Jackie and I both kept watch on the back door. Did he follow us?

I knew there had to be a better place to hide. We were not even hidden, but my body refused to move from the soothing chill of the floor. The 911 dispatcher said it would be all right for Jackie to cut the ties off my wrists, as long as she did not touch the plastic with her bare hands. When Jackie tried using her kitchen scissors, they simply left pitiful grooves in the plastic. The scissors would break before they even dented the industrial-strength zip tie.

With the phone squeezed between her shrugged shoulder and cocked head, Jackie jumbled through drawers, seeking another solution.

She found a pair of garden shears. Still talking on the phone, Jackie frantically gnawed at the ties with the sharper tool. As I watched the slow progress, I noticed that her hands trembled. Absorbed in surgical concentration, she cranked on the shears' handles as the blades slipped around the thick, white tie.

The dispatcher encouraged her to keep trying and assured us that help was on the way. It did not occur to me to talk. I kept watching the back door. Jackie pried and squeezed without cutting my skin or touching the evidence. Finally, my wrists were free, as the offending tie landed on the floor. Jackie left it there and continued her conversation with 911.

Apparently, angels also carry garden shears.

I stared at the deep red welts circling my wrists, not feeling a thing. I had no sense that those wrists belonged to me. The dispatcher must have asked Jackie if it was a case of domestic violence. Jackie said yes, she thought so; she thought he was my boyfriend. I shook my head vehemently and said, "No, no, I have never seen him before." Jackie put her free hand to her mouth and breathlessly relayed this to the dispatcher. "Oh my God—he was a stranger? He was a stranger!" That probably scared her even more. I felt sick. I wished the floor would stay in one place, and mumbled something about lying down.

I curled into a fetal position on the floor. It felt as though one-minute epoxy suddenly gripped me to the concrete. Even lifting an arm seemed impossible. The room and Jackie continued to orbit me. Those magical, pounding adrenaline spurts that had fueled my escape drained out of my system. No slow leaks. More like the sudden dump of power-steering fluid on a driveway at the same moment the old hose splits—nothing left in the reservoir.

My head weighed a thousand pounds, as though I had become a rag doll. I willed myself to stand. Nothing happened. It seemed important to stand. I wanted to show Jackie I was okay. The epoxy held me down as I waited for The Guy to press his face against the sliding glass door.

Two police officers arrived. Jackie let them through the front entrance and led them to the back room. Both men stood above me, six-foot towers in uniform. Coiled tight on the floor, I felt sawed off and diminished. I shivered as I peered up to see a triangle of worried faces, Jackie and two cops, bending and staring at me, three concerned stalks of wheat.

I tried to collect myself and tell them what happened. I described the man who attacked me, his clothing, that he had a gun. The officer who carried the radio asked me what the gun looked like. I admitted that I did not know much about guns, so could not tell him what kind it was. He asked if it had a revolver, and I said no. A swift, stricken look betrayed his alarm. He lifted the radio and spoke in hushed, worried tones, warning his peers that the man was carrying a semiautomatic.

I relayed more details, telling them I did not see or hear him leave through the front door of my house, and assured them I had never seen him before. Jackie held her hand to her mouth and paced the room.

An ambulance arrived, and Jackie let two EMTs into the house. A young, handsome (why only young and handsome at times like this?) EMT reached down and touched my curled shoulder. I instinctively cowered, even though he was there to help. At his next attempt to approach me, I winced again. In tune with the situation, he backed off and removed his hand. I said something like, "Before you touch me, please just tell me who you are."

The EMT eased farther back on his haunches. In a gentle voice, he slowly told me his name, which of course I do not remember. But that was not the point. I said, "Okay, you can touch me now." He shyly gestured down so I would look to see my exposed breast, poking out at a wild angle from behind my tight sports bra. I tucked it back in, all eyes still staring down at me. Just when I thought it was impossible to feel any more vulnerable.

The EMT rubbed the angry, red ridges on my swollen wrists and shook his head, sadly. I knew they would go away. That was the middle-aged voice of experience. I was familiar with those despicable signs of aging—deep red sleep lines creased and settled into my forehead and cheeks every morning. They used to take minutes, and now take hours to disappear.

He wiggled my fingers, flexed my stiff wrists. I knew those parts were okay. Gingerly probing my scalp, the EMT said it was time to go to the hospital. It finally occurred to me that I was on a cool, dark floor, and I was alive, surrounded by people who wanted to help me.

I have a surreal memory of lying on the sloped stretcher in the ambulance. They parked in front of Jackie's house, and I could see what was going on across the street. My favorite mail carrier stopped to speak to the police. I knew he would keep his eye out for anyone in the neighborhood he did not recognize. It was that kind of neighborhood, and he was a safe man who watched out for people. I found a sense of comfort seeing him; he was a gentleman.

Police cars scattered on each side of the road and in my driveway. Dark-blue uniforms and crisp white shirts swarmed the house and yard. The second EMT, the driver, asked me which hospital I wanted to go to.

I asked him which hospital was closest. When he told me, I asked if he would take his wife there if she needed a hospital. He grinned and nodded. A female police officer opened the ambulance door and held up her camera to take my picture. Really? Right now? I am not a fan of photos of myself and knew that one would be a winner.

On the slow ride to the hospital, without flashing lights or sirens, I remembered again to breathe. A whoosh of exhaled air released a storm of panic, marvel, anger, and amazement. Turning to the EMT riding beside me, the words "I am so blessed!" rushed out of my flabbergasted mouth. The EMT considered this. He leaned back in his seat, tipped his head a notch, and held it to the side as he nodded thoughtfully.

"Blessed?"

Pause.

"Huh."

His smile was melancholy, the smile of someone who had seen a lot of tragedy.

"I guess it is all how you look at it. I'm glad you got away."

We both fell silent and looked out the window. It is all how you look at it. There is a mystery to blessings, and why I would consider that time to be one of them.

The EMTs wheeled me into the emergency room at the South Austin Hospital. I overheard them telling the staff about my great escape and about a gunman on the loose in Travis Heights. The doctor patted my hand and said, "Good work. That bastard—I hope they catch him."

After poking around on my scalp, he injected several shots of Novocaine and waited about five minutes for the numbing to take hold. While we waited, a nurse came in to assist, and he coaxed her to sew me up. Obviously used to that, and happy for the professional experience, the RN readied herself for the task. In an assured voice she ordered, "Novocaine."

The doctor winked at me and said, "No need. This girl is tough. Just stitch her up."

The nurse looked up in surprise and dropped her implements on the tray. "*No way,*" she exclaimed, and we all laughed.

"You were kidding? I will so get you back!" she smiled and looked down at me kindly. After the nurse (expertly) stitched me up, they sent me through the tunnel of an MRI machine. After that, an X-ray tech folded my body in strange and painful positions. I began to notice that everything hurt. Nurses and doctors see rough stuff in the ER. Reviewing the results, we all agreed that my injuries were miraculously minor—a slight concussion, about ten stitches in my scalp, and multiple bruises.

The doctor prescribed and administered some Ativan, a form of benzodiazepine used to treat anxiety. Fifteen minutes later, a satisfying sense of safety eased into my cranked-up muscles. I did not know how much I would grow to love that stuff. A nurse stood next to me, holding my clenched hand, generously encouraging me by saying, "I cannot believe you did that. You were so *brave.*" I did not feel brave; I felt shaky and scared. A spinning world, the frenetic buzz of disturbed thoughts, sparks of fear, and a thumping headache did not feel like bravery to me.

Within a few hours, the nurses moved on to other patients. A social worker spoke with me about available counseling options, as well as financial assistance from the state. She provided a grainy copy of an information sheet listing services provided by the Texas Crime Victims' Compensation Program. The information, intended to be helpful, was TMI, overwhelming and confusing, something I wanted to put off for later. I had yet to identify myself as a victim. I hate that word.

A plainclothes detective stood next to my bed for at least an hour and a half, tape recording our conversation. He was thorough and well-intentioned. Before leaving, he used some rather large tweezers to deposit my bloody shorts and T-shirt in a plastic bag. Lucky for me, as I had climbed into the ambulance, Jackie handed the EMT a neatly folded pair of pants and a shirt. She had thought of everything.

BB had come and gone by the time the detective left the ER. I had my phone—a police officer had brought it from my house to the idling ambulance. The cop wanted to know if it belonged to me. I said yes, so he let me keep it. That was handy because I was too flustered to remember any phone numbers. Speed dial has simplified my life and ruined my memory.

I wanted to call BB right away. She had planned to drop off flyers that afternoon to prepare for Sunday's open house. I was frantic to warn her to stay away from the neighborhood and prepare her for the bevy of police cars and officers surrounding the house. I reached her on the phone. She had hurried over to the hospital and marched by the front desk, informing anyone who might ask questions that "family had arrived." BB always knows the right things to say to cut through red tape. She held me, and we both strained to keep from crying. I could tell by the way she looked at my face that it would be a good idea to avoid mirrors.

BB left, promising to pick me up as soon as I could go. The hospital door shut behind her with a heavy *thunk*. I could hear the click-click-click of her rhinestone sandals diminish down the hall. The room's atmosphere was sterile, impersonal, aching with prior traumas, and now mine. I usually love silence, but the room felt like a fluorescent-lit tomb. For the first time since The Guy pulled his gun, I had time to gather my thoughts. It hurt to think.

I doubt that anyone knows ahead of time how to prepare for that sort of event. We can plan for a trip, a funeral, even an operation, yet I am left to wonder how one organizes thoughts after such a blow? The silence in the lonely room haunted me. I did not want to be alone. So I did what I consistently do when at a loss: I pressed the speed dial for my best friend.

Christie lives in Seattle. When she answered the phone, she was walking around Green Lake, admiring all the puppies. I left space for her to describe a cute pug in a sequined tutu before spilling the news. How do you introduce this kind of information? We talked for a long time. Before we hung up, Christie told me her palms were sweating, and she was having difficulty absorbing the information. I understood.

Aside from a low cell phone battery, I was not ready to call my family back east. They were celebrating at a wedding shower for my nephew and his wife-to-be. I could put the call off for a day or two. Before calling my brother, Don, I wanted to find my bearings and figure out what had happened.

Everything I could think of to do had been done.

I hated the silence of the room, as I inspected the lumps and bruises forming on my arms and legs. Their colorful emergence confirmed what I suspected. What I thought might have happened, actually happened. I tugged the starched hospital sheet up to my chin, folded my knees close to my chest, and remembered again: when all else fails, breathe.

I felt a welcome wave of relaxation from the pharmaceuticals and recalled my words to the EMT about feeling blessed. Those words seemed distant, a mirage of gratitude. I managed to break away from an armed robber, so sure I felt blessed.

In the next breath, I remembered my financial troubles, all of the problems I faced before that day. Agony dropped from my throat to my gut with the sudden realization: Diana, you are so screwed.

I spent the next few hours lying back with my knees up, trying to reframe those four words: You Are So Screwed. I tried to put a positive spin on things. It did not work. The phrase repeated itself, subliminally. Those four fucking words replicated, in chant-like fashion.

Along with bright, buzzing lights, space-age medical equipment hung off the ceilings and walls. Those contraptions really freak me out. They scream bodily intrusion. I expected George Jetson to walk in the door, turn a knob, and jolt me with harmful light beams.

I closed my eyes.

I find it helpful to look at engineering problems and personal problems in the same light—from all angles. Often I will imagine "the challenge" as a physical thing, sitting in a high-backed chair in the center of an empty room. I, the solution seeker, have the ability to circumambulate the obstacle, to literally view it from all sides. Then I can reframe the problem in a new way, thus finding solutions previously unavailable to my frontal lobes.

In the past, I had used that process to select the "perfect" plumbing fixture, solve engine problems, design kitchens, mend relationships, and decide whether I should go to the doctor. I wanted to reframe the four words, so I could feel better about all of this. The drugs were working. I was fairly relaxed by then and had nothing else to do. I pulled the bleached hospital sheet up high, around my ears, and snuggled my arms into a full-body hug.

I was born with a rich imagination, which basically means I daydreamed all through middle school. I enjoy using my imagination and practice using it every day. For me, picturing a large wingback chair is a no-brainer. I squeezed my eyes shut and conjured a formal-looking piece, perhaps for sale at an American Heritage Furniture store. Upholstered in delicate paisley fabric, the chair seemed a bit pretentious. I came to terms with that. I did not have to *own* the chair, I told myself—I just needed to imagine it.

I closed my eyes again and continued the reframing exercise. I had only begun to formalize my acquaintance with the chair when I imagined two nondescript people walking into the chair's otherwise empty room. Their appearance took me by surprise, but experience with the chair game has taught me to roll with it.

The two people carried a wooden sign, about five feet long. They carefully placed the sign on to the chair's arms, leaning it against the wings, so I could read the message: YOU ARE SO SCREWED.

I have a friend who knows how to use an expletive. She often refrains, out of deference to others. As an alternative, she discovered that it is easy to turn all sorts of words—as a matter of fact, most words—into expletives. She might be sorting through piles of contracts on her desk and exclaim, "Sheets and towels," with a strong emphasis on the first syllable.

We all get what she is saying. However, no one seems to be offended. She can turn "God Bless America" into a respectful expletive.

I took one look at that sign and thought of her.

"Sheets and towels," I said, emphasizing the first syllable.

In the past, when I did those reframing exercises, I generally walked around the chair with the problem sitting in it, in order to see all sides. Since the world was spinning, and I was not, I decided to walk in a counterclockwise direction, hoping that might even things out. The drugs were efficiently taking the edge off, so I believed I was thinking clearly.

I kept my eyes closed and walked counterclockwise around the room. When I walked in that direction, every time I stopped to look at the chair, no matter where I was standing, the sign faced me, with its big, bold letters in full view. I stood still; the chair stood still. I walked in the other direction, and the sign followed me.

At six in the evening, BB came back to retrieve me. By then I had been involved with the chair for a couple of hours. No matter the angle, I saw that nicely painted sign. I was glad to abandon the exercise; the reframing project's failure deflated me. That time I discovered no solutions, simple or complex. I had a pile of troubles, and I knew it.

Jackie's pants were far too small. I wrapped a sheet around me and shuffled, unceremoniously, down the hall to check out. A chipper young woman ushered me into her cubicle. There was still, after all of this . . . paperwork to complete.

"Oh! You're all red," she said.

I thought she was kidding and then remembered my decision about ignoring mirrors. I looked down and sure enough, there was even blood on the bed sheet I was wearing.

"Yeah, kind of a rough day," I said.

She was genuinely concerned. "Why, you poor thing! Are you sure you're okay?"

Now I was concerned, mostly about my appearance.

"Yeah, I'm all right. I had a tough go with a stranger today."

She got excited. "Are you the one from Travis Heights? The one *on the news?*"

Good grief. I hadn't even thought about the news.

"It's on the news?" I said, weakly.

"Oh my, yes! This is exciting! I can't believe you did that."

I tightened the sheet around my torso, wondering how long it was going to take to sign the papers, so we could leave. And wondering what she thought I had done.

Cheerfully, the woman went on to tell me not to worry about the hospital charges. In cases such as mine, the state of Texas would pay for it out of the Crime Victims' Compensation Fund. That word again. I was relieved to hear about the help and told her so. As I tripped over my sheet on the way out, she eyed me.

"Are you sure you're okay?" She seemed doubtful.

I was at a loss to reassure her, having tried my best.

"Thanks—I'll be fine."

I turned to leave and noticed the sign, now in the lobby, leaning against the ugly paisley chair: YOU ARE SO SCREWED.

BB's car smelled of leftover tamales. Her sister rode in the front, and I rolled, mummified by the sheet, into the back of BB's Honda wagon. I was incredulous that anyone could eat. Didn't everyone in the world know how bad the day had been? A spark of rational thought allowed me to forgive BB and her sister for eating. It was not such a bad day for them.

It felt as though a grapefruit was growing out of my skull's right side. The image startled me. I still had not looked in a mirror. I pulled my right arm out of the twisted sheet, tentatively tapping my palm on the right side of my sticky head. I was relieved to find nothing of that size, only several bumps the size of lemons.

We were all in a quandary. Who knows what to do after something like that? I was in no shape to make any tough calls, so I waited for BB to take the lead. She had all those kids, and so I told myself BB would know what to do.

We agreed that a trip to the pharmacy would be a good start. BB dropped her sister off at home and drove me to Walgreens. I rode in the backseat because it was too much work to move to the front seat.

The medication the doctor gave me in the ER was wearing off. I had not eaten since breakfast. Everything hurt, even my eyelashes. We walked into the store. The pharmacy was packed with people dropping off pre-scriptions. Every woman in the long line held a crying UNICEF baby. There was loud, tinny music and snot everywhere.

BB knows me well. I believe she would describe my demeanor as socially prudent, and definitely patient. Imagine her surprise when I practically shoved one of those sick babies aside to reach the front counter. I grasped the cashier's hand, begging for "emergency pain killers." She recoiled and pumped on a bottle of hand sanitizer. BB retreated to the potato chip aisle, where she could keep an eye on me, at the same time disassociating herself from the "psycho lady in the Halloween costume" at the cash register. The pharmacist, no stranger to difficult people, quickly attended to the problem. She even escorted me to the door. BB followed at a distance.

I wriggled back into the Honda. BB handed me a bottle of water and suggested I take some of the pills. She avoided looking at me. Most notably, she did not say anything else. BB is rarely at a loss for words, especially encouraging ones, so I understood that she had no idea what to do with me.

Watching friends and family over the years, I have observed something interesting about marriage: it provides people with the option to drag a loved one into super-difficult situations. We drove back to BB's house in search of her husband.

The three of us drove back to the First Martini. BB's husband, Juan, is good-natured about participating in his wife's super-difficult situations. We made a plan: we would all go into the house. I would take a bath, pick up a few essentials, feed the cats, and leave. There was a long conversation about taking or leaving my car. From the backseat, I was not tracking the entire debate, and I was unsure about the location of my car keys.

I enjoy the protective feeling of male friendship, especially when I feel intimidated. For example, I have learned that in dealing with people like the cable guy, the dynamic is easier when I have a male friend with me. Poor Juan was now my default protector because he was BB's husband.

By the time we reached the front door, I was not intimidated. I was downright scared. I wanted an army of men by my side, packing heat. I assumed Juan was not carrying a weapon. Just his presence helped tremendously. BB and I would not have attempted this alone.

Juan opened the door. We made him go first. Pierre rushed to our sides, scolding me for leaving him outside too long, oblivious to what Spartacus and I dealt with that afternoon. Poor Spartacus was still cowering under the sofa.

"Where's my food?" Pierre demanded, tail straight up, absorbed in his mealtime. Spartacus refused to come out from his hiding place, even turning down food, which was unheard of.

The three of us stood in the kitchen and looked around. Pierre whined persistently for food. Juan spoke first, in his smooth Peruvian accent. "I think we need to clean this up." BB got busy, as she is prone to do, looking around, pointing out the clouds of charcoal (used for fingerprinting) rubbed into the doors and around cabinet handles. Ever tactful, BB did not mention the bloodstains, which appeared to be everywhere.

Walking into your own crime scene is spooky. Maybe eerie is a better word. Juan and BB were quiet. For some reason, if we spoke, it was in a whisper. We followed a red swath of proof, marking an *O* through the house—dark blood on a straw-colored floor, charting the path from the kitchen sink, around the circle of worry, and the race to the front door.

Returning to the kitchen, I bent to scoop out dry food for Pierre and Spartacus. The world was still spinning, so I crouched on the kitchen floor. I reached for the cats' small food bowls, Pyrex custard cups, filled halfway with my dark, almost black, blood. The image of those red glass bowls still leaves me heavy-hearted.

For the first time, I cried.

They never show that part in the movies, people cleaning up their own mess. Now, it is an obvious "duh." It isn't the responsibility of law enforcement to hire a cleaning service after an investigation, so who else would do it? That cleaning detail had not dawned on any of us until that moment. BB and Juan took charge. Collectively, we found rubber gloves, a bucket, cleaning rags, and a stack of bath towels. They swooshed me off to the bathroom, assuring me that raising five children trained them for that sort of thing.

Juan and BB handed me a bath towel, using the other five towels to sop up blood. Later they told me that after the towels, they used a bucketful of cleaning rags and finished off with a roll of paper towels.

The hot water in the tub pulled me back to earth. I found myself repeating, "Did that really happen? Did that really happen?" The stitches in my scalp pinched the lemon-sized lumps. Shock radiated from my heart, volts of electricity darted through thousands of neural pathways. This was a new level of feeling on edge.

I sunk down and swirled my hair through the water. A crimson ripple radiated from my body, turning the bathwater red, as though the entire tub filled with blood. I drained the water and ran another bath. With time to think, I reviewed the day. I had survived something savage. I traveled to a primal state, behaving as an animal, stung with the drive to stay alive. I shook my head. I lived through the day. I was okay.

Okay is a relative term, but I was alive and moving. After two baths, aside from miscellaneous bruises, my injuries were invisible. Because I refused to face the mirror, I do not have a memory of what I looked like before the bath, which turned out to be a good decision for me. After the bath, I looked the same as I had the day prior, to the rest of the world. However, from my perspective, on the inside looking out, everything appeared and felt different. I felt transplanted into a different body with a new, slightly lopsided, set of eyes. I was beginning to learn that life feels entirely different after a head injury.

Every dial in my system inexplicably turned in odd directions. Every internal gauge recalibrated, all sails set in an entirely new angle. I entered a new matrix, with an entirely novel set of conditions, sensations, and perceptions. It was too early to understand that.

At the time, I simply felt disoriented, reeling and rolling in waves of new territory and the effects of Vicodin and Ativan. I walked to the front door, fully dried and clothed, which felt like a big accomplishment. The floors swabbed clean, BB and Juan stood on the deck. I stepped out the door before I saw they were speaking to a young woman holding a microphone. Two vans loaded with cameras and mounted disks advertised the local news stations as they slowly coasted up and down the road in front of the house. I know the reporter saw me before I turned around quickly and hid inside. Backing off, retreating, moving away—that was my instinct, and I trusted that BB and Juan would protect my privacy.

The young newscaster left after talking to BB and Juan for about five minutes.

With those TV cameras cruising up and down Alta Vista, I was pretty sure The Guy would not return that night. That was the only positive I could come up with in terms of the news. I had a decision to make about the press; however I was not ready to think about that.

Cats fed, house cleaned, I grabbed a toothbrush and a few things from my closet. Juan removed the open-house sign from its post. No one was going to be in the house, hanging out alone, until the police found The Guy.

BB drove my car as Juan followed us back to their house in her car. I was grouchy and abrupt with BB. The bulges on my head pulsated, and I had passed the hypoglycemic tipping point hours earlier. I hated leaving the cats and my home. I hated that my favorite house did not feel like home.

We climbed the rickety spiral staircase up to BB and Juan's apartment. Juan unfolded the hideaway bed, and BB put on sheets, fluffing a few pillows for me. I was lucky to have such good friends. I recognized this, despite an overwhelming desire to bite their heads off.

It had been a rugged day, I muttered to myself.

Sleep would help.

Easing under the covers, I wanted to escape to that planet my stepson, Chase, went to for a few years. Maybe I could live in a Tibetan cave for the rest of my life. Anything seemed better than this new version of reality.

I rolled onto my left side, away from the stitches, and reviewed the circumstances one more time:

This had been a bad day.

Surely tomorrow would be better.

What was the worst that could happen?

As I drifted off to the sweet escape of slumber, the last image I remember popping up was the wingback chair and the sign with those four prophetic words.

CHAPTER TWELVE

THE NEXT FEW DAYS I DRIFTED IN AND OUT OF SLEEP ON THE foldout. I was in the way; the bed took up most of the room. I remember lying in a tight curl between naps, waiting for the meds to kick in. Escape felt terrific. That was all I wanted.

To say that BB's phone rang constantly is not an exaggeration. The news reports said a realtor was holding an open house in Travis Heights. They said a gunman attacked the realtor, and he was still at large. On television, they held a steady camera shot of the for-sale sign at the First Martini. The sign included a good-sized photo of BB and her phone number in large print. Every realtor in Austin thought BB was the one holding the open house.

This is how rumors start. Most of the information was accurate, though we know that details can make all the difference. Her phone ringer was loud. I was in the next room, listening to her explaining. No, no, she was fine—followed by several strategies aimed at minimizing the fact that her client was lying in a heap a few feet away.

I was upset that The Guy now had her name and phone number. I worried for her safety; we did not know where, or who, this man was. The thought of something terrible happening to BB sent me over the edge. The realtors were calling, and so were the news stations. Word was out. Christie started a phone tree, so a network of people knew what had happened. They all called BB, so she ended up in customer relations. I felt as though BB started out with a client and ended up with a patient.

Her distant voice in those conversations drew me back to a world I wanted to ignore. I woke long enough for a stop in the closest bathroom, a glass of water, and more meds. I do not remember eating. Knowing BB, she forced something nutritious down me. I ached everywhere. Something was wrong with my back, along the spine. It was noticeable, but I was not ready to figure it out.

If I kept sleeping, all of those problems would go away. I found no reason to wake up. On the day of the attack, when I told Jackie, "I just want to lie down," I had no idea what that meant.

It never occurred to me to quantify how long a person could lie down in one spot, or if a bad day could actually last for several years.

CHAPTER THIRTEEN

I MANAGED TO GET OUT OF BED, SHOWER, AND DRESS FOR A MEETING with the detectives on the case. They were from the sex crimes unit. In a nondescript beige room, I went over the entire story with one of them. He asked good questions, and I trusted him. We spoke for over an hour, and then the second detective came in to question. He asked me if The Guy was wearing any jewelry. I said no, and mentioned that he did have a pair of wraparound sunglasses in one of his pockets.

He asked me if I had ever seen the man before.

"Absolutely not," I said.

Within several other questions, he mentioned a Travis Heights blog that was teeming with active entries. People in the neighborhood were shocked and wanted to find the guy who entered my home. The investigator said he learned from the blog that a break-in had occurred on that same Saturday in Travis Heights. They were following up on the lead to see if there was any connection. It was reassuring to know the detectives were on it.

After that, I met with Camille, the police department's social worker. Camille ended up being my main contact with the police. She was gentle, smart, and sensitive. Camille asked questions and helped me remember details as we met with a sketch artist. By then, my body was one big ache. The room was spinning again, so I closed my eyes and tried to focus. I needed to remember something I did not want to remember.

Once I settled down, it was easy to recall the details. Unfortunately, the image of The Guy's frigid face at the other end of the barrel burned a hole in my memory. That picture endures, popping up in a haunting, random, and powerful way.

I concentrated, trying to send an image from my mind to the artist's fingers. I strained to recall the subtleties of the stranger's features—roundness of chin, length of five o'clock shadow, precise eye color. It was a difficult and tedious process. I wanted to lie down. Camille urged me on, appealing to my desire to get an *A* in everything. She encouraged me, saying that many people cannot remember anything (or were not around to describe their assailant.)

After a few hours, the sketch was close enough for me. I knew there were some inaccuracies, though I could not pick out what was wrong. The artist did a remarkable sketch, in light of my vague verbal acuity. BB picked me up and took me home to lie down.

Later that evening my brother Don was flying in from upstate New York. I perked up in anticipation of his visit. Sometimes, there is nothing like having a big brother around. I cut down on the meds so I could talk and drive. In hindsight, I should not have been driving. None of us realized how zonked I was—far and above the effects of medication. It was not apparent on the outside, certainly not to me as I drifted through the experience.

I sat on BB's folded-up bed, waiting for the five o'clock news. I was showing more interest, although it still seemed like a distant story. I saw a call coming in from Camille and answered right away. She said a lead in the case was blossoming—the police had a photo lineup for me to review. She asked if she could come over with two investigators. I gave her the address, and she said they were on their way.

BB and I waited anxiously for their arrival. In rare form, a pummeling rain poured out of the sky above Austin. It was a hard-driving Texas rain, loud and slick. Three figures hustled through BB's garden and up the winding stairs. The four of us sat down at the kitchen table as BB left the room. One of the detectives slid a photo composite out of his rain-splotched briefcase. He shook it carefully to remove any drops.

I watched him position the page so the three rows of photographs faced him upside down before placing the paper in front of me on the table. Camille and the two men looked at me intensely. The one with the photos asked me to look carefully. Did any of the pictures look like the man at my house?

I lifted the paper, hungry to look. I scanned one face, then another. Top left, top middle, top right, bottom left. One face resembled Craig the Crazy Cowboy, only sleazier. I knew he was not The Guy. Middle left, The Face. Number seven—that was The Guy! I pointed at his picture. There was no doubt. He looked a bit like Michael Keaton.

I refocused my eyes to catch any facial expressions from the people watching me. All four of us swallowed hard. My heartbeat jumped, sped like an engine gone wild. The detectives looked like two teenagers with a new computer game, trying to act unexcited. They had a suspect. Their smiles broke as they leapt for the door to leave.

Camille, perceptive social worker that she is, could see I was about to hyperventilate.

"You okay? Need a few minutes to breathe?"

I nodded.

Both the detectives sat back down, tuning in, staying with me. I wanted to puke from seeing his face, and I wanted to jump with joy.

Five minutes later, BB and I watched all three round back down the spiral stairs and disappear into the slippery night. They were going to the courthouse for a warrant. That was all they could say right then.

CHAPTER FOURTEEN

MY SPIRITS SOARED, INFLATED BY HOPES OF CATCHING THE Guy. I focused on my brother Don's arrival in three hours. I went for a cheap *mani-pedi* at the Korean place near the First Martini. My hairdresser gingerly washed and dried my hair. I mentioned an accident. She did not ask for details.

I was coming back to life. Sometimes clean hair and polished nails can do that. Once Don's flight landed, we drove by the house, not going in. I needed sleep and going inside would rev me up. I had filled Don in on the photo lineup. We were excited. He kept telling me how great I looked. Everyone I ran into said that. I guessed they were expecting something more head-gauzy.

I was telling Don how relieved I would feel, probably in the next few hours, when we knew The Guy was behind bars. We were on our way to Don's hotel, where I would join him for a few nights. My cell rang, and I saw a restricted number—APD, the police department. I pulled over to the side of Travis Heights Boulevard. It was dark inside the car. The dashboard's cobalt-blue lights lent a shock effect against all the black. He smiled as I repeated the news: they got the warrant. He raised his right fist in the air. Victory.

There was a pause on the other end of the phone. I detected a deflated tone in contrast to our spark and realized the police were not telling me something. I waited. Don watched my face as the detective explained the current situation. They figured out that The Guy was not from Austin. He lived in Abilene, Texas, a six- to eight-hour drive to the west. He said they'd decided it was probably not an attempted sex crime, maybe more like a robbery. Turns out The Guy needed money.

The detective said that state troopers and U.S. Marshals convened on his home in Abilene with the warrant. His family answered the door, but he was not there. An hour earlier, The Guy had blasted off in a Lincoln Town Car. He absconded with a large sum of family money and lied to his wife and children, concocting a story about a religious pilgrimage due to much-needed solitude. He had turned his cell phone off before leaving Abilene.

The Guy slipped out of their fingers. That was a letdown, to say the least.

I hung up the phone feeling dejected, and drove to the hotel. Don turned on the TV once we settled into the room. I tried to stay awake but fell into a deep sleep before the eleven o'clock news.

The next morning, Don told me about the news report showing a face shot of The Guy. We hoped that would lead to something good. Don rode along as I met with my doctor and a few close friends. In the afternoon, we went to the First Martini. I fed the cats and watered plants. I gave him a play-by-play account of the ordeal as we walked the circular floor plan, the path of escape. He noticed a damaged drawer handle below the kitchen sink. It was bent in half, digging into the drawer. He asked me, "How did that happen?"

I was unsure. Had I fallen against it during those jumbled moments I cannot remember? Was that why my back hurt? Maybe I had rammed my spine against the drawer handle. Now that I was waking up, it was becoming more difficult to ignore the back pain.

We walked across the street to see Jackie. She opened the door and stared at me blankly, shifting a confused glance from my face, over to Don's, and back. Jackie was ahead of me by a few days. I had yet to understand the stress of hearing a knock on the front door, after the ordeal we had shared. I am still unsettled by the sound of someone knocking on my door.

She recognized me, but not really.

"Jackie, it's Diana." Her eyes widened. "And this is my brother, Don."

It took a moment for this to register. "Oh my God!" Emphasis on the third word. "It's *you*! Oh my God! You look so *whole*!" Jackie has a cheeky British accent.

Her hand flew up to her pretty face. "Come in! Come in."

Ever the gentleman, Don touched my shoulder to allow me through the door ahead of him. I detected water in his eyes. Jackie offered us seats in her front room. I was relieved she did not lead us to the back of the house. We sat, and she said it again, in disbelieving tones, "You look so whole!"

It was nice to know that was how I looked, but I was not feeling whole.

Don collected himself and thanked her, genuinely, for helping me. Jackie was our hero in all of this. I shuddered to think what would have happened if she had not been in her garden, and was not the kind of person willing to help someone, even if she thought I was someone other than her neighbor.

"Of course, of course," she said in her wonderful accent. "Diana, I cannot stop thinking about you. I can't believe you are here!" She faced Don, saying, "She fought for her life! It was amazing. I still cannot believe what she did!" I wriggled uncomfortably in my seat. I was not feeling strong or brave, and my back ached as much as my head.

Being the center of attention can make me shy and self-conscious. The praise was a bit overwhelming. On the other hand, I did get mileage out of it. Growing up, my brother was the big, tough football player, and I was the cheerleader. I will admit to some pleasure in the role reversal. Our visit was short, knowing there would be more visits later. As we walked back to my place, neither of us spoke. I felt comfort knowing that an angel with spectacles lived right across the street.

By the time Don went home at the end of the week, there was nothing new on the case, not even a detected ping from The Guy's cell phone. I wanted to go home, too, to the First Martini. No one thought that was a good idea, including me. Don, BB, and Juan all wanted me to return to BB's living room.

I went back to the First Martini anyway, which scared people, including me. Going home felt like the best decision within a series of imperfect solutions, a state of mind I would soon know well. Yes, there was a minute chance The Guy would be back, yet I doubted that would happen. He was not after me, just my money, which still hits my funny bone. Staying with BB and in Don's hotel room worked at first, but I wanted the familiar. I needed to stabilize.

It is difficult to say if losing The Guy or sending Don off was more of a downer. I would say it was a dead heat. I sat in my car and watched Don's back pass through the airport's revolving door. He turned and waved before disappearing. Yikes. I felt *alone*. I had another observation about marriage: after a super bad day, there is someone to go home to.

On the way home from the airport, I let go of the inner debate and turned left toward the First Martini. Pulling into the driveway felt normal. That was reassuring. Stepping over the bloodstains on the deck felt abnormal. Pulling out my keys and selecting the hot-pink one felt deliciously normal. Walking in to see if there was a stranger hiding somewhere did not feel normal.

Pierre greeted me with enthusiasm. Spartacus was still under the couch whimpering. Everything in the house seemed to check out okay. It was a beautiful, sunny day. I loved the light at Alta Vista.

Nothing is like home: familiar dish soap, wrestling kitties, thirsty plants, and the same old noisy refrigerator. I needed familiar. A taste of normal felt great. I was tired, and I longed to be still. I phoned BB to let her know I was going to take a nap.

"There?" She said, alarmed.

"Here," I said.

"Are you sure?" Loving tone.

"Yes, I'm sure, BB. Thank you for your help. I just need to lie down . . ."

I wilted like a dry, drooping potted plant, cautiously lowering my bruised body onto the couch. The sun through the window lent heat to the scratched-up leather. My eyes melted toward sleep, as my queasy, cranky heart flapped its wings. My heart would pound and buzz for a very long time; I just didn't know that then.

The kitties tucked into the *Z* of my frame. As the three of us tangled up in a soft nest, I fell asleep, my heavy arms bathed by the movement of hot sun and dappled shade.

I was home.

I sighed and snuggled in with my hand on Pierre's fur, telling myself that all I needed was a nap.

PART TWO

Living on Tenterhooks

CHAPTER FIFTEEN

I CONKED OUT FOR EIGHTEEN HOURS UNTIL THE DISTINCT CALL OF A mourning dove startled me. I leapt off the sofa, flying from a dream state to hypervigilant alarm. My heart buzzed. I looked around to see where I was and if anyone was there. I was a child afraid of the monster under my bed. A disturbing jolt from sleep into a startle reflex became my norm. Sleep offered a holiday before waking up triggered irrational and cruel anxiety.

A slow, insidious, unraveling occurred. Any sense of strength had long since drained out of my adrenalin-soaked system. My body parts hung heavily, either rag-dollish and limp or terrified, with no in-between. The Guy's face stared at me, whether I was awake or asleep. When I did rouse myself, I could not find one single thing I wanted to think about. Thinking triggered memories of The Guy in my home, and the chair with its sign. Why wake up for that?

A tenterhook is a small, sharp nail used to stretch fabric across a frame. *On tenterhooks* is an old-fashioned term for living in a state of anxiety and apprehension. I found myself feeling like a piece of cloth stretched across a crooked frame, tightly bound by sharp, rusty nails. I was living a life on tenterhooks, twenty-four seven.

After a few days of avoidance sleeping, the mourning dove's *whooo hoo hoo* brought me back to the reality I sought to ignore. I dripped a small cup of coffee and shuffled to the couch. After fidgeting for a while, I found the precise angle for simultaneous coffee intake and reclining. Once settled, I noticed a spider above my head, cheerfully showing off by defying gravity. I coveted the few heavenly sips of coffee, knowing my nervous system could only handle small bits of caffeine, and focused on spider woman, swinging ably in the gentle HVAC wind.

That got me to thinking: What would an animal do in my situation? Aside from the obvious man-made financial complexities, my body had experienced a trauma. How do animals deal with trauma? Life in the wilderness is full of that. I looked at Spartacus and considered his past actions. Whenever he was injured or sick, he slept more.

That resurrected the memory of a story I had read in *Reader's Digest*. Right then, I could smell the pages of the old magazine and see the large print. An everyday house cat, content on his thirty-seventh-story ledge, was enjoying a rare summer breeze in New York City. Perhaps he relaxed too much, or something startled him. We will never know for certain, but somehow his center of gravity moved in the ill-fated direction of out, with a free-fall to the unforgiving sidewalk below. When his horrified owners got down to street level, they found a squished cat, and no signs of blood. Unmoving, the cat wiggled his whiskers and gave them a pleading look.

Distraught, the owners carried the cat back upstairs and laid him on the sofa. A veterinarian came by to poke and prod at the poor guy. Puzzled, the doctor said she could not see anything wrong with the cat. The owners did not see much *right* with the cat, so they decided to leave him on the couch in peace and see what happened.

The cat lay still for six months. I know, I know—there are holes in this story. Did he drink water? Did they feed him? What happened to the food and water post-ingestion? I did not recall those details. What I did remember was this: the cat stayed put for six months. One morning, he stood, stretched, rubbed against his owner's fuzzy bathrobe, and demanded food.

I decided that was what I would do. I would lie down until I was ready to get up. If it worked for the cat, it could work for me. I mean, Forrest Gump ran around America for a year or so until it was time to stop. In the same spirit, I would lie down until it was time to get up. I pledged to recline on my couch until it was time to stop. Relieved to have a solid plan, I went back to sleep.

The First Martini's living room featured a white leather sofa. That couch was so utterly spectacular, she required—no, *deserved*—a name. We called her Marilyn.

Marilyn oozed femininity. She was sleek and curvaceous, soft in all the right places, saucy and firm in other places, unashamedly exotic. I bought her on clearance, when I had first moved to Austin. She ended up in the bargain basement because her right arm flopped, asymmetrical to the other side. I regarded the defect as good fortune, a beauty mark on perfection, at half the price.

For several months after the attack, as families ate, slept, loved, and fought, while church members gathered on pews, while lovers wove magical moments, while researchers doggedly pursued a cure for cancer, while teachers went to school every day, and mothers stayed up nights with sick children, I became a potato on Marilyn.

The phone rang almost every day. I altered the ringtone to vibrate and chose soft chimes for calls I might be willing to take. Numb and insular, I let it ring, ignoring pleas from the outside world to participate. I had enough to talk about with myself. Why speak to anyone else?

My thinking moved in circles as the ground continued to spin clockwise. I repeated questions to myself: What happened? What should I do? Those words woke me up, and they put me to sleep. Waking became the nightmare, while sleep kept me alive.

Other questions pressed against my wish to avoid thinking. Would he come back? Would they catch him? I watched rerun after rerun of my encounter with The Guy. Who was he? Often I thought of *Martini Homes* and the chair with the sign. Vertigo became a familiar state. I floated, swimming for a sense of equilibrium. Even the view through the lens of my eyes was strange, tilted, blurry, and rheumy. Nothing made sense, except for being home with the cats and sleep.

The worst flashes from sleep to fear occurred during the night. I would stir from a deep sleep and within seconds, my mind geared up to high speed. No matter what I tried, I was unable to stop the thoughts. One night I awoke with a jolt and began another review of my situation's complex circumstances. I felt the sensation of landing, with a *thunk*, on the bedrock floor of an old crater. As I looked up from the floor, climbing to the top rim seemed impossible, utterly overwhelming.

I wanted to "hand the keys back to the bank." It was disappointing to know that is not how it works. I knew deep down in my sorry heart that it would be a long, slippery, tedious crawl out of that hole. How would I work? What would I do for income? How could I come back from this? When would I physically be able to work? Would my head hurt for the rest of my life? I needed money. In another way, money seemed to be the least of my problems. There were still no pings or new words about The Guy.

Income meant work. I had to go back to work. Going into a stranger's home was out of the question. Thoughts of entering a room with someone I did not know sent me reeling. Besides, a friend from work had said the estimating business was drying up.

By November 1, less than a month after The Guy entered my home, I stopped making payments on all my credit cards. I paid for my cell phone, health insurance, and the mortgages for the Second and Third Martinis. My remaining checking account funds would buy food. The rentals would have to carry themselves from then on. I had nothing in reserve for an emergency, so if one of the houses needed a repair, I was out of luck. I knew better than to think that was not going to happen eventually. Owning real estate costs money.

I spent days swimming between blurred states and flashes of exquisite clarity. I looked at the world through thousands of separate, rectangular, clear snapshot memories of a hazy experience. My thoughts' range and flow went wild, from irascible, tenacious, second-by-second reruns of the random assault, leading to fear of the future. Sickening worries and ripe emotions filled me. My head hurt from the outside in. Inside my skull, a hidden labyrinth of nasal passages remained in a state of ice cream headache. The pain ran from the top of my head, through my right eye and sinuses, straight down to my front teeth. Bruises on my shins and arms turned banana-yellow with strands of blue-brown and ran in patches up and down my limbs. My back felt twisted, slightly cracked.

I felt lousy and lucky. He could have killed me, raped me, or both. It was strange to hurt that much and feel so fortunate at the same time. I continued to stare at the ceiling. Where is The Guy? Is he going to come back? Is he hurting someone else right now? Why can't they find him? Why did he do this? Will my head stop throbbing? Will I end up out on the street? What am I going to do? How am I going to pay my bills? How long will it be until the bank forecloses on the Martinis?

As I was swiftly learning, brain injuries and trauma are invisible to the eye. Several weeks after the attack, I attended a work meeting. One of the owners looked at me and said, "You don't look that bad to me." Two close work friends were standing by my side, protectors and empaths. When she spoke, they inched in closer to me and stared at the floor. She had no idea how bad her words sounded or felt.

My brain and mind were different, but to everyone else I must have looked the same. My life stopped, and my body was coated in fear. I felt like a different person, one I had not met before. From my new brain's point of view, life was depressing. My shoulders felt loaded down with dread. I could not find a way to stop feeling frightened or alarmed.

My body's unchanged shell housed an entirely new nervous system, alien, touchy, and jumpy. I felt exquisitely sensitive, as though fine, new tissue lay on glass shards. The subtle change in those neurological settings affected my physicality's coarser mechanisms. My hand-eye coordination was different. It felt like someone had converted my operating system. I ended up with Vista instead of XP, and I didn't like the change.

I lay awake, watching busy mental images as my dendrites and neurons fired until they were raw. My inner wiring had a brownout, involuntary shock therapy. One disconcerting aspect of that heightened sensitivity was my enhanced sense of other people. It felt as though I understood more about them than they knew about themselves.

My right eye felt puffy and watery, as though wincing inside the socket. From my vantage point, it felt as if my eyeball moved in closer to my nose, which distorted my point of view looking out from the inside. My head injury was only minor, and it radically changed my life. I could only begin to taste what people with major head injuries must endure. Constant headaches were intense and sickening, intensified by some medications I was taking.

My doctor and I were trying different meds to help with the anxiety and numbing pain. I stopped taking a few prescriptions immediately, because they worsened the headaches. I benefited from my meditation practice. I knew my mind well enough to notice it was going off on a negative track and could rein myself in. I cannot imagine how confusing and disorienting this must be for children, or anyone who suffers head trauma and cannot articulate the changes.

My back felt twisted, off kilter. I wondered if my roll and flight off the bed had relocated a few vertebrae. The initial X-rays did not indicate anything more than a minor twist, but I knew better. I could feel the exact point in the center of my spine, where my spine locked stubbornly in a twist. A bony hook of one vertebra locked tight against another. And a strand of soft, tender tissue, perhaps a nerve or slice of tendon, lay trapped between the intricate bones, like fabric pulled by a tenterhook.

My spine felt tweaked—like a broken zipper, nothing aligned. When I moved, any back stretch pulled the hooked, delicate tissue tight, and immediately my mind flashed to The Guy.

CHAPTER SIXTEEN

A FEW YEARS PRIOR, I HAD GIVEN UP THE QUESTION "WHY?" FOR Lent. I am not a practicing member of the Catholic Church; however I like the idea of giving something up for a predetermined amount of time. When I was deciding what to renounce, I asked myself, "What are some of the least constructive things you do?" I don't drink much, and sugar is not my thing, so giving up a food or beverage would not serve much purpose—with the exception of ice cream. That's a sacrifice I am not willing to make. Let us be clear on that.

I decided that wasting time was one of the least constructive things I did. I thought about all of the hours, days, probably years, I had dedicated to asking "Why?" with no visible or viable return on the investment. So I gave up "Why?" for Lent, and after Lent, I never turned back. I have observed loved ones, strangers, and acquaintances wading through tunnels of tragedy, asking why. Why me? Why did this happen? In my own life, I had dedicated years of evenings wondering why so-and-so had said that, or why I hadn't gotten the contract, or why I had chosen to live in a place where the weather behaved miserably.

The more I examined the Lent challenge; I had to admit I found no satisfying answers to "Why?" I began to see "Why?" as a way to invite emotional torture into my home for a cup of tea. I gave up the futility of "Why?" and replaced it with "What?" I find "What?" to be a stunning query. It has pith, teeth to it, and forces my pulse on reality. To answer "What?" I leave aside conjecture and look at the facts. Once I face the facts, a bit of "Why?" is useful to discover the root of the problem, but for me, "What?" needs to come before "Why?"

The facts were grim from my new, lopsided, self-conscious point of view. I hated asking "What?" because that triggered the twenty-four-hour movie of The Guy's face and what happened, frame by frame, repeating endlessly. I began to understand that was the result of trauma and its devious, repetitive ways. No matter how strong the effort, I could not turn off the movie. I liken this state of mind to listening to a Good Humor ice cream truck playing the worst ice cream truck music ever, driving up and down your street all day and all night. That is how irritating it feels to experience the aftermath of trauma.

Days when I was on Marilyn, dozing, not sleeping, I found glimpses of solace. I stared at the ceiling for hours on end. Over the years I have learned that something wonderful usually happens when I allow visits with quiet. On Marilyn, I could tell that the longer I stayed still, silence soothed and slowed every second. As my body and mind found consonance, the visual world inside Alta Vista intensified.

I lost myself in the spectacle of dancing light brushing across the oak floors. Each window offered its own patch of illumination, ever changing. At once brilliant, then instantly fading into the mottled shadows of fluttering leaves. My Austrian leaded crystals hung from clear fishing line where they swayed lazily in a row of small, square windows. The crystals magnetized direct light, which blasted astonishing prisms against the chalky ceiling and Navajo-white walls. I fixated on the crystals' exquisite, moving chunks of rainbow. The rainbows ran scattered, random pathways, changing in tune to the sun's position.

As I bonded with Marilyn, I watched gradual, glacial strings of moments. Moment, random moment, after moment, all lined up like DNA strands. Some days I succeeded in easing my heart rate. At those times, I could begin to look at things philosophically. When life circumstances are going well, humans have a tendency to take credit for this, and when things are not going so well, we tend to blame others or ourselves. I decided that was counterproductive thinking that reeked of self-absorption.

I contemplated the options for shifting my view. It occurred to me then that maybe life is simply moment after moment. Many minutes string together, forming a smooth symphony, and the music is unaffected by my personal efforts to get what I want. Before then, I had spent much of my life pursuing tomorrow's goals rather than living moment after moment. Now life moved like an old turtle. Nothing was happening; I was simply lying there. In that slow, nothing-happening afternoon, I saw that my mind was the only thing moving.

Life on Marilyn felt marginally protected. My stressed and overwrought mind had a greater range—I began to appreciate beauty. As my uncharted mind wound in relentless, speedy circles, a new chunk of rainbow would seize my attention, bringing me back to the phenomenal world. Other times, I would experience wonder, exclaiming to myself, "I actually got away from him! I escaped! I lived! I am the Bionic Woman!"

I was still amazed that I managed to get away from The Guy. In hindsight, I attribute my escape to the years I spent skiing. I was physically strong and fast—but more importantly, competing with men did not intimidate me. I suspect that is a huge benefit of coed sports. Men are not the strongest and fastest all of the time, even though most assume they are.

In the myriad napping/waking hours, I reviewed the empty bank account dilemma. Unemployment insurance was not an option. As an independent contractor, I did not qualify. I felt paralyzed and awed at the quick turn of events. I filled out some paperwork with the Victims' Compensation Program, hoping for some financial support through the rocky transition. As it turned out, I never qualified for help. My employer was not obligated to disclose my income because I worked as an independent. That was the excuse the agency used. In stronger times, I would have fought the decision. For then, I was too overwhelmed to take on another battle.

Weeks earlier, I had readied myself to convert the Second Martini's garage into a bare-bones apartment. The one-room studio would provide me with a place to live when the First Martini sold, or when the bank took it back. I had a collection of bits and pieces, leftovers from past building projects. Between four French doors, a large utility sink, light fixtures, and a few walls, I could piece together a rustic living space. The garage apartment was no longer a possibility. I needed to bag the original plan and come up with something else. That required thinking, just what I wanted to avoid.

I lay with an ice pack on my head, watching dust motes shuffle and dance in long, even strips of daylight. Rainbows from the crystals bounced from the floor to ceiling and along the walls, as my cell phone vibrated incessantly, mostly with calls from creditors. I still cringe at the sound of a vibrating phone. I felt lousy and underhanded, dishonest. For the first time ever, I could not pay my bills. Moreover, I had no idea when that would change. My head throbbed, my heart sank and pounded, while my back creaked and howled. The phone buzzed, insistent.

Don, Sue, Christie, Kathi, and BB called me daily. Camille from the police department phoned regularly. Her calls consoled me. She was a pro and knew how to relate to my state of mind. She often reminded me to take this one breath at a time. Camille made some calls and helped me schedule time to meet a counselor.

The day of my first appointment, I rose from Marilyn, reluctant yet determined to go. While gathering my purse and keys, I paused to visually devour the darting movement of a burst of colored light from a window crystal swaying across the room.

It would be dark when I got home; the flying rainbows would drift into the ethers. I didn't want to go anywhere. Leaving the house seemed like a tremendous chore. I strained to push through the resistance, promising myself I would return soon to my lifelines: Marilyn, the hot water bottle, Pierre, Spartacus, and locked doors.

While driving to the appointment, I marveled at the outside world's vigorous pulse. A few weeks earlier, my world stopped for a few seconds, then started spinning. Everywhere I looked, other people seemed to be moving on in regular patterns. Everyone in the world appeared to be moving on, except for me. I wanted to turn back and drive home. A lump in my throat signaled a problem. Home, the place that used to be my sanctuary, suddenly frightened me. I knew therapy would require more concentration and effort than I thought I had in me; I needed help.

CHAPTER SEVENTEEN

I KNOCKED ON THE COUNSELOR'S OFFICE DOOR, AND AS IT OPENED, I noticed a bank of large windows behind her. She stepped forward to greet me, and I think we shook hands. Her name was Stacey. We settled into chairs across from each other before I met her eyes. I tend to do that when I am nervous. The office was on the second floor, so the full-size window to my right faced straight into the fat belly and strong limbs of a live oak tree.

It did not take long for me to feel comfortable in Stacey's presence. Camille had shared enough with her that she knew the essentials of my situation. That saved me from having to rehash the details. We talked more about how to face the aftermath.

Stacey explained to me that many people who experience events such as mine struggle with PTSD, an acronym for post-traumatic stress disorder. I'd heard the term many times, with only a vague understanding of what PTSD meant. It was something *other* people struggled with. My life moved on after theirs had stopped.

I noticed a black clock with red digital numbers, also to my right. I watched the minutes turn, ready to get out of there. It had nothing to do with Stacey or the purpose of the visit. I felt worn out after fifteen minutes of talking.

I pulled myself from the red numbers back to Stacey, who was explaining that everyone has his or her own response to a violent event. It was Stacey's task to help me learn how to manage my response. She said these things do not go away by taking two aspirin and going to bed. Amen.

She went on to say that people with brain injuries and traumas could be compared to a file cabinet that has been knocked over. The cabinet crashes onto its side, and the drawers' pop open, releasing all the folders and files across the floor, under a desk, or out in a hallway. The organization is gone, but the thoughts and memories are all still there, albeit sitting in different places. Some folders end up empty, or one page might stay in the folder, while the following ten pages slip into the wastebasket or in the wrong file.

Post trauma, we go back to that file cabinet, finding only chaos and disorganization. No wonder I felt disoriented. I could not access files and assumed they were lost. It did feel as though my brain were stuffed and cluttered with inaccessible documents I could not find. It was, and continues to be, frustrating, disorienting, and often embarrassing. For instance, I might call my friend Jessica "Rebecca" without realizing the mistake, until I see a puzzled expression on her face. I realize her name is not Rebecca and panic. What is her name? I cannot describe it any other way. I missed my mind, and the way it used to think.

Stacey practices a specific trauma therapy called EMDR. I had friends who worked as therapists and trained in this technique; all spoke of its effectiveness for healing trauma. It was not talk therapy during which we spent the entire time discussing the crime, the gnarly details, or latent problems with my mother. I was relieved to know that. Rehashing was the last thing I wanted to do. I find some forms of talk therapy strange. But let me tell you: EMDR is much, much stranger than that.

Stacey began by explaining the process. EMDR stands for Eye Movement Desensitization and Reprocessing. No wonder they gave it an acronym. Francine Shapiro developed the technique for helping people after a traumatic or distressing event. The event can overwhelm usual cognitive and neurological coping mechanisms. The memory and associated stimuli of the event are inadequately processed—in other words, the file cabinet fell on the floor and dumped the files.

I agreed. My mind's filing system was splattered all over the ground. My functional thought processes hid out in an isolated memory network, far from my conscious mind. The goal of EMDR is to process distressing memories by using specific eye movements to evoke neurological and physiological changes. It sounded odd, but I was willing to try.

During our second appointment, I positioned myself in the same chair, about four feet across from Stacey, who sat on a dark couch. I leaned back in her thick, cushiony chair, the kind you can sink into. Stacey began explaining the first step in the process. I needed to identify a "safe place"—an image or memory that might elicit comfortable feelings and a positive sense of self. I said, "You have got to be kidding."

Stacey continued, explaining that I needed to identify that sense of safety, and use it as an anchor to stay calm in the face of wild emotions and sensory perceptions. I faked the "safe place" for that appointment, so I could try the technique. Safety was a far-fetched idea.

Once I told Stacey I was ready, she asked me to focus single-pointedly on a disturbing image of something about October 11. I described his face, and my stomach tightened. Then came the strange part: Stacey asked me to stop speaking and concentrate on the sensations in my body. She raised her right hand slowly and asked me to move my eyes, following the back-and-forth motion of her hand. I was to move only my eyes side to side, not my head. The first time I did this, I felt like a cartoon character watching a Chinese Ping-Pong match.

We practiced this several times. After a set of eye movements, fifteen to thirty seconds in length, Stacy would ask me to report briefly on what had come up for me—a thought, feeling, physical sensation, image, memory, or a change in any one of the aforementioned. After responding, we would do another set of eye movements, and she would again ask me to describe what was happening in my body.

After each set of these exercises, she would ask me how distressed I felt on a one to ten scale. According to the literature I read, the (alleged) desensitization phase ends when the one to ten scale has reached zero or one. The thought of feeling a zero seemed out of reach.

Week after week, Stacey and I stuck it out together on that rather bizarre path. I had the sensation of following someone I barely knew yet trusted on an unfamiliar trail in a dark forest. Outside of Stacey's office, the majestic live oak wrapped its branches around the span of the window, standing as a protector from heat and fear.

Sitting in the pillowed chair across from Stacey, she would check in with me and see how I was managing and then ask me to go to my "safe place." Her instructions were clear: close your eyes, relax, take time to picture a place that feels safe. I was still unable to get that part right.

The safe place process felt so tree-huggy. As a distraction, I thought of Barbara Walters. Would Stacey ask me what kind of tree I would be? I thought that was funny but held it in. It took multiple sessions for me to buy into the process. I had to ignore my inner critic. An honest attempt required complete buy-in. I had to relax and use my imagination, with a commitment to feeling vulnerable and silly. I needed to suspend all commentary and analysis.

My attention span was weak, so I wanted to skim over the hard spots. Stacey was asking me to go deep, to feel and be authentic. I felt ridiculous and did not want to go that far, so I fidgeted in the smooth, gray chair, negotiating with myself. I made an appeal to my inner adolescent, promising—just get through this safe place thing, and I will buy you a pint of ice cream on the way home.

Each week with Stacey, I made earnest attempts to find the "safe place." My first idea for this mythical place made me cry. I pictured a bright spring day in the mountains above Juneau, skiing with my friends. I saw smiles—cheerful wedges below wraparound glasses, our bodies navigating through dense, smooth, and untracked snow. I missed those friends, and the unequalled escape of powder skiing.

The broken zipper on my back pinched and returned my thoughts to reality. I wondered if I would ever get to ski through untouched snow again. The possibility of a lifelong injury shook me. Stacey said that picture would not work; there was too much emotional attachment. I nodded, my face cradled in a wet wad of Kleenex.

"Could you find another?" she suggested, patiently.

I pulled fresh tissues from the box by my side. Crud, this was hard. I longed for Marilyn.

How was I supposed to feel safe until they caught The Guy? I felt crabby; it required too much effort to be creative. Stacey persisted, although tenderly. Again, I could not find any thought or place that seemed safe. I fought the urge to behave like an impudent child and throw a temper tantrum. "This is stupid!" I wanted to shout.

We agreed to try again the following week. What did it mean to feel safe?

CHAPTER EIGHTEEN

I RETURNED TO MARILYN'S SOFT COMFORT. THE DAY AFTER MY COUN-
seling sessions, I found myself in a fog of exhaustion. As I dozed, I
pondered safety—what it means, what buys safety. Money in a savings
account would make me feel safer, but not truly safe. Who, if anyone,
could provide safety for me? I replayed Stacey's soft encouragement:
"Diana, take baby steps, tiny ones. Try a five-minute walk every day.
That is enough right now."

Spending my days on Marilyn between appointments, the more I
broke things down, the more I noticed that my life appeared to be one
choice after another after another. Then, and for the rest of my time on
Earth, life was nothing more and nothing less than one frame of the
picture after another. I got all philosophical, lecturing myself: either I
could decide to lie there and cry, or I could *jump up and move on* with
zest and enthusiasm.

With zest and enthusiasm, I remained nailed to the couch. Low

November light revealed dust beams leaning away from small square windows. I lingered on Marilyn, the room's quality of light captivating. I had to admit, the randomness of life sure got me this time. It felt as though a cosmic iron skillet bonked me on the head and sent me to the bottom of a volcanic crater. Was all of this the result of random molecules, jumping electrons, God particles, and plain old, crummy luck?

I worried about everything—including coming up with a "safe place" by my next appointment with Stacey. It sounded like a wonderful idea; I *wanted* to feel safe. In reality, my main concern seemed to be about pleasing my therapist. I was afraid to get an *F* in trauma therapy.

A spontaneous giggle erupted from deep inside; it felt good to laugh. Maybe someday I would have a sense of humor again. That was encouraging, my own thinking making me laugh. Self-deprecating humor has always been my favorite. The absurdity of wanting to please my counselor was rich.

I laughed again, thinking if that kept up, I could be my own source of distraction. I sucked air into my diaphragm. Man, that giggle had felt good. At least I cleared up that absurd notion. This was not about getting an *A* in therapy or gaining Stacey's favor. I wanted to heal and get my old mind back. The rest of that was useless thinking.

I lay there long enough to feel the afternoon sun wane. I was learning an important thing. Life is one moment after another, and I am along for the ride, so I might as well make some choices regarding outlook. Everything else appeared to be out of my control. Nothing was actually happening as I lay still on Marilyn, moment after moment. However, in *my mind* it felt as though everything was happening. Life on Marilyn turned out to be all about my thoughts.

That day, I came to what I call "radical acceptance." I was in the middle of my life situation, whether I liked it or not. I might as well learn how to embrace things as they are, because what I saw was what I got. I could at least try to laugh about my circumstances and find a way to experience joy, even if it lasted only a few seconds.

I decided that spending the rest of my life laughing, or having everything go my way, held sparse appeal. I never thought I needed more character, but it was building organically, thanks to the pressure of adversity. I could begin to see the benefits of not getting what we want.

Choosing to embrace calamity and discomfort sure sounded a lot like accepting life on life's terms. Accepting my pain and fear wasn't easy and certainly not much fun. If levity could build balance within hardship, I wanted to try. I was having some off days; however that did not mean laughter should be crossed off the menu.

I perked up at once. The idea prompted me to swing my feet to the floor. Laughing more often seemed like an excellent idea. I decided to practice cracking myself up, intentionally doing small, stupid things every day, anything that might spark some gaiety. I saw the folly in attempting to live by slick "motivational speaker rules" or raising champagne toasts to the end of crying, the extinction of worry, or lack of fear. That would be close to using a Band-Aid to cover a gaping hole after heart surgery. I needed to do this stitch by stitch.

Letting go and deciding that I would "be positive" about this bailiwick seemed illogical, and far too much to expect of myself. However, if I could find a way to sprinkle a few laughs into those days of recovery, the situation might improve. I added an action item to the baby steps rule: walk at least five minutes, and try to laugh at least once a day.

Camille from the police department continued to check in with me frequently, without any new breakthroughs on The Guy. On one call, she reported that investigators detected his cell phone pinging, somewhere in West Texas. The next week, Camille told me law-enforcement agents found his Lincoln Town Car, wiped free of fingerprints, ditched somewhere near Oklahoma City. Camille thought that sounded like someone who did some research and knew what he was doing. Either that or he was a *CSI* junkie.

At my next appointment with Stacey, I told her about the car. I continued to struggle with the safe place thing. The news from Camille unsettled me. I was feeling desperate, as though I would not ever find a way to move through the first step of EMDR. I semi-pleaded with Stacey, "What if I locked him up in a metal box?"

"Maybe," she said, turning her pretty face to watch my nervous, wringing hands. "It's worth a try."

Saturated in self-consciousness, I closed my eyes, willing the inner critic to step aside, determined to find a way to lock The Guy into a metal box. I visualized a bulky, industrial-strength padlock, one that would never allow him to break free. I added a second combination lock, because it made me feel better. There were small windows for air, but I placed them on the opposite side of the metal box, so I could not see them from my fluffy chair. I visualized someone handing him food and water, intentionally noxious provisions—fish-head stew in curdled milk.

This was easy. I relished the thought of locking him up in a big, metal box; it generated a small sense of security. After a few minutes, it was fun. I could make anything happen! I watched him, casual and unaware, as he walked into the box. As soon as he entered, I made the heavy door hinges groan and snap shut behind him. I heard keys rattle against the door with a metallic clink.

It worked. The gray chair felt comforting all of a sudden. A spontaneous sigh rumbled up and out of my lungs. It felt as though he were really in the box. That simple mind trick, creating an image of The Guy locked away, felt great, for a minute. I found a way to contain him, then it was back to finding that place that felt safe. I strained my imagination, finding fault with every idea.

The session with Stacey dragged. I wanted it to end—thirty-five minutes remained on the digital clock. I sank further into the chair and closed my rolling eyes. I hated this and felt my childlike impertinence emerging. Stacey was quiet.

My mind wandered through a composite of memories, as I wondered where I might feel safe, now that The Guy was constrained. For some reason, I flashed on a National Geographic photograph of a statue of an enormous, golden Buddha. His round, bare belly seemed politically incorrect in this millennium, which made him slightly vulnerable. The Buddha's giant, smiling face and giddy, gentle eyes seemed to me a symbol of perfection. In a way, the statue was a symbol of enjoying the perfection of things, exactly as they are, even if you are a bit chubby. I liked the plump, golden Buddha. Maybe if I hung out with him, I would feel safe.

I opened my eyes long enough to see that Stacey was still there, waiting for me to process. She was good at allowing quiet time to work through things. I felt a flush of appreciation for Stacey's tender patience. Closing my eyes, I rested the back of my head against the chair.

Carefully, respectfully, I crawled and pulled myself up and onto the grainy surface of the statue's pedestal. I shimmied over the Buddha's knee, climbing into his large, wide, upturned hand, which rested on top of the other one. As I positioned myself to meditate, the session ended.

I felt better walking out of Stacey's office that day—no *F* in therapy for me!

In the following days at home, as you know, I had plenty of time to practice. Even from a horizontal position on Marilyn, I became used to pretending to sit cross-legged on the great, golden hand.

My baby steps stayed small, then over time they multiplied. Some days my walk lasted ten minutes. Other days, I could barely pull my body up and outside to walk for five minutes, I persevered. I set up a

Scrabble board on the dining room table, playing both sides, not keeping score, looking for ways to exercise my befuddled mind. I studied new words, paging through brittle sheets of my father's dictionary. That helped me feel close to him. I missed my dad, yet felt relieved and grateful he was not alive to see me in such a mess.

In sporadic phases, I made a word play or two, as I waited for the water to boil in the teakettle before I filled the hot-water bottle that my back was addicted to. Long strands of light hit the oak floor as I sat at the round glass table, playing with words. Those were pure fleeting moments of escape from the incessant, nagging question.

In my next appointment with Stacey, we agreed that the safe place issue was resolved, so it was time to talk in depth about the assault and practice EMDR. I told Stacey my doubts about the eye-moving thing. She smiled and agreed the whole eye-movement process sounded wacko. She assured me that it often helps people, so why not see for myself? I had to admit, there were subtle shifts in my thinking, moments when I felt a relative sense of stillness. I settled in across from her for several minutes, until I could see myself gently climbing up and sitting comfortably on the Buddha's steady, gilded hand.

After I nodded my head to acknowledge that I was in the safe place, Stacey asked me to walk back inside the First Martini. She instructed me to recall any aspect of October 11 that came to mind and then describe what I was seeing and hearing, including any noticeable scents or sensations. Suspending belief, I stood at the kitchen sink, turning to face the nudge below my ear. My heart flopped in a giant leap, shocking every nerve. The Guy. I recalled his even stare, his primal stance, and steady, egotistical eyes—the Dominator. I strained to describe the sensations in halted sound bites until Stacey's smooth voice instructed me to stop speaking.

"Okay, now stay with that, and watch my fingers."

Steering my eyes to her raised hand, I concentrated on the ping-pong movement of her fingers, back and forth, a living metronome. After a short while, she set her hands in her lap and asked me to describe what I was experiencing. When I let myself go with this, it turned into a wild ride. I smelled potent cigarette smoke one minute, experienced a headache the next, felt fine a moment later, then shrank with alarm in the next heartbeat.

Stacey explained that people who experience trauma have shifts in their brain. I was not imagining the changes. My files were truly scattered all over the floor. The eye movement slowly helped me reorganize the filing system. Over time, I found it easier to think clearly. The Guy remained in the stainless steel box, while I sat on the Buddha's hand. I felt like a baby bird in a sturdy nest, relearning how to use my mind.

The holidays were approaching; spending them alone would have been self-imposed torture. I scraped together the required airline miles to spend Thanksgiving in upstate New York with extended family. The pre-travel logistics and flight took every ounce of energy I could muster. My back was sore by the time I landed in Syracuse. On the ride to my brother's house, I had to lie in the back of the station wagon, with a blanket and a large dose of Ibuprofen. I fell asleep on the one-hour drive to Don and Sue's house.

Once there, I enjoyed remarkable tranquility and security in my brother's home. Austin, the container of my troubles, seemed remote, as though the town was orbiting thousands of circular rings away from the snowy winter in New York. To Sue and Don's alarm, I slept most of the time. Between naps, I watched heavy snowdrops descend to the cold ground. The snowflakes fell straight down, determined to follow the law of gravity. I remembered a pilot friend in Juneau who wore a round button that read, "Gravity: it's not just a good idea. It's the law." The thought of him made me smile. A visceral surge of love for my friends who made me laugh brought cheer to the dark day. Laughter is potent medicine.

For at least a week of thick clouds and frigid days, I sat in the cool sunroom, where my Dad loved to nap. I wrapped myself in quilts, reading and watching a gang of wild turkeys hobble through thick, wet snow. Their brown bodies worked hard to break track in the blizzard's stores. They looked depressed. I figured they were fine; I was the one with the blues.

Sleep was, and continues to be, the ultimate escape from trauma. Waking still included a bolt of alarm and worry. I despised the nighttime zaps of sweat, the pulse of my banging heart, and nervous, sickening thoughts of The Guy's crazed, self-assured face.

I slept and ate and slept some more. Sue said that Don told her to hold a tissue over my nose to make sure I was still breathing. We laughed, and I understood they did not know what to do with me. We would figure it out. I loved being there, feeling safe and familiar. After joking with Sue, I hid upstairs behind the bathroom door and cried. Foreclosure and bankruptcy sat stewing, waiting, in my future. I was not ready to talk about that, suspecting my family had no idea how dire the circumstances were. I faced too many systemic failures, more than I could digest. There was no comfort in talking about it, and my beastly inner critic roared, "We Martins don't go bankrupt—we pay our bills."

I adore holiday food, but a sensation of black tar pooling in my stomach left me without an appetite. Dread took up residence in my chest. Each night and every morning, Sue and Don turned on the television to hear about the latest heave and buckle of the mercurial stock market. Of course, it concerned them. Don had retired in 2007; Sue was still heavily involved in her real estate business. Bile churned in my belly. Their investments were at great risk, while my business and bank account had died.

Two days before Thanksgiving, I assumed the horizontal pose on their plaid sofa. I missed Marilyn and the kitties. My cell vibrated—an unknown number. I ignored it, as usual, feeling sullen familiarity with the creditors' ongoing autodial systems. It would ring again shortly. A *bink!* signaled a voice mail's arrival. The credit card company's autodial systems did not leave voice mails.

I eyed the Samsung, considering never checking my messages again. Don and Sue were both out running errands. Alone in the house, I privately contemplated "cell-phonicide." Snow poured from a listless sky, the outside world a monotone, gray oil painting. The wild turkeys bobbed in unison through fresh snow. They looked the part of hunched, caped, Charles Dickens characters on a lonesome holiday night. Their lives looked hard. I dialed my voice mail as the turkeys changed direction to head east toward barren brush.

An unfamiliar voice relayed a brief, excited message: "Diana, Officer Black, U.S. Marshals here. We arrested Danny Lott fifteen minutes ago. He is now in custody. Call me."

My hair stood on end.

They had him.

CHAPTER NINETEEN

A SQUIRT OF ADRENALINE EJECTED ME FROM THE COUCH. MY heart bounced as I galloped from the living room to the kitchen and back. I willed Don and Sue to come home, so stunned I couldn't navigate the cell phone. I was breathing fast, yet something felt different. I inhaled from a new sector further down in my lungs.

I wondered how they caught him as I took the first breath of a new chapter. I released a long exhale, realizing I had been holding my breath for six weeks. On the next elongated draw of oxygen, I saw that a large part of me did not think they would ever catch him. I exhaled, feeling the whoosh of a pressure cooker. They caught him. I pounced and pranced around like a puppy until my brother came home.

I heard Don's car crackle up the driveway. Before unzipping his parka or removing his boots, Don took a peak into the kitchen, where I stood. His facial expression personified a question mark. Why was the plaid couch potato behaving like a Mexican jumping bean? My wool socks slid and pulsated up-off-down hard on the wood floors as I repeated, "They caught him! They caught him! They caught him! Oh, wow, they caught him!"

Genetics played their funny dance as our body language mirrored one another. We both threw our fisted hands and elevated arms back, sighing massive bellows of air. We stopped to hug each other. Don pulled off his jacket, and then both of us paced and pounded our fists in the air repeating, "oh wow, oh wow, oh wow, what a relief, what a relief," as though we had practiced this spontaneous duet of victory.

For the next two weeks, we gorged on familiar Thanksgiving comfort and celebrated my nephew's wedding. The days were exciting and festive. I danced like the Energizer Bunny at the wedding. I remember several martinis (I was not driving). My back ached for days after, demanding penance for dancing with my niece all night. It was worth the pain. I could have missed the party, if The Guy had had his way.

When the parties were over, everyone went on with their lives. It was time to return to Austin and my big fat mess. I noticed that I enjoyed calling the First Martini "home" again. It was no longer a waiting room for news on The Guy. He truly was in a metal box.

At the same time, I struggled, feeling bound and trapped in the recession's obscure financial net. Sue's father was a retired banker. When I was in New York, he and I discussed the current economy. Ever practical and intelligent, he shook his head and sighed, saying, "Diana, I just do not see how this could have happened. It is as though it had been orchestrated. It had to be an inside job."

CHAPTER TWENTY

I GRADUALLY LET MY GUARD DOWN IN THE FIRST MARTINI, KNOWING The Guy was in the box. Despite or maybe because of a sense of liberation, I was too revved up to sleep. Incessant, redundant mental pictures repeated in rough, glaring squares. My cells cringed as though the bad ice cream truck music had played nonstop for several days. I could not slow down or defuse my mind.

The economic news became more gruesome. Rampant lying and cheating within our "financial services" industry hit the news. We now know that was right before Bank of America lied to their investors and acquired Merrill Lynch. In 2008, tens of millions of Americans lost their homes and livelihood, while 1% of the population reaped staggering advantages of wealth.

While I wallowed in despair over the economy, more information about The Guy surfaced. Earlier that month, I had received a call from a producer of *America's Most Wanted*. He called to say they were interested in the case and considered doing a reenactment in Austin. I agreed to speak with him again in December. That was a surreal phone call.

In the meantime, *America's Most Wanted* loaded information to their Website with The Guy under the "Wanted" tab. The profile included his by-then familiar driver's license photo and a brief description of the attack. I purposely stayed away from the Website so I asked a few friends to describe it to me.

In the pursuit of pleasure, some people monitor Websites like *America's Most Wanted*. Entertainment of that sort never occurred to me, but I am glad there are people who pay attention to these things. Apparently someone in Dallas recognized The Guy from the Website and called in the tip, and that's how the U.S. Marshals arrested him in Lewisville, Texas.

I take this opportunity to thank the anonymous tipster for doing the right thing.

As I continued to recline on Marilyn, I uncovered new layers of paint on the canvas of The Guy. I had more facts, so there was less to make up; solid information replaced speculation. The Guy was in trouble with the law before he had arrived in Austin. He was facing felony charges in Abilene that November for interstate sale of child pornography.

The Guy needed money to defend his case. He lied to his family, said he was leaving home for a religious pilgrimage. Instead, he drove to Austin, packed heat, duct tape, and zip ties in his pockets, and found me, the solution to all of his problems. How do people come up with this stuff? It serves him right to have picked a woman with no money.

Prior to that bright idea and those child pornography charges, Danny Lott was regarded as a pillar of the Abilene community. He was a devout Christian man who played guitar and sang in the church band. He even served as a youth football coach—all the stuff that gives you the woolies, if you have a moral code and read between the lines.

Acid etched my stomach as I learned more about The Guy's trouble with the law. Child pornography charges. How did he end up coming to my house? Had he followed me? Was it a random thing? Was he checking out open houses to prey on someone who was alone? What if I had not run? What would have played out that day? My mind was stuck in a massive, circular labyrinth of unanswerable questions.

I continued my weekly visits with Stacey. During one appointment, I felt particularly antsy. By then, sitting on the big Buddha's palm felt safe and familiar. That open space encouraged my inner prankster. I wanted to go home and hide. It was too much work to process the tough stuff. I felt bored and disinterested in Stacey's fingers. I wanted a diversion.

My thoughts were worlds away from Stacey. I thought levity might help and decided it would be fun to tickle the Buddha's solid hand, hoping to get a rise. I watched myself laugh, with an open mouth, acting impish and devilish, with a baby's pure delight. It was silly and reminded me of people who attempt to provoke a Buckingham Palace Royal Guard to smile. I was messing with the golden Buddha, and it was fun, even if the statue stood still.

Stacey brought me back to the exercise when she asked me to return to the motion of her fingers. I burst out laughing.

"I feel ridiculous!"

Stacey giggled too, and then directed me back to our exercise.

According to the red digital numbers, we had twenty-five minutes left, and I was ready to go home. I did not want to do the work; I just wanted the positive results. I could see that the strange process helped ease the sting of my anxiety and dread. Therefore, I left the Buddha's unmoving palm alone and focused on Stacey. I needed to pay attention and trust the process.

My one-hour sessions with Stacey routinely left me exhausted. The next morning, after tickling the Buddha's hand, I wandered around the path of worry, feeling disoriented and wretched with headaches and nausea. I wondered how I could feel so worn out when most everything I did was in a horizontal position.

I had a strange sensation that I moved into a new body, as though I received replacement parts, without requesting them. The experience is challenging to explain. I wandered in unknown territory: My inner body felt raw, as though I had undergone a transplant of my nervous system. My mind felt mushy as it wrestled with disorganized files. I forgot names, something I used to be good at, and often lost the details of an earlier conversation. A clear, loud videotape of October 11 still scratched deep grooves within my clenching muscles and nerves. The grooves prevented me from remembering anything except every detail of the encounter.

My days on Marilyn coalesced into a blur of free association, with extended gaps between anxious speculation and worry. The gaps were pleasurable, lacking the frenetic chatter that colored most every phase of my existence.

Following one of these pleasant openings, thoughts drifted to a comment an acupuncturist had made almost eight years earlier. Treating me for back pain, he studied my palm while feeling my pulse. "Huh," he said, which never sounds like a great utterance from a healthcare practitioner.

"Look at this: your lifeline is extensive, but it's broken right here, and then it continues over there. And the new line goes on for a long time. It is about in the middle of your lifeline, almost as though you will jump over something and land in another life."

Ever articulate, I said "huh."

Pause.

"I wonder what that means," I said.

He puzzled further on my palm. "I really don't know."

Remembering the conversation, I studied my right hand in the light one of the square windows provided. Sure enough, there was the leap. To be exact, the two lifelines ran parallel for a while. The first line rose up in the center of my hand to its finish line, as the second one got a running start before passing the first line.

That was exactly how I felt: in the middle of two lives, leaving one and hopping on the caboose of the other. I was moving toward something new and unknown, in a different physical body. It did not matter whether I believed in palm reading or not. The symbolism in those lines felt predictive, as though destiny might be real.

The concepts of fate and destiny were far too heady for me. Instead, I looked at the lines on my hand and decided that I liked the new line. It was lengthy, deep, and as strong as the first one. Maybe there was a good, strong life ahead of me. Life felt overwhelming and heavy; a happy, healthy life seemed an abstruse fantasy. I decided to be patient with this new body and mind, and to treat it with delicacy. If this was my new life, I wanted to be vital and feisty again. It would take time to have another equally strong life; however if I made any other choice, The Guy would win.

CHAPTER TWENTY-ONE

T HE GUY WAS BEHIND BARS SOMEWHERE IN TEXAS, WAITING TO GO
to trial on his pornography charges. Camille and Stacey warned me that
it would be a year or so before my case went to trial. I decided I would
not talk about the trial until one was on the docket. Thinking about
it was enough; discussing it only served to increase my heart rate and
attract unsolicited advice.

I cannot resist another critical conversation about uninvited counsel. I
wish saying, "do not give it" impeded people's urges to offer such guidance.
Unsolicited advice creeps around in many forms: "Why don't you . . .?"
"You should . . ." "Don't you think . . .?" "Why didn't you . . .?"

How freely we humans dispense recommendations regarding things
we know virtually nothing about. In saying "we humans," I am aware
and horrified to reflect on all of the nosy, useless advice I spouted over the
years. Mea culpa. I tried fixing people and things, coming up with the
right platitude or homespun wisdom to make *myself* feel better.

Advice does not help the recipient of those unsolicited pearls of wisdom to feel better. Providing advice allays the anxiety of the one who does the providing. Free advice is often based on a few facts, heavy on conjecture. I have a favorite quote, by John Galsworthy: "The level of idealism grows in direct proportion to one's distance from the problem."

I was positioned to receive a great deal of well-meaning and unwelcome advice. I noticed how quickly the words poured out, so many people righteous and sure about "what I should do." I stewed alone in a difficult and unsavory pot. I didn't know anyone to turn to who had a similar experience.

With this, I learned to count to at least ten before I speak. In other words, take time to confer with the critical thinking department prior to opening my mouth about someone else's problems. I decided to ask myself questions when someone else is upset: Is what I am about to say true? Is it helpful? Am I tempted to say something here to make myself feel better?

I wanted to learn how to be like Stacey. She accepts and acknowledges my pain, rather than attempt to talk me out of it. At that time, I was not in the mood to act all positive and gay. Life sucked right then, and I wanted to be allowed to feel it suck before moving onto a different view. I noticed this made some people uncomfortable, so they coached me to look at things with a positive spin. If you want to be positive, send casseroles, not advice.

I parboiled on this advice thing, grinding it over in my mind. One night when I could not sleep, I reran someone's opinion about my situation. I don't remember the specifics of the conversation, but as soon as I heard the person say, "Have you seen *The Secret*?" I wanted to run for the hills. Why did this get under my craw?

The answer to that question required time to fester. I had zero answers and abundant questions. My fiery irritation was an arbitrary annoyance, nothing that decreased my love for the people who mentioned *The Secret*.

Could I stretch myself enough to feel gratitude for the well-meaning reminder that life will turn out all right?

The advice-givers exposed my easy-to-press buttons, so I tried warming my heart into a state of generosity. After all, people were sincerely trying to help, and I was edgy and grumpy about it. It felt like everyone has wanted to fix me ever since I looked up from the floor to see Jackie and two police officers peering down at me. I felt like a cracked porcelain bird splattered on the floor, in need of repair. Something only requires fixing when it's broken, right?

Even when I feel okay about myself, if someone starts to fix me, I suddenly feel broken, as if I am doing something wrong or need to improve. As I considered this, a rainbow from one of the crystals settled on the kitties, asleep at my feet. I wished I could speak with someone who would listen and ask good questions before "sharing" advice. I thought of Lucy in the *Peanuts* comic strip, sitting alone in her psychiatry booth with a sign advertising Free Advice. For the first time, I grasped the depth of the joke.

Laughing about Lucy's psychiatry booth led me to think about Dr. Phil. When I watched him on television, I thought he gave some decent advice to people *when they asked for it*. I liked it that Dr. Phil gathered facts before spouting off. I seemed to be getting heaps of uninformed, unprofessional advice from people I cared about, and I did not want to hurt them. I was pretty snotty by then, so I knew delivery about my insulted feelings would have been less than silky.

My longing for good advice (not the stuff I was getting), led me along a deeply embarrassing path. I decided that if I wanted more Dr. Phil conversations, as opposed to listening to the Lucys of the world, it was up to me to make that happen. It was close to three in the afternoon, so I rolled onto my right side and clicked the remote to watch Dr. Phil.

I turned the TV off at the end of the program and went back to staring at the ceiling and listened to Spartacus purr. I determined that talking to Dr. Phil would be my ticket to survival; he would be the one to provide common-sense strategies for moving on. Christie was my number one sounding board, but I was wearing her down. That was the last thing I wanted to do, so it felt important to find other sources of support.

The phone vibrated. I bristled, choosing not to answer. I was too intrigued with the Dr. Phil idea. So with crossed arms and furrowed brow, I itemized my motives and intentions. I was not seeking notoriety or a fifteen-minute spot on Dr. Phil's show. Dr. Phil often sends his guests for a full physical and psychological examination at the PNP Center in Dallas. If he sent me there, that would be fantastic, and probably much needed. However, that was not what I was looking for.

I wanted extensive conversations with Dr Phil right there, in *my living room,* while I bonded with Marilyn. I wanted to talk to Dr. Phil as my friend and confidant—hours of deep communication, no magical thinking, no silly advice, no muting through commercials, just straight talk.

Pierre stretched, intentionally batting Spartacus in the eye. I uncrossed my arms, resting them along the sides of my new and thinning body. I transferred my gaze from a cat fight to the evening shade on the ceiling. I always had my doubts about motivational speakers. They manage to get me all pumped up. Set goals! Go for the dream! Be the cause for what you want in life! Work smarter, not harder!

And then it all loses its charm. The seminars' effects were often lost on me in a couple of weeks. Right then, I resented that self-help approach. I noticed the tone of my inner voice, so prickly and defensive, sarcastic. A squeaky bird-voice thought peeped in—okay, you don't want schmaltzy, I get that. The question remains: How can you get the help you want?

I clearly needed to talk to Dr. Phil. I could come up with no other solution. I used the base of my thumb to scratch the stitches on my head, itching as though a thousand ants crawled on my scalp. I stopped scratching and moved to rest my head atop the back of Marilyn, where I could see out the back window. A whole world existed on the other side of that glass. That side was vague, disorienting, and far too big for me. I lived on a white couch, in my mind calculating, scheming, figuring out, and literally scratching my head. In a way, I did not actually live in the world; I lived in my imagination.

A late-afternoon rainbow shot across the painted kitchen cabinets. I backed up to the words . . . lived in my imagination . . . and remembered how much better I felt after pretending to lock The Guy up in a metal box. Why couldn't I do the same thing, pretend to talk with Dr. Phil?

I decided to pretend to talk with Dr. Phil. I knew it was nuts. If anyone found out, he or she would—or should—shove me into a straitjacket. Maybe that was what it meant to be delusional, as in popping a rivet or living with an unsound mind. I was losing it. Would I ever feel sane or safe again?

I resolved to do whatever it took to regain or reinvent myself. I prepared to speak with Dr. Phil.

CHAPTER TWENTY-TWO

I SLEPT THROUGH THE NIGHT, FEELING A SENSE OF PLEASURE ABOUT my decision. The next day, after a walk and some Scrabble, I melted back onto Marilyn. I closed my eyes and decided to have fun, as though readying for an adventure. I strained to concentrate and keep my mind from wandering. I remained still for a long time, determined to visualize a conversation with Dr. Phil. Finally, it began with a loud knock on the front door.

Folksy and gracious, Dr. Phil and Robin McGraw sat in my cheerful living room, which was miraculously clean. Hey, why not?—this was my story. I wanted to relax. Dr. Phil's mass was bulkier than it looked on TV. He squeezed into one of the leather chairs I had bought on Craigslist. It was a cramped situation, but he was polite about it. Dr. Phil deferred to Robin for the pleasantries. She radiated, like on TV, and I could tell she does adore the mountainous Dr. Phil. Robin fit perfectly in the matching charcoal-gray Craigslist chair. It was more her size.

A young Latino butler, who looked like Mario Lopez's twin, served each of us lemon water and then exited soundlessly, stage right. It was perfect. I was getting into this.

Dr. Phil crossed his legs and steepled his hands against his chin. He scrutinized my face. A kind heart projected through his eyes as he spoke.

"Well, you sure got your hair caught in the wagon wheel, didn't you?"

I nodded as tears rushed to my eyes. He reached over with a fresh handkerchief so I could dab at my dripping mascara. The gesture made me feel special. We spoke for hours. I was freed from looking for red numbers on a clock saying our time was up. He asked me relevant, pragmatic questions, with professional skill. He acknowledged my loss, grief, and fear. He did not tell me to buck up because there were people in the world much worse off.

Dr. Phil said it was not my fault "some nutcase decided to sweet-talk his handgun into my life and whack me over the head with it." He had a point. The Guy's choices were not my responsibility. I was involved in this mess, but it was not all my making.

Dr. Phil stuck with nuts-and-bolts questions, guiding me along a logical path, leading me through things I could not see. He held the flashlight while I shuffled along, bumping into rocky places, straining to hear his plain-speak insight. He gave me homework, asking me to examine my particular tipping point. What pivotal decision might guide me toward overcoming the challenges? Or the other way around, what decisions might lead to my demise?

The Mario Lopez lookalike ushered Phil and Robin out the front door. Spartacus stretched and used his "I want to go outside" voice. I asked the butler to let the cat out too. Spartacus remained in the living room, so I drifted back to domestic reality, in which I was the cat's butler. Extracting myself from the sofa, I considered Dr. Phil's questions. Was it possible to determine one point of no return? Could I identify one deciding force that propelled me to the point of living on a couch that had a name and pretending to talk with a TV personality?

I needed a few days to think about all of that before scheduling my next appointment with Dr. Phil. Outside, the ground rustled with dry leaves drifting in a waterfall of soft sound. The chocolate-brown leaves remaining on trees fluttered, dancing in shadows and light inside the living room. I stared at the white ceiling, spellbound by the playful light, and looked for hints based on past decisions or actions. Could I pinpoint one fundamental juncture, a single fleeting decision that rested on my shoulders? All of this had to do with my thoughts and actions. What part did I play?

I ruminated on this for a week before identifying the root of the matter. The pivotal point teetered on the day I became a business owner and started *Martini Homes*. If I had not become an entrepreneur, I would not have been an available target for The Guy or the banks. The desire to realize my professional and artistic dreams, and the subsequent largest investment of my life, became my demise. What I thought was the best life decision I could make resulted in an empty bank account, life on Marilyn with Dr. Phil, and a splitting headache.

When I started *Martini Homes*, I jumped into my dream like a wild gangbuster. I invested every ounce of my time, money, and talent, as every business owner must do. You have to dive in and go all the way. There is no halfway point, unless you have Paris Hilton's bank account. I did not say every *successful* entrepreneur jumps in all the way, because every failing business owner does the same thing.

I took that chance, and I had to live with the consequences. When I opened *Martini Homes*, I speculated that I might get X, A, or B, but definitely not Y. And I had gotten Y. When I made that fateful decision to open *Martini Homes*, my examination of the market and calculated potential growth was based on incomplete and fraudulent data. I thought the U.S. economy was healthy, and I believed Alan Greenspan's treatise on capitalism. He said it made sense to build capitalism on the assumption of social integrity, while the financial services industry thrived in a growing soil of deceit and greed.

The recession hit, and The Guy entered the equation. I began *Martini Homes* in the house where The Guy changed everything. I put myself at risk hundreds of times when I met with strangers in homes. I decided it was time to stop doing that. One thing was clear: *Martini Homes* was no longer a dream come true. The business was unsustainable and unsafe.

I stewed in the juice of sorrow and a rotten sense of failure. It did not take long to see this was taking me down the unappealing road called "feeling sorry for myself." I thought about what I learned on the couch, about life being one picture frame after another. I reframed my thinking to an almost scientific, data-driven study of each moment, examining each separate picture frame of life. I focused on each moment, broken down into separate split seconds of existence, frame by frame, moving forward. Each frame was actually a snapshot of the present moment. And I'll be darned. Despite my emotions, in every snapshot, everything appeared to be fine.

It occurred to me that if I could train myself to view life in this way, frame by frame, as if taking a still photograph every second of my life, I could live in the present moment. *Thinking* about moments is what got me into trouble and a stinky state of gloom.

I became fascinated with each moment. I noticed that when I paid close attention to the color, quality, tone, and smell of the air around me, or when I paused to feel the friendliness of sun on my skin, I was in the present moment. How many moments string together in bondage to construct a lifetime? How many moments could I learn to notice that everything was actually okay?

Details around me sharpened into focus. Months after The Guy incident, I continued to find tiny dots of my dried blood on the otherwise soothing Navajo-white walls. The specks jumped out at unexpected moments, waving multiple arms. I would wipe the wall clean and find more dots on the floor. Other times I ignored the precise, round spots; they offered too much room for drama.

I had no desire for more drama. There was plenty right there. I remembered Dr. Phil encouraging me to think about Act Two of my life. I had managed to live through Act One, so how did I want to continue living? What would I choose to cultivate and what would I choose to avoid? I had a blank slate. Not much remained of my "past life." This was an opportunity.

I remembered how Dr. Phil leaned forward in that tight chair and slapped the back of his right hand into his upturned left palm for emphasis.

"Look, Diana, life is either a *yes* or *no* scenario, not a whining *I don't know* scenario. Start by telling yourself that if anything is not a wholehearted *yes*, it is a definite *no*."

CHAPTER TWENTY-THREE

I STAYED FAITHFUL TO MARILYN, IN HONOR OF THE NYC CAT I READ about in *Reader's Digest*. The room dozed with me, containing low, sheer shafts of cosmic dust and angel light. I began asking myself questions. How could everything feel so bad, when this moment is so utterly beautiful?

I suspect I naturally fit the profile of a hermit. At that point, the circumstances pressed those tendencies into a full-time practice. I had become a full-fledged recluse and wanted to stay that way. I needed to step away from society to recalibrate. For some odd reason I thought of my friends who are Mormon. They would never choose to spend this much time in pain and alone. Green Jell-O salads aside, the Mormons I know are loving, sincere, and of the group mentality. Being with family and community is their greatest value. I respect that and honor those beliefs.

However, I would be sending church members away with damaged feelings if that level of socializing was expected of me. I watched a documentary on public TV where they interviewed a man who described himself as a fringe monkey. He said fringe monkeys are loners, hanging out on the edges, the first to warn society if danger is on its way. They live near the outer rim of society. I am a fringe monkey.

Marilyn coddled and supported me. Spartacus and Pierre kneaded, soothed, purred, and peered directly into my eyes. I imagined them wondering if I was going to lie there forever. It was a good gig for them to have me around as their first responder and heat source. I had some new material to digest. The banks acted quickly in those days. I missed two mortgage payments on the First Martini, and the bank began a foreclosure process. Soon after, the same thing happened on the Second Martini.

In December, two months after The Guy's visitation, the renters in the Second Martini broke their lease to move back to Chicago. BB bought another St. Joseph statue and listed the Second Martini on the MLS. When the rental income dried up, the mortgage payments had to stop. Dulled by the thought of two sets of foreclosure notices among the unpaid bills stuffed in my east Austin post office box, I rarely picked up the mail. I was exhausted from the creaky wheels of night. I traveled in circles of worry, twenty-four hours a day.

I did not have a man, which seemed to bother some people. Fortunately, the "no man" thing did not trouble me. Some friends and family lamented that "I would never love again." Oh please. I know and love fantastic, honorable, generous men. I was not going to allow a bad seed to change my bonds with the good ones. Everyone wants romance to save the day. That is why Hollywood spices up the movies with something sexy-wexy to keep our attention. I was not up to that, vowing to crawl up and out of that formidable crater on my own. This was not going to be a story about a big, tall, and handsome knight on a white horse coming to the rescue. I would be the administrator of my own recovery, at my own pace, in my own way. This allowed me to be clear about one more item on the agenda. Romantic fantasies would not be my form of salvation.

As the days, weeks, and months passed on Marilyn, I performed mental rewrites of my résumé. I searched for an angle to help me read like something other than a down-and-out, self-employed loser. BB flapped her perfectly manicured nails in the air. "Just tell them you're a cross between Annie Oakley and Betty Crocker. That'll get their attention." Leave it to BB to provide the day's laugh.

Between bouts of mental cover pages, résumés, and a sense of financial panic, I experienced long periods of grace, deep relaxation, and a tinge of bliss. I began to accept the unexpected changes. My brain had changed forever in subtle ways, which I could not articulate. Everything looked and felt different. Pieces of life seemed to break, crumble, and splinter. Yet I was astonished and pleased to be alive.

I was alone with Marilyn and the cats, but I was not alone emotionally. Support poured through unseen, magnetic lines. I knew people far and wide were rooting for me. Close friends and family members called every day, often talking for hours, lamenting or laughing with me. On the phone, I often kicked around strategies with Christie when I felt lost. My breath would be shallow and timid as I faced the task of accepting my new reality. Christie and I spoke every day. She stuck with me through years of confused, troubled conversations.

Christie is one of those skillful people who knows how to listen and how to avoid lending advice or steering all conversations back to her. She is a wise and generous friend. Early on after the attack, a wise friend warned me that losing friends was a likely outcome. He cautioned me against taking on hurt about this. Some people do not know how to deal with tragedy, so they exit stage left. This turned out to be true. Instead of feeling hurt or angry, I was grateful to the people who departed from my ramp. In the same light, I recognized relationships that needed to go.

By then I knew who my allies were. The ones who remained formed my post-and-beam structure, which held me together and encouraged me to find the joke in every day.

My cell rang incessantly between the legal hours of eight a.m. and nine p.m. Each unpaid creditor knocked repetitively on my cell phone door. I watched the black phone vibrate, squirm, and hum as it sat next to Spartacus on the ottoman. Guilt, shame, and sorrow seeped through the phone into my body. Those companies deserved their money, and I could not pay them. I signed contracts for houses I could no longer afford. Debts stacked against me at a furious rate, while I lay there doing nothing. My real estate that was valuable six months earlier now represented debt, not equity.

Kathi called most every day and listened with understanding and empathy. She still lived in Juneau, the place I used to call home. It was Christmas Day, and I was sick with sorrow and blinded by migraines. I had a small, potted pine tree lit with a string of white lights. The dots of each light beamed toward my eyes like sharp, pointed spears. I unplugged the Christmas cheer and turned off the lamps as we talked.

Kathi would soon have hip surgery, to be performed by Dr. Gorgeous, a few days after the New Year. We decided to share our forces of misery, companionship, and resources. I had enough airline miles to get to Juneau and back, and the ability to stand long enough to cook. Kathi walked with crutches, and had the need to eat and enough money to feed both of us. A friend in Austin agreed to housesit the First Martini. Shortly after the holidays, I flew north, to towering snowbanks and Kathi on crutches.

Put two strong, touchy, physically limited, and mentally stressed women in the same house for a month and expect misery. We had our moments; we knew how to navigate through them. Kathi was hell on crutches the first few days, until the pharmaceuticals wore off. I watched her whisk over shiny ice, in and out of the car, zooming around, and thought, "I am not going to be able to keep up with this." Her vigor was miraculous.

Then the drugs evaporated from her system. She slid down the continuum from high to low functioning in one day. She began to experience a great deal of pain. Fighting over the flowered sofa became our main pastime. We laughed, griped, sassed at each other, ate plates of delicious food, regrouped, philosophized, and snarked some more. Kathi and I do share a sardonic edge.

I have known Kathi for about thirty years and continue to be fascinated by her natural tendency to look at everything through dark-colored glasses, while I fall far and hard on the side of the rose-colored lenses. She is all about the severe, macabre details of illness, emotions, and social issues. These details must be processed intensely, to find the absolute darkest, worst-case scenario—and *plan* on that happening. I consult with Kathi before making any decision. I rely on her to come up with stuff that would never cross my imaginative mind. I love that about her. I don't really make my decision based on what she says; however, I always throw her perspective into the mix.

Our friendship is the play between a balloon and a porcupine. I bounce around, enthralled and buoyant over the heavens' changing light, while Kathi leans toward death, dying, illness, and hospice work. Kathi's relationship with the shadow keeps her quills sharp and tough. This works for us because deep down inside, she is an extremely kind and funny porcupine, and deep inside this balloon is one tough babe. The balloon consistently bounces close to the prickly quills, risking the quick ouch of an acupuncture needle, atomic holes in thin, delicate skin. I remain alert as I lean in close, but not *too* close, to my wild, wily friend.

A record snow year resulted in frozen snowbanks looming above Kathi's Subaru. Thick heavy snow then turned into a few more weeks of dark, cold rain and gloomy skies. I do not do well in low, gray weather. Adding depression to the scenario reminded me that wet, dark weather had a lot to do with my deciding to leave Alaska in the first place. For the first time, I said no to skiing while I was in Juneau. My ski friends were astounded and gave me grief in a fun, teasing manner.

In a way, saying no to skiing felt like saying no to life. Carving through powder is, without a doubt, my favorite activity in the entire universe, galaxies ahead of coffee Häagen-Daz and the thing men wished we thought was number one. I wondered if this state of mind would carry me forever, a river of new existence, saying no to doing my favorite things because they were too expensive or painful. Would I regain the strength and drive to ski uncharted, steep slopes? I reminded myself again about life as one snapshot after another, and baby steps. Maybe that is what wise ones mean when they say, "This too shall pass."

My stubborn, relentless streak held strong. I pressed hard against the agonizing day-to-day angst. This too shall pass. This too shall pass. While I was in Alaska, BB took care of the Second Martini and sent my mail to Juneau each week. Those envelopes full of bills and foreclosure notices left me in a pit of despair, so I rarely opened them. I suffered from a neurotic need to "be on top of things," until my life became all about unpaid bills, foreclosure notices on two houses, and tax collection notices, with past-due interest plus a daily penalty. I was drowning in those envelopes.

About two weeks into my stay, BB called to say I had received two offers in one day on the Second Martini. She was breathless with excitement. We turned it in to a bidding war. What an unbelievable shift of grace for me. Before I left Juneau, we were set to close on the Second Martini in early March.

The nine-hundred-square-foot garage behind the house was filled with interior doors, windows, bathroom sinks, French doors, chainsaws, paint cans, flowerpots, furniture, and spider webs, to list the larger items. I prepared myself, knowing it would take a mountain of effort to sort and sell all of that in a month. If clearing that garage out meant a bit of cash and one less foreclosure, it was time to extract myself from Marilyn and get to work.

CHAPTER TWENTY-FOUR

I FLEW BACK TO AUSTIN IN EARLY FEBRUARY 2009, LEAVING JUNEAU with a rested body and a churning, busy mind. It felt wonderful to be home in Texas's balmy air. I would always love Alaska, but the somber weather and effort it took to live there tested all of my strength. I uttered these words as the jet lifted off from Juneau: "Alaska, I love you, but you ask too much of me."

Home again, I puttered through the First Martini, pulling dead leaves from houseplants, taking pleasure in the inviting, muted light. I reflected on my Alaska trip. The contrast in environments left me relieved to live in Austin. I was grateful for the years of my youth up north, but by then, I was flat-out finished with the place.

As I snapped a dry leaf off my spider plant, Spartacus busted a move, throwing Pierre to the hard floor. Both cats screeched for added attention as a startling knock, knock, knock threw all of us into a wide-eyed stare at the front door. The sound of loud thumps on vibrating glass set me on alert, a resonance of The Guy. I turned toward the front door to see a shining gold star within an expanse of brown polyester. It was the constable, grasping a brown, official-looking envelope in his crossed hands.

My body flushed. It felt as though a dying fish flopped in my belly. Was this about The Guy or my financial troubles? I opened the door and greeted the man in the large brown uniform. He asked for me by name and said, "Ma'am, I am sorry—lots of folks in your position. But I gotta give you these papers. The bank is taking your house back. You have thirty days to get out. If you don't leave by March 9, your life's gonna get a whole lot harder."

The final eviction notice for the First Martini had arrived. I fought the urge to make excuses for my situation; he did not need to hear about my personal problems. I was sure he had heard and witnessed enough stories in the span of his career to do without mine. I also knew that no one at the bank wanted to hear about my troubles. I was out of luck if I thought talking about this would change anything. I owed money I could not pay back. The fact that I had no idea where I was going or what I was going to do was of no concern to the bank or the constable.

I assured him that I planned to leave on time, wondering to myself where I would go. He looked tired and kind as he said, "I been doin' too many of these lately. This is a terrible time, ma'am, for lots of folks. Yesterday I had to kick out a family with six kids. They had nowhere to go. I hate doing this. These are rough times."

As I closed the door, panic triggered a harsh case of the jitters. I didn't open the envelope before placing it on top of the Scrabble board and started laps in the circle of worry. I noticed a few more blood spots on the walls. I wanted to throw up and throw myself on the floor like a toddler.

The day was beautiful, sunny and clear, just like Saturday, October 11 had been. My path of worry was routine and worn as my path through life, hidden behind clouds of doubt. I was unsure where to begin. I had no plan, no work, and in thirty days, no home, no money, no clue.

I kept pacing until I realized that was wrong. I did have a plan—actually, two plans. Everything needed to be out of the Second Martini's house and garage by March 1. Nine days later, I had to move out of the First Martini. So my workload doubled. Moreover, at the same time, I had to figure out where to go from there. My siege on Marilyn was truly over. It was time to stand up, stretch, demand food, and move on.

The new scenario forced me to expand from taking only baby steps. On top of the five-minute walk and daily laugh, I set to work on the Second Martini's garage. I took on selling, bartering, and giving away every item related to *Martini Homes*. During breaks, I piled broken branches from pecan trees in the backyard and cleaned the house. In February, while in Juneau, I had received the first foreclosure notices for the Second Martini. However, I refrained from opening the envelopes. With a solid offer, if the Second Martini sold that would cancel the foreclosure; we were running against the clock.

I trudged through the moving chores every day until I was too tired and sore to continue. In the evenings, I still found plenty of time for Marilyn and a continuing generation of mental spam. I created scattered, chaotic lists, real and imaginary, of to-do items. Selling and moving from one house is enough of a challenge. I had two places to clear, business inventory and household furniture to sell, with a major life decision taking place at the same time.

I began to generate some cash by selling business inventory. It was not a lot, but enough to relieve a bit of pressure. A forced change was in the air. The phenomenal world began making decisions for me, and there were plenty more decisions to make.

Since I was unloading the business (ironically once considered the dream come true), I grappled with the eternal question: What would I do next? The proceeds from the Second Martini would be minimal, enough to pay the past-due property taxes, with a small sum of cash left over.

I had not earned a paycheck in four months. I struck out in the social assistance game when it came to actual financial benefits. However, the state paid for medications, physical therapy, and counseling, so I have no complaints. The government is not my daddy. If I stretched every dollar, I had enough food and gas money for one month. The Second Martini would close in three weeks, so I was sure I could make it. I know how not to spend money. It was time to stop paying the premiums on my medical insurance.

One evening, after a full day of sorting through dirty buckets of nails, paint, and miscellaneous tools, I assumed the Marilyn position. It was after dinner and dusky outside. Dr. Phil showed up, unannounced. Robin was shopping down the hill, on South Congress. So Dr. Phil and I, just the two of us, hung out in a relaxed, almost family-style approach. I sprawled, physically tired, yet content, in Marilyn's firm grasp. We caught up on a few pleasantries, and then he asked me if I understood that time was up. I absolutely had to make a decision.

"Yeah, I got that."

I locked my eyes on the ceiling, looking carefully for a possible blood spot.

"Do you have *any* idea how you are going to make a living?" Dr. Phil leaned further forward and tilted his large head, which gave me the impression he had no idea how I was going to make a living. That was disturbing. I thought Dr. Phil had all the answers.

I continued my fascination with the ceiling. After an uncomfortable silence, I lifted my palms, fingers spread, and I rolled my head from side to side.

"I got nothin'."

A fat, lethargic sigh farted out of my mouth. Before this debacle, I was the consummate planner, the logistics person, the one who was making lists and working my plan. I was embarrassed to feel so confused and hopeless.

Dr. Phil got right to the point. "Do you understand that for a very, very, verrrry, long time—as long as a snake's breath stays on the track of a wagon wheel—you will need to work to make up for what you have lost over this past year?"

A late-evening shadow streaked across the ceiling. I considered what a snake's breath might smell like. It was inconceivable to list all of the losses; I did not want to count them. Contemplating snake breath was more enjoyable.

He proceeded, "Who are the people you want to associate yourself with for the rest of your, ummm, ah, most likely lengthy . . . working life?

I wanted to buy some time before responding. A thoughtful answer would require hours on Marilyn. I knew he was onto something important, so I thanked him for stopping by. Sitting in the tight deco chair with his knees together, Dr. Phil appeared confined, almost seat-belted into the economy seat of a small airliner. I wondered if he ate those morbid little packages of airline peanuts as I continued to stare at the ceiling. He did not get up to leave, as I had hoped. He was not finished, and there is no dismissing Dr. Phil.

Tipping his head to the left, he quizzed me.

"What do you have to build on?"

And "What is it you want to do?"

A blast of raw electricity sputtered through my ragged nerves.

"I want to do exactly what I tried and failed to do—run *Martini Homes*, which I am unable to do anymore. It took me decades to decide on a career. I loved it, and now I can't do it; it is not even an option. I feel trapped, beat down, and defeated, okay?" I stayed still, reluctant to move because I wanted the surge of fire to explode. I was bitter, freaked out, angry, confused, bewildered, and boiling-point pissed. I was livid, at The Guy and my financial conundrum.

"I get that," he said, and then the pisser: "How's that working for you?"

"I know," I whined, "But this is such an unexpected reinvention."

My blank slate stayed blank. I could not think of one single thing I wanted to do for the rest of my life. I wished I had died on October 11.

He paused, leaning back into the dwarfed chair. "If you had died, what are the things you might have wished you did more of? What activities, people, or interests do you think you would miss the most?"

Absolutely nothing joyful or remotely interesting came to mind. I felt locked in place, unable to move or come up with anything other than a quart of premium ice cream or a million dollars. Even those images lacked a sense of joy or comfort.

"Do you consider yourself second class? Do you feel like the underdog?

That caught me off guard. It was true. Being unemployed and feeling unemployable was taking its toll on my self-worth. It felt as though the entire economy froze as we all stood still and waited for the other shoe to drop in the uncertain future of our new economy. I did not hold myself up to be first class. That being said, I did not want to feel second class either. He hit the nail on the head; I felt downgraded, limited, stumped, and helpless.

The gray chair released its hold on Dr. Phil as he unfolded exponentially into an imposing yet gentle giant. He pulled an ironed handkerchief out of the inside of his suit jacket and handed it to me. His eyes held mine. I could only imagine what my mascara looked like.

Before turning to go, he warned, "I'm gonna leave you with these questions, and I'll be back in a week. By then you'd best come up with some answers, girl. Because as sure as a toad has bumps, you've got to get off that fancy white couch and put some verbs in your sentences."

CHAPTER TWENTY-FIVE

T HE NEXT DAY, I STOPPED AT THE LIBRARY AND HALF PRICE BOOKS on my way home from the Second Martini. I began an earnest search for a new career. I was in my fifties reading college catalogs; at least I knew well enough to skip *What Color is Your Parachute?* I selected books on "undergraduate options," thinking I might be able to learn a trade or skill to enhance my experience, because Dr. Phil asked me what I could build on.

I carried a profusion of books home and dumped them on the ottoman, relocating Spartacus to less comfortable turf. I sat up straight on Marilyn, eager for information. Time flowed as I absorbed the stack of books over the next four nights. I soaked it in, speed-reading, searching for clues. It seemed too late to attend school for two years to become a dental hygienist, or ten to become a doctor. I wondered how to build on my work experience and education without completely starting over again.

After I finished reading the entire pile of books, I closed the final paperback, pulled out a bath towel, and wept. I slumped on Marilyn and soaked the towel with fountains of shame. The reality of forming a new life filled me with discouragement. Not one page in all of those books held any hope for me. I did not want to do or be anything. I was in second class, easy to feel in a society in which profession defines us. A part of me felt so worthless. I moved through a few minutes of wishing I had died that day, quickly deciding there had to be a better option. That was crazy talk.

Thinking there was one trillionth of a chance in finding a career on Craigslist, I logged on. Five minutes online reminded me that thinking a solution awaited me on Craigslist was more delusional than talking to Dr. Phil. This was serious. I needed to move toward change. What I was doing was not working. I had to make a decision.

Eyes bleary and worn from weeping, I reopened one of the books, entitled *101 Careers*. As I sipped a cup of tea, I shuffled the pages as I would a deck of cards. One word popped out at me on the top right side of the page, so I stopped there: paralegal. I didn't know what a paralegal did, and I never knew anyone who did that. I read the paralegal section in each book and learned that they perform various roles, beyond working in law offices. Corporations and government agencies use paralegals for document preparation and contract work. Nonprofits and businesses use them for general organization and legal review. The more I read, it sounded like something I could learn, and it could fit into a variety of situations.

I remembered Dr Phil's question: What do you have to build on? Maybe I could build a credential like this and open a door to something new.

I had a month to go before it would be time to leave the First Martini. Between phone calls about appliances and every object under the sun that I had for sale, I scoured bookstores, libraries, and Websites to gather information. The paralegal idea sounded interesting; I could specialize in real estate or contract law. Again, I would need training, and most of the programs took two years. I wanted to stay in Austin, however the educational options were poor. If I wanted to attend school, it would require leaving Austin for a while.

I found a program in Houston that was accredited by the American Bar Association. The school offered an eight-month program for people who already had a four-year degree. I called the school and found out that the next program started on March 9, my last day at the First Martini. I got goose bumps.

The next day, I took the three-hour drive to Houston, toured the school, signed up, procured a government student loan, and drove home. I pole-vaulted from having no plan to a multifaceted fast track. I had thirty-two days to close up Two Martinis and move to Houston.

In hindsight, this decision made itself for me. I went along for the ride, feeling unsure and tentative, hanging on tight. I never imagined living in Houston or becoming a paralegal. Neither ever skimmed across my radar. I view it as one of the most sound, life-altering decisions I have ever made. This certainly gives me pause about my own judgment. I should pay less attention to my own desires and more to the organic unfolding of time.

I knew of no Alaskan who thought he or she would ever live in Houston, Texas. That, in itself, was a shock. The sudden decision and swift change of direction involved less analysis, rational problem-solving, logic, and cost analysis than I would use to purchase a car. It just happened. A major life change rolled out on its own. Seeing no alternative, I chose to ride along rather than scrutinize the strange new direction of my life.

While mysterious conditions shoved me east to Houston, I still had to do the grunt work. I had to be the cause, the one to make it happen, and I faced an epic task involving the less cosmic elements of life. I immersed myself in garage sales, the dump, Habitat for Humanity, and thoughts of moving to Houston. I drove back to Houston for one day and found an inexpensive apartment close to school. I used garage-sale cash for the deposit.

Back home the next day, as I took breaks from dissolving *Martini Homes*, I sorted through personal belongings at the First Martini. By American standards, I lived in a small house, yet I owned far too many things. I felt like The Ugly American, spending the afternoons contemplating all of the stuff I retained in my homes. Was it worth all the work and money? Was it worth anything?

I sorted through musty boxes of family photographs, even finding a few juicy (and ancient) love letters. I worried about the Second Martini; the conditions of the sale made me nervous. The closing date continued to move back further because the bank required more and more paperwork from the buyers. BB and I trudged through each delay, becoming more concerned.

I had a bad feeling about the deal's tight corners. I needed the money from the Second Martini to start school on March 9. If the sale did not close, I could not go to school. I had to move somewhere, and I was almost out of cash. BB and I had a circular dilemma on our hands. March 9 approached, and the lender continued to stall on closing the Second Martini. What if I moved to Houston to start school and the sale fell through?

CHAPTER TWENTY-SIX

T HE CHALLENGES REFUSED TO LET UP. I FELL TO THE ILLS THAT flesh is heir to. Fine sediments of stress settled in layers, a tiramisu of human emotion. I remembered a profound saying, origins unknown: Faith is the willingness to move forward in the face of despair. I printed that in block letters on a hot pink sticky note and pressed it to the bathroom mirror.

The Second Martini's buyers continued to reassure us that they wanted the house, but the mortgage company persisted in throwing obstacles their way. As we passed the second closing date, the bank requested a certain document. Once they delivered that paperwork, the lender demanded another piece of information.

The loan's underwriters wanted to see a completed 2008 tax return, even though April 15 was a month and half away. The buyers jumped through hoops to have their CPA finish the tax return early. They were business owners, so it was not a simple 1040 return. Feeling victorious, they submitted copies of the tax return in less than a week. The bank said that would be inadequate; they wanted an original copy. Details like this went on. It was as though the bank was searching for every possible reason to prevent the sale. I knew the signs.

So did BB and the buyers. On Friday, March 5, the sale was still in limbo. I pushed forward to leave for Houston the next day, and I barely had the money to get there. It is interesting to note that the mortgage company offered me one thousand dollars if I vacated the First Martini by five p.m. on March 6. I imagine this expense made their lives much easier, because it was an incentive for the homeowners to get out. I counted on that money to get started in Houston. I still faced the fact that if the Second Martini did not close, attending school was out of the question. The buyers knew this. In good faith, they offered me more money down, so I could get to Houston. Nervously, I kept asking BB: what if the sale doesn't go through, and I spent the money to move to Houston? I wouldn't have the money to return to them. I was not eating; BB could not sleep. The knots pulled tighter. I had to move somewhere in four days, and I paid a deposit on a place in Houston, so I continued to pack.

I rented a sixteen-foot moving truck and hired two movers to arrive at one p.m. on March 5. By three p.m., the moving company called me to say they would be there any minute. By the time they arrived an hour later, it took me five minutes to see that I had more years of experience loading trucks than the sum total of their ages. Immediately, rooster-like, the young boys proclaimed with an air of expertise that everything would not fit in the truck. I assured them it would. They argued. I looked at the clock. We would make everything fit, and we did.

However, we missed the five p.m. deadline. The mortgage company representative came by and reminded me that he could not pay me until the house was empty. I would not get my check for a thousand dollars that day, which threw another wrench in the works. He did stop by the house on the last day, and mailed me a check, but I had counted on that money to get to Houston.

At the last minute, I sold the refrigerator on Craigslist for two hundred dollars; it was the last thing to go. I had gas money to get to Houston. After we packed the truck, I left the cats in the house and drove to BB's office to continue the ongoing conversation with our buyers. They were frantic, and so was I. The foreclosure notices were coming in for the Second Martini, as my school plan seemed to be falling apart.

By nine p.m. we gave up on any hope of news, and I drove home for my final night at the First Martini. I slept on a foam pad, the last piece to go, and remembered my first night there on the same foam pad. I was not sure how to leave and say goodbye to the place I once called home. An odd mix of great good fortune for having time there and numb sadness hovered behind the stone in my chest.

It seems that when a family moves, their home reverts to a house. The space mourned with echoes as I swept up dried lavender, fine Texas soil, and cat hair for the last time. The smell of herbs, dinner parties, and ginger baths remained, enshrouded in the walls, concealed from the next inhabitants. There would be no more lead crystal rainbows against the ceiling, no friendly, square patches of light, no loud refrigerator buzz, no more loads of laundry. Home is where the cat's hairballs land and where the phone rings at seven a.m. with a dear friend on the line. Home is where the coffee grounds splash far past the wastebasket and where chips in the enamel ooze rust in the bathroom sink.

By six a.m. on March 6, we were on the road. The truck felt huge, long, endless, towing the car behind. By then I had sold the old Ford Ranger to a man who eyed it at the metal recycling center and asked me when I was going to sell it to him. Talk about perfect timing.

As I labored to lift the cat's kennels into the cab of the rental truck, they made enough noise to wake the neighbors. Spartacus pooped before I unblocked the rear truck tires or turned the key to start the engine. Big, healthy boy—it proved to be the winner of stink. I wrestled with the kennel door, attempting to clean the poo without letting him out. I managed to complete that task in time to watch Pierre tear off his kennel door hinges. I grabbed and crammed him into the bigger kennel with Spartacus. They snarled and hissed at one another for a minute and then calmed, huddling together, somehow finding reassurance in each other's misery.

Four hours later, I shook out the tension in my hands as I turned the truck off the busy freeway toward our new, quiet city block. I pulled up to the new digs, a funky, fifties kind of apartment complex. Nothing fancy, however it had a certain charm. The best part was the neighborhood, made up of older bungalows and kids riding the streets on bikes. It seemed like a safe place, in relative terms.

As my left foot pressed the pedal to engage the emergency brake, relief poured through my veins. Driving a sixteen-foot moving truck towing a car tested my confidence. I made it in time to meet the Houston movers. I have a tendency to feel sorry for the people who move other people's stuff around, because just dealing with your own stuff is a pain in the butter dish. They carry beds and boxes all day, every day, bless their hearts. It was a hot and humid afternoon. They huffed and groaned moving my stuff up a flight of stairs, complaining the entire time about the rubes from their company who had packed the truck in Austin.

They were helpful souls, though, and led me through traffic in their pickup to the lot where I needed to return the truck. Houston is a big place; I would have been lost without their help. I was happy to back my VW off the truck dolly and wend my way back to the new apartment. It took a few hours to make the bed and unload some kitchen boxes onto the countertop. The cats were more than happy to be out of the kennel; they sniffed and explored every inch of the place.

Once I unpacked the important things and shoved the rest aside, I decided to venture out for a grocery store I remembered seeing earlier. It was dark by then and raining hard. I poked through dark, wet, unfamiliar streets, windshield wipers on high, looking for familiar signs or buildings. I marveled at the hands of fate that threw me down in Houston, Texas, of all places. I would not have come up with that idea on my own.

As I passed under a bridge with railroad tracks that I did not know about, a train thrashed overhead and blew its horn. Whhhaaaannnnkkk! I jumped out of my skin. My heart pumped frantically; my hands trembled for hours. I wanted to turn around and go back to the apartment and Marilyn, even if I was hungry. I was learning the hard way what a raw experience it was to live under continual stress in a tense, hypersensitive body. Reinvention is not an easy thing.

CHAPTER TWENTY-SEVEN

Histoly tells us now that Monday, March 9, 2009, my
first day of school, was also the day the U.S. stock market bottomed out.
Classes ran from eight a.m. to noon, Monday through Thursday. I found
an easy freeway-free route to school on Google Maps. It felt good to have
a place to go, even if I was unsure how it would all play out, and if I could
stay in school.

BB emailed me to confirm the closing of the Second Martini on
Wednesday, March 11. That never happened, so I continued to go to
class and study. By Thursday afternoon, BB and I could barely speak to
each other. This was not from anger, more from a place of mutual wear
and tear. We both knew the deal was about to implode and did not want
to admit that to each other.

On the morning of Friday, March 13, I called her, "I think this is the
end. It's not going to close, is it?"

I counted on BB to look on the bright side. She spoke with caution, knowing I was tetchy and falling toward defeat. "I don't think the bank is going to loan them money."

I figured the same. Hearing it from BB confirmed my worst fears. I would not have the money to go to school, and the bank would soon foreclose on the Second Martini. I knew how bad the first foreclosure made me feel, and now, I was facing a second one. I stood on my apartment balcony, looking down into a shaggy attempt at a community container garden. I leaned my head against the chipped paint of a wrought iron railing. My eyes traveled up to notice a budding tree rising above the roofline of our building across the narrow courtyard. The old, barren tree held hostage a twisted, shredded kite, flopping and puffing, snagged within tight, sharp branches. My first Houston friend appeared to be waving a downcast hello.

Following Stacey's instructions, I set out on a five-minute walk, which turned into a full tour of the new neighborhood. Even if school did not work out, I wanted to stay in the apartment, so I decided I might as well learn the lay of the land. I was in the same position in a different city. I needed to find some sort of work, anything, to keep a roof over my head.

The walk helped me digest the probability that the house would not sell. There was nothing I could do to change the course of events. I knew BB would try to find another buyer for the Second Martini; time was running out. I missed two mortgage payments on the First Martini before the bank began foreclosure. I missed three on the Second Martini. Those were the days when the banks were tanking and scrambling for every dollar possible, evicting owners quickly. Soon the inventory of foreclosed and underwater homes would become so immense that people stayed in their houses for months, even years, before the banks dislodged them.

After the walk, I opened the door to the apartment, and my cell phone rang.

It was BB, panting. Her words sounded muffled, perhaps from moving her head close to and then away from the phone. "Diana, get in your car and drive to Austin, *right now.*" I heard more puffing. "The buyers are driving down from Dallas, *right now.* They said screw the banks and their stupid rules. *They are paying cash for the house.* Today. Diana, get here now!"

I splashed dry food in the cat bowls and a few grains misfired into the water bowl. In disbelief, I swiped a glob of peanut butter on two stiff pieces of Ezekiel bread, grabbed a banana and a big bottle of water, and turned the wheels of my car down the street toward the freeway, on my way to Austin. I pulled into the parking lot at the escrow company at three p.m. The buyers arrived around four, so we sat together and waited for some last-minute paperwork. This was unorthodox. Closings are usually scheduled so that each party goes in to sign at separate times.

I met the buyer, a woman who wanted the house for her sons, who were musicians. They planned to convert the Second Martini's huge garage into a music studio. She was frustrated, to say the least. She and her husband had enough cash to write a check for the entire sum of the house, yet the bank denied them a mortgage. A year prior, the banks had given anyone with a pulse a mortgage. Then they simply stopped loaning any money because they were too big to fail, while the rest of us did.

Both houses were gone; that was that. The fall of my business was over. Now I only had the Third Martini, and my renters covered that mortgage payment. Eventually I hoped to go back and live in the house when I finished school and found work back in Austin. At least I was going to end up owning one of the Martinis, even if the others had to go.

Although I sold the Second Martini at a loss, there was enough equity to pull some cash back out, which provided a bit of breathing room. The relief was astounding. I had money to pay a few months' rent and continue with school. I felt sure I could find a part-time employment in such a large city. I would clean up the mess and eventually recover from the loss of *Martini Homes*. I committed my efforts to the end goal: get through school, find a decent paying job in Austin, and get back on my feet.

I enjoyed school because it forced me to focus. After a dim four months on Marilyn, I had to switch gears and concentrate on longer tasks than a few Scrabble moves. I tackled my studies in a meticulous, painstaking, and determined manner. When I found myself perseverating on The Guy or how I would pay rent, I roped my mind back into homework. It did not matter what I was studying; anything would have helped to refocus my mind, and happily, I enjoyed learning about law. I studied at a narrow glass desk by the apartment's front window where I could see the kite almost hidden behind thickening summer leaves.

Houston's palm trees, mirrored buildings, traffic, humidity, fancy homes, and tree-less suburbs left me feeling like I was in an isolation bubble. I had never lived around so many people before, and I had never been so lonely. I think there is a striking distinction between being alone and feeling lonely. For me, being alone does not mean something is missing; it means no one is around at the time. Feeling lonely implies a loss or lack of something. I knew how to be content alone, yet I was lonely in the midst of eight million people.

The apartment's layout was in a narrow rectangle with two windows, one on each end. The window above the desk opened my view to the kite and the courtyard, while the window in the east-facing bedroom looked out to a massive tree in the backyard. Under morning sun, the cats rolled and tucked into the bottoms of billowing, sheer drapes in the bedroom. The cats were so content, it somehow felt that we would be all right. When I was not at school, I studied all day and read John Grisham novels at night, as I acquainted myself with the voices and stirrings of my neighbors on each side.

I missed Stacey and made an effort to remember her encouraging and simple instructions: keep it slow, be satisfied with baby steps. I held myself to a strict regimen, in bed at ten every night, up at six a.m., eat throughout the day, keep going, and nap if I needed to. The rhythm of school set the metronome, the hours building into the structure and a taste of stability. I began to ease my way in and out of sleep, misty layers of serenity intermixed with dark, rumbling clouds of flashback dreams.

Each day as I walked from the parking lot to school, I limped past a chiropractor's office, wondering if and when I would allow a stranger to wrap his or her arms around me to wrench violently on my spine. The broken zipper still seized a nick of nerve or tendon, holding it in the same pinched twist. There was too much risk of tearing the soft tissue. Besides, I had no health insurance and barely enough money for rent.

Within my strict cocoon of routine, I gathered strength to begin the fruitless search for a part-time job. I bet half of the people in America were looking for crummy part-time employment in 2009. In hindsight, I regret my tenacity in this area. The results proved so disappointing, I should have dedicated those hours toward walking, studying, attempting to meditate, or napping on Marilyn.

Some days I felt a strong urge to feel sorry for myself, so I allowed a few full afternoons of that. In the end, feeling sorry for myself only deepened the shades of darkness to an intolerable degree, so I let it go. It would be nice to say I accomplished this due to my Herculean effort and indomitable strength of human will. In actuality, I did it because not letting go felt so much worse.

When I say the words "letting go," I mean that I let go of some degree of emotional charge, not of the actual problem. I used to think the best solution to a problem was to get rid of it. I could not get away from the current dilemmas; my only choice was to learn how to tone down the emotional charge. So to me, "letting go" means releasing my own strong reaction to something, not the thing itself. That soothing of my reaction was a wonderful idea, not so easy in practice.

Everyone is different. For me, it doesn't work to decide, "Well, poof! I am not going to let this bug me." My gears turn slowly. While living on Marilyn in Austin, I learned a great deal about my mind. I watched myself peel off one strong reaction after another until I felt a glimpse of harmony. That is how I managed to let go—one thin layer at a time. The going was slow.

My relationship with Marilyn continued in Houston, and she did offer economic advantages. It costs nothing to lie still. One day after school and a short walk, I curled up to take a nap. April light danced on the tile floor. A sense of clarity filled the room, similar to some of my blissful moments at the First Martini. I fell into a deep, dreamy sleep, fully relaxed. At times like that, my tense body savored the escape from the frothy sea of thoughts and emotions. As I let go in sleep, I rolled over gently from my side onto my back. As my hips settled, the constricted bones in the broken zipper snapped, with a grind, and suddenly the pieces lined back into place. Liquid bliss surged from my tailbone to the base of my skull. A whole, full breath emerged in a gush of relief. I felt an ebb and flow of healthy fluid filling every fissure and crevasse in my spine. The gush preceded a zing of low-voltage electricity that sizzled up my back.

I stopped moving to savor the rush. When watercolor painting, it is difficult to control the direction and pattern of wet paint. If the artist is lucky, that lack of control results in some of the most delicious swirls of color in the universe. This form of artistic miracle is often referred to as a "happy accident." The untwisting of my spine was one of those happy accidents, when I sub- or unconsciously moved in the right direction to free up the coil and bite in my spine. The experience beat any chemically-induced state of mind I have ever known. I felt whole and structurally sound.

A shred of tissue remained snagged by the zipper, leaving a slight tattered sting of tenderness. Overall, the pinch felt uncomfortable; so the urge to complain decreased. My back felt much closer to the right track. This encouraged me to put the walking shoes on every day, building up time, but taking it slow. Those were short strolls compared to my previous life in the mountains. However, I walked longer and loved it. That was a welcome change.

CHAPTER TWENTY-EIGHT

I N LATE MAY, THREE MONTHS AFTER MY MOVE TO HOUSTON, I decided it was time to declare Chapter Seven. I drove to Austin for my day in bankruptcy court. Forty-five minutes before I arrived at the courthouse, I stopped by the Third Martini to visit with one of the renters. He sadly shook his head as he gave thirty days' notice. He lost his job and could not afford the rent. I felt for him, and it totally altered my plans. Earlier that day, I made the mistake of wondering if things could get any worse.

I met my bankruptcy lawyer in the courthouse foyer, just beyond security. My attorney believed in the lowest common denominator method, lazily pushing me through to the inevitable end of any bankruptcy: a stripped bank account, pitiful credit rating, disgrace, embargoed options, and fear of the future on top of feeling like a schmuck. I shirked my responsibility to pay a few credit card companies for many thousand dollars' worth of building materials. Admitting to bankruptcy felt like the mother of all failures. On the other hand, I was grateful to live in a country where signing the rat's nest over and beginning anew is possible, without jail time, entering a house for paupers, or watching my hand get sliced off at the wrist.

In court, I fidgeted while the bankruptcy judge reviewed my tax return. Officiously turning through pages, he commented with a slight smile that it was the thickest pile of papers he had looked at all day. I now understand he was trying to make a joke. I was not feeling very funny as I stared at the bottom line, the figures impossible to read, turned upside down; but I knew one number by heart: the net operating loss, *my* net operating loss.

Mentally, I tallied up a few more numbers: I had recently paid the basset-hound attorney next to me three thousand dollars. I had paid seven hundred more to my CPA for that fat stack of papers in front of the judge. As I totaled this in my mind, I heard the judge telling me to set up a payment plan with the court. I owed another six thousand dollars to cover various technicalities, too painful and lengthy to explain. My attorney had missed a few details, so I owed more money, when I thought I was getting rid of debt. I walked out of court holding about fifty dollars in cash, with enough gas to get back to Houston. All I can say is, it sure costs a lot of money to go broke.

I put a few quarters in the parking meter and, of course, called Christie. She was at work, so we only spoke for a couple of minutes. When I hung up, I made the unprecedented decision to avoid a visit with or call to BB. I looked at the Jetta's dashboard. It was nine thirty a.m., and I was ready for the day to end. I drove east on Sixth Street and swung a left toward Houston. I felt so low. What I didn't know at the time was that I had joined millions of Americans in the beginning of a social and financial epidemic. We composed the wave of people suddenly forced to figure out how to crash with grace. We learned what peasants have known for centuries: anyone who says, "Money doesn't matter" has money.

Naïve to the ways of bankruptcy, I hoped to hang onto the Third Martini until I graduated at the end of October. I had still not found work in Houston, and now I had lost a renter. I held no cash reserves to cover a missed rent check or routine repairs on the Third Martini. I had six months of school to go. Experience pointed its crooked finger. I could lose the Third Martini at any time. I knew how fast that wheel turned.

I sold my last asset, the car, on Craigslist. A man and his wife flew all the way down from Oklahoma City to buy my diesel Jetta. I owned it outright, so the sale gave me enough cash to finish school. You know things are bad when the best investment you've made in two years' time is a car.

After a month of riding the city bus, I bought an old, hail-battered Honda Accord. I have witnesses to attest: people moved to the outside of parking lots to avoid that car. It had rough karma written all over it. Forty-nine hail dents scattered the Honda's body, forming a galaxy of rusted stars. At least no one was going to steal it.

The time came for me to call BB and enlist her to sell the Third Martini. I had to lower the price and my hopes before we started getting bites. The house was smart, efficient, and beautiful. It took a month or so before BB and I were finally involved in another bidding war. We closed the sale in late August. The house sold at a massive loss. However, I made enough to honor my obligation to the bank and walk away with a minuscule amount of cash. *Martini Homes* was over.

CHAPTER TWENTY-NINE

SCHOOL WAS THE BEST PART OF MY LIFE, AND LIFE IS USUALLY SIMplified when you don't own anything valuable. I tackled assignments enthusiastically and began to sleep better at night. My memory and problem solving improved one nominal step at a time; still, I could focus for longer periods. I enjoyed thinking and dreaming in the language of law, becoming absorbed in the dialect of legal briefs. It felt much like learning a new language. I looked forward to going to class and to my late afternoon study session at a nearby coffee house.

The protracted Houston summer boiled in sticky, ferocious heat, a world away from Alaska. By late September temperatures cooled, so my walks increased in length and regularity. I loved the balmy evenings, with shocking, raw orange-rose sunsets blazing in reflections on the mirrors of Houston's buildings. A breeze filled my walks with sweet moisture and the tickling sounds of palm trees.

By September, the sticky weather subsided, and my walks had become the best part of the day. I walked and studied, using the time to see how many of the elements of the U.S. Constitution I could memorize. My mind was still slow and uncertain, but I continued to work it as though I were training a horse, one lesson and task at a time. I worked for those *A*s. Nothing came easy.

In early October, three weeks before the end of school, I accepted an offer of employment in Houston. The school set me up with an interview at a law firm located in far west Houston, in the realm of box-store/suburban hell. Ironically, my drive to the interview helped land me the job. At the end of a pleasant interview with the hiring attorney, he asked me to send him a writing sample within a few days. He did not care what the sample was about; it could be about anything, and shorter than one page.

The situation was not ideal because it was not in Austin. However, it was real-life experience in the field I wanted and needed to pursue, so I drove home, changed my clothes, and sat at the laptop. I crafted the following piece and hit the send button the next morning.

WRITING SAMPLE

Yesterday on my way over to your office, the air conditioner in my car went out. I sat in direct contact to blasts of suffocating heat while rolling down I-10. Checking the dashboard, cheerful green lights still indicated a successful flow of refrigerated air. Mechanical disappointments are a way of life, not to be taken personally. At that moment, this was feeling personal. Fully dressed in a formal, partially polyester suit, this ride was feeling more like wearing a black garbage bag while sitting in a Finnish sauna.

It would be easy to ask myself rhetorical questions: Why me? Why now? Is this God's idea of a joke? Instead, I focused on pragmatic issues. Is the Dove deodorant doing everything as advertised? Are my Googled directions accurate? My thoughts drifted in a more philosophical direction. To rely on an automobile is to know mechanical malfunctions. "I break down at the most inconvenient times; therefore, I am a car."

My Accord is an ignoble beast, pockmarked from hail, worn down from twelve years on the road, and lacking the slick style of today's models. Nevertheless, it starts, stops, blinks, and passes inspections, so how can I complain or justify an upgrade?

My online research is alarming. Perhaps replacing the compressor will cost more than my property taxes. Maybe it is just time to roll down the windows and let my hair fly wild! I smile, knowing that is the Northerner in me saying silly things. No self-respecting Texan would settle for that. Air conditioning in Houston is a lifestyle, not a luxury.

The attorney called a few hours later and laughed about my writing sample, then quickly offered me a position to "handle dockets for homeowners' associations." That sounded fine to me. Once I knew I had a job, I practically levitated above the ground as I walked my favorite loops. My relief was intense, palpable. The plan had worked. I found a way to build on my skills and found a decent work situation in a scary economy. I could see some of that light reflecting off Houston's mirrored skyscrapers, finally shining back on me. It was the proverbial light at the end of a long, murky tunnel. Or, should I say I *thought* it was the light at the end of the tunnel?

CHAPTER THIRTY

A FTER SEVEN MONTHS AND SIXTEEN DAYS OF SCHOOL, I BEGAN MY new career as a paralegal. It is curious how some memories remain clear in every detail, while others from the same episode are vague. Images of this particular employment opportunity separate themselves in framed boxes like a comic strip in the Sunday paper. The snapshots are clear, yet nothing about them seems real.

I learned an important lesson from my interview at that law firm. Once I see the sophisticated lobby and the artwork in the conference room, I should ask to take a look at my potential office. The first morning I arrived for duty, I walked down a long, fluorescent hallway with about ten open doors. Each doorway exposed a paralegal's back, facing a dark beige wall behind a small computer monitor. These were not cubicles; they were more like closets. Each paralegal hunched over a desk, surrounded by stacks and stacks of bulging file folders.

What I did not know on my first pass down the hallway to my cubicle was that each one of those manila folders on all of those depressing desks contained the documented history of someone who was about to lose his or her home. I was handling the dockets of HOAs, otherwise known as Homeowners' Associations. What had not been discussed was that ninety-five percent of those dockets were involved with people like me. They were about to lose their homes because the HOA was suing them for unpaid fees. I was suddenly in the business of "collections."

On the fourth day, the first pile of folders began to form on my empty desk. My cubicle had a window; however, the third wall of desk furniture covered it. My first independent task involved the preparation and delivery of "demand letters" to homeowners who were going into foreclosure. It was my job to tell them to either pay up or move out.

God certainly does have a sense of humor, which can be quite annoying.

For the first five days, I cried on the way to work, in the Dentbucket during lunch hour, on the way home, and at home in the evenings. They paid me to send the same dreaded white-and-green envelopes I used to pull out of my east Austin post office box. Those envelopes used to fill me with the urge to die. They were the ones I just didn't open.

On Monday morning of the second week, I resigned. Quitting anything feels like defeat to me. Relinquishing the only job I could find over the past year seemed illogical, slightly insane. It was also necessary. I hated myself for sending those letters. I already felt like the old gal beginning a new career; I didn't want to hate myself on top of that. Staring at my image in the bathroom mirror, I noticed new and undeniable lines of sorrow, fear, and exhaustion creasing my face.

We all age. However, I blasted through an accelerated dress rehearsal. After quitting at the law office, everything seemed to wrinkle overnight. An adorable four-year-old girl in our apartment complex ran up to me one day and peered into my face. With force and conviction she proclaimed, "I don't like you! You're old!"

This same young girl used to talk to our gray-haired neighbor named Virginia every day. Virginia was at least twenty years older than I was and bound in a wheelchair. I told Virginia about the young girl's comment and asked if the child ever said that to her. No, that had never come up but that sweet baby girl sure pressed my internal vanity buttons. It didn't matter so much that I was aging. It was starting over after fifty that depressed the tears out of me.

I tuned up my résumé and sniffed out leads for work in Austin and Houston. I used my unplanned free time to continue studying, after deciding to take a national paralegal certification exam in early December. I knew I would never take the test—or pass it—if I put it off. My best shot at passing would be right after school. The idea of picking up books and taking the test in a year or so was fantastical, at best.

November brought rain drizzling from dreary skies. Inside, I existed in a compartmentalized world of résumés and flash cards. I wrote thousands of terms on 3 x 4-inch index cards, listing the six elements of a contract, the fourteen amendments, and Latin terms embedded in the language of legal terminology. I broke up study periods with walks and eating lunch at noon while watching *The Ellen DeGeneres Show*. It was getting close to the holidays, so Ellen was giving all sorts of valuable stuff away. I cried when she did that, not for want of the stuff. I wished I could be the one gifting it all away. The foggy weather and monotonous routine left me feeling blue and unemployed.

It snows in Houston on rare occasions. Local legend says if it ever snows, that only happens in January or February, never, ever in December. The long-awaited paralegal exam arrived the first weekend in December. On test morning, plump, wet snowflakes plunged from the skies and stacked up on the Houston streets. Although confident in my own winter driving skills, I was terrified of Houstonians swerving on the road. The Dentbucket performed fine in the snow; I made it to the testing center safe and on time.

All ten to fifteen of us in the test room whispered to each other about the snow and our tales of travel. One of the women in charge entered the room and announced the decision to reschedule for another day. Crestfallen, we argued in force: Why were they sending us away after we managed to get there? Eventually, the administrators relented and heeded our pleas to let us take the test. A histrionic forecast predicted the possibility of snow throughout the day, so they rescheduled the second test day for the following weekend. In due course, the sun blazed on dry pavement the next day. Nothing felt simple or favorable anymore. I dragged through the week, sending out the rays of hope and delusion called a "résumé," while studying enough to keep the momentum flowing.

I finished the test the next Saturday. Before receiving the test results, I rubber-banded the stacks of flashcards together and packed them in a shoebox, storing it on a high closet shelf. Studying for the test was a satisfying achievement, and I hoped worthwhile. If I passed, I would never have to take that test again, and the flashcards would remain on the top shelf. A letter arrived in the mail three weeks after the test. I passed. The flashcards are still in rubber bands, although I do refer to them from time to time.

In December, I tended to my prized Meyer lemons. The now voluptuous lemons were mere minor-league blossoms when I moved them from Austin to Houston nine months earlier. I had managed to cultivate two Rubenesque, sunny yellow globes of beautiful fruit. For many, there is nothing exotic about growing a lemon or two outside; nonetheless to an Alaskan that was a unique and exciting experiment. By Christmastime, the lovely pair of hefty lemons had ripened on a small tree in our narrow courtyard below my apartment.

I had spent months in joyous anticipation of presenting my prized lemons as a Christmas gift to my family. The homegrown fruit would be a small and loving, personal gift to everyone. I imagined we would drink iced water with fresh lemons at Christmas dinner.

In the courtyard, my neighbors would walk by, gazing appreciatively at my lemons. The plants became a shared pet project for the apartment building, with me doing all the work. I enjoyed the opportunity to meet most of my neighbors, who took an interest in the bright luster and progress of the plump and noble fruits. I was proud of those lemons and couldn't wait to share them with my family.

Several days before the trip north, it got chilly, and the media broadcasted a frost warning in Houston. To protect the lemons from freezing, I moved them to a more protected corner of the courtyard. As soon as I woke up the next morning, I checked the outdoor thermometer; it was above thirty-two degrees Fahrenheit. Pacified by the above-freezing temperature, I got dressed and padded down the stairs in my slippers to check on the lemons.

The lemons were gone. Someone picked my lemons.

My mouth formed a big *O* as I digested the sight of the lovely lemon tree without her golden treasures. I turned and trudged up the stairs to the apartment and commenced a paper towel cry over the phone with Christie. She too had admired the robust lemons during her recent visit in October, apparently forming a bond, because she also cried with outrage and a sense of loss. Later, she and I both tried to explain such high emotions around the fact that someone had stolen my lemons.

People were like, what? You two cried over a pair of lemons? We understood their response, which did nothing to allay our sense of outrage. Of course they did not get it, because *it* was not about the lemons. It was about one more act of unkindness toward humanity. I still think about those sunny yellow orbs and wonder if they ended up as lemonade or smashed in aromatic clumps on a neighbor's porch.

Christmas with family was wonderful; no one else missed the fruit. After the festivities, my brother reviewed my résumé, and we discussed strategies for the new employment paradigm. We were unsure how to navigate the new economy. My throat tightened, and my head ached. As we discussed theory, the stock market continued its blasé performance.

After a rough goodbye at the airport, I sat down in the waiting area to regroup. As my brother Don had walked with me to security, he broke down and cried. My brother is not a sentimental man, and I took his tears to mean that even he was scared about my future. I dried off and began to read a silly novel as I sat near the gate. I realized it felt as though I lived in a permanent waiting room. My phone pinged to notify me of a voice mail message that must have gone through as I navigated through security.

I pecked through the steps to retrieve the message and heard the voice of an attorney in Houston, looking to hire a paralegal. I called him before boarding, and we scheduled an interview for the next morning. Fifteen hours later, I was driving to his office, suited and coiffed, with no need for real A/C in January. I was nervous and excited to be on my way to an interview that would result in a new and much improved situation.

After fifteen months of unemployment, I finally had work. It was not just a job; I was excited about the assignment. I assisted two attorneys who represented clients suffering damage from exposure to toxic materials. I enjoyed both of the people I worked for and the others in the firm. It was a delightful fit, including a relatively easy commute into a beautiful area of the city and interesting, challenging work.

I gushed to my closest family and friends: "I finally made it through that one . . . over a year of unemployment, but it is all good now!" What a rush to finally relay some happy news. I spent hours at my glass desk by the front window, calculating how long it would take to pay off personal debt and save for a Dentbucket upgrade. The calculations did not point to a handy solution. I knew it was going to take a long time to crawl out of my murky financial and medical mess.

A week into the new commute, the Dentbucket refused to move. The transmission was kaput, as they say in places other than Texas. Every mechanic I spoke to said Honda transmissions never go out, except for this one. Desperately trying to maintain a cheerful view based on my new state of employment, I wanted to face the obstacle straight on. I added money to the balance on my bus pass and spent the first paycheck on that obstinate car.

For me, the first month of any new work gig involves unease. At night, I ran through classic nightmares, such as showing up at the office without the benefit of clothing, forgetting how to type, failed alarm clocks, and irrational bosses. The dreams were tense yet manageable compared to lying awake worrying about not having work.

At the office, real-time tension took over as I stared at the copier's nine-hundred-page manual, wishing for a psychic connection to the machine. I think the first month of any new occupation should be all about locating the best bathrooms in the building, knowing where to find extra TP, and learning how to log on to the server. It is also about hoping the phone will not ring because you have yet to master transferring calls. A new job means there are no excuses for failing to follow your boss's unclear and purposely vague instructions. You figure it out.

Christie says it takes her three years to feel comfortable in any new office. I adjust slightly faster, in degrees, and usually a month into the learning process, everything feels at least familiar. I begin to syncopate with the system. Sure enough, the fifth week of work found me at ease, my desk cleaned of old projects, ready to take on the next layer of complexity. The unemployment angst was finally behind me. I emailed my friends. Life is good! I love my job!

The Dentbucket continued to lay dormant in the shop, waiting for parts and sweating mechanics to perfectly align with the stars. On the Monday of week five, I rode to work on the city bus, which smelled like stale popcorn. As the bus paused for a pedestrian, musty, gray fog floated past my smudged-with-who-knows-what window. I reflected on the tightness of urban space, the expensive parking, and people living on top of people. The notion of settling there shocked me. How in the world did I end up in such an unlikely place?

I smiled, thinking that the Gods of Life were playing tricks on me again. I may think I want one thing, but the winds of life often deliver something surprisingly different. I was fine with learning how to adapt to a life in steamy Houston. I had friends and cousins who lived there; it would be easy to make a life in the city. Popcorn smell, questionable auto mechanics—so what? Life felt fantastic. *I had a great job.*

I opened the office at seven thirty with another paralegal assigned to the early shift. We chatted while sliding our lunch bags into the refrigerator. The office kitchen had one of those fancy "make a decision and push one button" coffee machines, so we each made a cup of our choice. I liked her and grew to enjoy our five-minute visits at the start of each day. I walked the hallway in semi-darkness, stopping first to flip on a double light switch before turning toward my office located at the end of the line, in a file room. In the interview I had asked to see my desk and given it a stamp of approval. Although it did not have a window, when I looked straight through the doorway, I faced the office that belonged to an attorney named Milton. We had become friends, and I could see the skyline through a wall-to-wall window in his fancier digs.

Milton and I agreed we were the outliers and took pleasure in our confinement at the end of the large, L-shaped hall. I still smile every time I think of Milton sitting across the hallway with his desk facing mine, finishing each phone call with his exceedingly slow, gracious,

Southern manner of polite goodbyes. Milton did anything with ease. It even took him a long time to hang up the phone. Once the receiver was back on the hook, he often glanced over at me with a smile that absolutely drawled and muttered one word: "nutcase." He would shake his head turtle slow and gently change his gaze to one of the many yellow legal pads on his desk.

That morning, I settled in to sort through papers and prioritize my list of action items. I knew it would be a productive day. Mike, my boss, would be out of the office for most of the week. I had plenty to do and looked forward to crossing off some items on an expanding list. The room was cool and quiet. Milton was not there yet. I stood from my chair to reach for a binder. As I turned back, Mike was standing in front of my desk, instead of in an airport security line.

"Hi! You surprised me. What are you doing here?" I was still not good with unannounced entrances. Mike was large, masculine, and imposing on any day. I noticed he didn't flash a brief smile before his normal, serious look. His face stayed straight on the serious side. He hung his thumbs in the pockets of his super clean, pressed jeans and shifted from foot to foot.

"Yeah, hey."

Just two utterances, and I could detect a tight pitch in his voice.

He continued, "I wanted to come by and talk with you before going to the airport." A banner saying, BOY HOWDY, THIS OUGHTA BE GOOD floated past, a digital sign running from left to right across my inner visual screen. Thumbs still in his pockets, his elbows moved up and out, inflating his already ponderous size.

"I, um, I've been talking to the partners all weekend and, um, I'm afraid I have some bad news. I've been fighting for your position, but they made a firm decision. I have to, you know . . . lay you off."

I have to lay you off. I repeated this in my mind a few times. Wow.

"Today? Like, right now?"

He nodded. "I'm afraid so. They are laying off five paralegals. I will write you a positive letter of reference and email it to you. You have done excellent work so far. I am sorry that I need to ask you to collect your things and leave your keys at the front desk."

I stammered something close to "If you ever need some help, please keep me in mind." He assured me he would, and we both knew he would not. We shook hands, and he turned to go down the quiet hall. Between the buzz of push-button coffee and incoming news, I shivered in a brew of caffeine, adrenalin, and shock.

I knew that familiar feeling: let down. Wow. I sat back into my chair to gain composure and assess the situation. I wanted to find a dignified way of removing myself from the premises, without crying.

A few people came in to say goodbye, including Milton. He was down with the news. On the way to the front desk with my key, I passed three suddenly empty offices. The second attorney I worked for walked me to the elevator. She appeared shaken too, wondering aloud why they hired me a month ago if they were facing layoffs. With ample time to wonder about that later, I shrugged, in a state of disbelief. My index finger pushed the star on the elevator button, as I watched her sweet, sad wave narrow down to nothing, closed off by stainless steel doors.

CHAPTER THIRTY-ONE

I WALKED BACK TO THE BUS STOP FOR THE 9:15 NORTHBOUND. The fog had dissipated, leaving vapor wisps in the tepid air. I noticed the current bus window also dwelled in a state of suspicious smudge. I recalled my state of mind last night, when I was looking forward to tomorrow. Then the tomorrow I was looking forward to was happening right then. It occurred to me that looking forward to anything is a form of illusion and recreation, another way to brush off the present moment.

Right then on the city bus, I wanted the present moment to go away. I could have wiped away the-who-knows-what on the window, but losing a long-awaited paycheck is not the kind of problem you can just *Windex* away. Swaying on my seat in the empty bus, I dialed BB's cell.

"You've got to be kidding," she said, and then without a pause "Your life is more unbelievable than fiction." I had to agree with the unnerving assessment. Everything in my stupid life felt weirder than fiction. BB gave me specific instructions: take a cool shower and apply new makeup—her remedy for all tears. I promised I would, knowing I would not.

The cats each rolled over in lazy stretches and yawned in response to my premature entrance. Sleepy, perhaps even put out by the interruption of their morning nap, they paid no attention to my mood. I dialed Kathi in Juneau. "You've got to be kidding." Without a breath or a pause, she groaned, "You're not kidding."

We spoke briefly as I flailed, at a loss for words. This was familiar territory. Once again, I found myself repeating the question: Did that really happen?

I slumped into Marilyn's soft curves and stared at the ceiling. "Holy cow," as my stepson Chase would say. I pressed the well-worn speed dial for Christie and shared the news. Her response included various descriptions of excrement. "Holy cow" did seem a bit tame; my life felt like a pile of steaming dung.

I proclaimed to Christie that it was an "ice cream and Ativan day," because those were the only two actions I was capable of pulling off. We giggled nervously, knowing how easy it would be to turn to Ativan and ice cream for the rest of my life. The ceiling in Houston was not a Benjamin Moore Standard White, like the Three Martinis. Knowing the property owner, the paint was Bargain Basement White. The dull, flat Bargain Basement White stared back at me.

Did that really happen?

I walked into the kitchen to find an Ativan and cut it in half. It was ten a.m., and I wished that alcohol worked its magic on me. I wanted a drink to feel like I had something to buffer the pain, a sure way to escape the bite. In reality, I knew alcohol would magnify my headache and make things even worse. I recognized the truth of Pema Chödrön's book, *The Wisdom of No Escape*. There is no escape.

I felt tired, short of breath, constricted, on the verge of hyperventilation. Rent was due in three weeks. I heard myself ask again, "Did that really happen?" As if to answer, my cell phone vibrated, shuffling on the coffee table. I answered without checking caller ID, assuming it was Kathi or Christie calling me back.

Liza, from the DA's office in Austin, was on the line. Marilyn stood still as my stomach flipped inside out. My jaw dropped back into the capital *O* formation. She spoke kindly:

"Danny Lott is here in Travis County. We are preparing to go to trial. Do you still plan to press charges?"

I nodded, which I knew did not make sense. She continued, "It looks as though he is not going to plead guilty. Mary, the prosecutor, is preparing to go to trial. Mr. Lott received a nine-year federal sentence for the child pornography charges. You know about that . . . right? Now he is here in Austin on federal extradition. We are looking at a trial date of April 26, about two and a half months from now."

February 8 was turning out to be quite a day. I spooned coffee Häagen-Daz directly out of the container. My father would have admonished me, so it felt as though I was getting away with something fun for a second or two. Lethargy followed in step behind the illicit ice cream. I called Stacey in Austin. We agreed to meet the following week. I repeated my joke about ice cream and Ativan. She did not think it was funny at all. "Are you having suicidal thoughts? Do you feel safe in your own hands?"

"I am not worried about ending my life," I said, truthfully. "I am going to be fine," I lied. It was not exactly a lie. I felt horrendous, yet I did not worry about my will to live. I was not going to hurt myself over The Guy and a bummer employment setback. I felt shaken, low, apprehensive, suspended in space, but I was not suicidal. Wishing I had died was different than killing myself.

For the next two weeks I lived in a directionless fog, too aimless to think about anything other than the trial. I joked that I was waiting for The Goddess of Inspiration to walk into the living room. I yearned for a visit from Dr. Phil, but he was a no-show. I spent most of my days trying to find the safe place, which generally turned out to be Marilyn.

The school I had attended held graduation ceremonies twice a year. Commencement fell on February 22, two weeks after that lonely walk back to the bus stop on Monday morning. The school has a tricky "attend graduation or you don't get a certificate" rule. Eating an old hairbrush sounded better than going to graduation. When I was puffed up about going to work everyday, the notion of going to graduation without friends or family attending was of no concern. In January, I actually encouraged Don and Sue to skip the graduation and opt for a Hawaiian vacation instead. It was an honest response at the time; however, as graduation neared, I wished they were coming down to Houston. Going to the ceremony alone and facing the trial instilled an unbearable melancholy in my bones.

CHAPTER THIRTY-TWO

WHILE I STARED AT THE CEILING AND LISTENED TO HEAVY METAL music pounding through the next-door neighbor's walls, my friend Russell traveled from Alaska to Philadelphia for a visit with his parents. He called me soon after his arrival; we shared our usual hour-long talk. Russell is one of my best friends. We are both single and make terrific friends, and we would be a natural disaster as a couple.

Our minds use diametrically opposite operating systems. I am a slow IBM, while he moves along with the elegance of an iPad. Russell's logical, empirical point of view is a constant source of amusement, but if he were my boyfriend (or worse yet, husband) his Mac mind would exasperate my every nerve. I find him hilarious, engaging, bright, generous, caring, intelligent—and insufferable. I suspect he would use similar praiseworthy words to describe me, replacing "insufferable" with "effete."

I was in a dreary, hopeless mood throughout our conversation. Russell committed the classic mistake of asking if there was anything he could do to help. I pounced and whined, maybe even groveled. Sweet

Russell cashed in a bunch of Alaska Airline miles and flew to Houston for the graduation ceremony. He cheerfully attended the event, treated me to restaurant food, and endured my shadow side.

I was a deadbeat. Russell patiently dragged me around town, acting as the good-natured tour guide for the most pathetic hostess in Houston. I tried not to be an Eeyore, yet admitted to the role in defeat. Always courageous and independent, Russell set off alone on walks each day, so I could have a few hours alone with Marilyn to fester in unemployed gloom.

The day after graduation was a relief. I had one less thing from which to recoil. The Dentbucket moved up to "possible operating" status after a hefty payment to the mechanic. We embarked on a drive south to Galveston.

On the drive down, I was relieved of graduation trepidation, yet it was hard to face the fact that all my friends from school were going to work every day and I was already on my third try. It felt as though I were walking through peanut butter, expending tremendous energy to move a few feet ahead.

Far from feeling happy and proud about the graduation, I was traumatized, shaken, defensive, angry, and hopeless. It was not fun being me. Thirty miles south of Houston I burst into big tears. I would rate it as one of my paper towel cries. This is why we make terrific friends—Russell is unshakably endearing and gentle with me. He is better than any man I know about enduring my brand of sniveling. As I cried, I glanced over to see his face bearing my sadness. Long, tremulous bouts of grief shook my body. And I was driving. In retrospect, a sobbing me barreling down Highway 45 in a rainstorm at seventy miles per hour in the Dentbucket was not even close to a sound idea.

Russell suggested, diplomatically, "Perhaps we could pull over and have a hug?

"No, I don't need to stop. I'm *fine.*"

Russell was ensnared in the painful position of being "the logical one," the voice of reason, the one who understood the need for the car and my madness to stop. I sailed beyond the smooth seas of reason, spurting monumental blasts of salty tears, while accelerating the Dentbucket over a slick concrete slab.

Knowing Russell as I do, I suspect his thinking went something like this:

1) He wondered why road crews used concrete slabs rather than asphalt on the highways in Texas, and 1a) if all southern states followed this practice.

2) He wondered if there were appropriate words to use with a wretch like me who was oblivious to the urgent need to stop the speeding car and get a grip on more than the steering wheel.

3) He gave up wondering and acknowledged that an unhinged mind WAS in control of the swiftly moving vehicle. Russell, a meticulous, law-abiding citizen, does not speed. I do. So my best guess is that he was giving himself a pep talk. "Just be calm, show patience, don't fix—she hates that. Remain buckled in, witness, do not say much, and do not try to coach her through this meltdown." As I said, Russell knows me well.

4) He probably prayed for life after the Dentbucket. He prayed the prayer of men who need divine intervention when dealing with hormonally imbalanced women turned terrorists. I could not blame my blues on spiking chemicals, having survived that particular cycle of insanity. I felt beaten down and wretched without the benefit of a hormonal excuse.

What meditation instructors call "my comparison-mind" overtook my heart and thoughts. When the influence of the comparing-mind comes to town, I devalue who I am and play the dim game of comparing my life situation to other people's circumstances. I define myself as a reflection of what I think other people have, which I do not have. At the time, I believed that everyone else lived in a parallel world, where paychecks flowed, and their cars started all of the time. I must have done something wrong to deserve a lower rung on the social ladder.

A seed of wisdom reminded the Drama Queen within that sliding into comparisons would only cause self-inflicted suffering. I recalled a recent conversation with my friend Bob, whose voice was exuberant with descriptions of a recent trip to Turkey. I felt envious and wistful, sorry for myself. And disgusted for choosing the route of self-pity.

Speaking of travel, Russell was planning his next adventure. He had purchased a bicycle for seventy-five dollars on Craigslist and mapped out a trip from Juneau, up into Canada, and south along the spines of the Rockies to Mexico. These were my friends—creative, vital, motivated people, living their lives to the fullest.

In the meantime, I continued to cultivate a strong and enduring relationship with my couch. That was my life. I felt pitifully small, which increased the lachrymose flow. I imagine Russell's blood pressure shot up a few points, as we continued to splash south on the freeway.

The rush of sorrow hit an all-time high as I remembered a particular look on Russell's face from the day before. His expression divulged a mix of confusion, pain, empathy, and "I must hide this" all at once. I caught a peek into the eyes of people who knew me before and saw me struggling then. The previous day, Russell had prepared for a walk along the Buffalo Bayou. I was not up to it. By now you know that I preferred Marilyn above all else.

I said, "Yeah, check it out, and see if you think it is safe."

I detected a spark of pain and frustration across Russell's face. In different times he would have said, "Jesus, Diana, you used to fly helicopters and ski down avalanche chutes, and now you are afraid to take a walk in Houston?" My embarrassment deepened. He was right. What was wrong with me?

We survived the drive. On the coast, we meandered along empty, breezy beaches, bouncing softly off each other's arms as we trudged through sand. Our heads bowed to the wind, Russell's presence served as a miraculous balm to my solitary existence. Before he left, Russell filled the Dentbucket's gas tank, baked a flourless chocolate cake with raspberry sauce, and left a pot of homemade French onion soup, cheese, bread, and an essence of love in the air. I shuddered to think where I would be without my precious friends.

Two weeks after Russell left, life seemed to change for everyone, except me. The only transformation I detected was a heavier case of the doldrums; my discouragement grew, while everything else shrunk. I spent the day sleeping and watching dumbed-down TV, weeping it up, letting the wet, salty moments be. I wondered about the trial, when and how it would turn out. In long hours of solitude, it is easy to see how thoughts work nonstop; random, far-ranging subjects pop up at the strangest times. I was, once again, on fire after a friend thought telling me how to feel would improve the situation.

I ranted on in endless bitter mental spam that I lived in a nation full of self-appointed motivational speakers, who think that telling someone to "just stay positive" is a sign of enlightened understanding. What *I* hear when someone preaches, "just stay positive!" translates into something like, "I think you should smear cream cheese frosting on your cow patty, and shut up."

As wacko as it might sound, I did not want to be positive. I wanted to be authentic and vulnerable about my situation. I felt like a giant carbuncle. Some people define this level of honesty as being "negative." When these folks launch into a predictable treatise on the power of positive thinking, I travel in spirals, down, down, to a lonely, misunderstood, and isolated position. I have learned at those times it is best to resist discussing the distinction between being positive and being real. I wanted to be chipper, but I was failing in that department. On the other hand, the result of all of this gushing positive thinking still seemed to result in a generation of eerily dissatisfied people.

Swift, jarring knocks on the front door interrupted my self-absorbed rumination. The knocking sound sent me into another skittish overreaction. My first urge was to head for the back room, avoiding the issue altogether. I tiptoed to the door's peephole to eye the compact circle of a tired postal worker's face, holding a green card for a certified letter. I opened the door, fast focusing on the return address for the name of a bank, lender, or courthouse. No signs of that, so I steadied my shaking hand to sign the receipt.

After thanking the mail carrier, I locked the door and examined the thick envelope, neat, packed tight. It was from Russell. I set the mail on a table and curled up on Marilyn to sleep. I chose sleep as often as I could, even before opening a care package from a dear friend. I despised this about myself yet remained committed to brutal honesty, moving beyond what I *thought* I should do, to what I had to do to get through the days.

After my nap, I opened the envelope, so Russell's texture and substance entered the room. Inside of a beautiful card, I lifted and unfolded an official-looking Word document with the following words: "I have loaned Diana Martin $2,000.00 interest free; the sum to be repaid when it is financially convenient for her," plus a check for $2,000. The image on the card was of a painting by his sister, which depicted frothy waves battering against a raw, rocky shoreline on Maine's coast.

I sensed that he understood the significance of this image, a metaphor for the place where I perched uneasily, grasping for a hold on the rocks. I felt tossed by waves like the ones in the painting. I was managing to hang on, yet at the same time I was tempted to indulge—to dive selfishly into the icy waves and float away.

I was way too chicken and determined not to jump. I knew this; so did Russell. He trusted me to reject the fantasy of floating away to an escape and make the choice to stay alive, maybe even eventually thrive. He gave me faith and the money, so I had no excuse to keep from moving forward.

That was a humbling place for me. My friends and family loaned me money without knowing when I could pay them back. I thought back to the day my nephew and his wife (twenty-five years younger than me, and both gainfully employed) sent me a one-hundred-dollar gift card for Whole Foods. I danced around the living room until I felt bashful, even though I was the only one there. It was difficult to believe that I would take money from my young relatives, and with such relish. I fantasized about the possibilities: thick Greek yogurt, fresh basil, black chocolate with sea salt. I stared at Russell's generous check without dancing, even though it was the lottery ticket that would keep me afloat until I found that next piece of driftwood called employment.

I put off that desolate search for "tomorrow" after some more sleep. For that to happen, I often used my best trick—deep belly breathing—while pretending to ski down a slope through fine, raspy snow. I imagined the sensation of floating, defying gravity, and of joy. This was my best sleeping tool, so I skied myself to sleep that night, allowing the rhythm of soft turns to do their magic.

The next morning, Spartacus decided, for the first time in his life, to chase his tail, which propelled his formidable body against the hollow, dangling closet doors. I popped out of sleep, jittery and distressed. At 5:54 a.m., I hurtled into obsessive thought. The force of anxiety felt as though a nurse injected one thousand CCs of pure caffeine into my veins. The rush was a familiar state, and entirely unwelcome.

I decided to get up, even though it was early. Strong, dark java in hand, I opened up my laptop to begin the blinding process of looking online for jobs. The ritual involved sending my cover letter and résumé into a nebulous void, where I was quite certain no one dwelled. After several minutes of reviewing employment Websites, I was ready for the day to end. I had yet to make breakfast and was already looking forward to watching *60 Minutes* and going to bed. I asked myself, "What is a reasonable amount of time to spend waiting for *60 Minutes*?" It felt wrong to be asking myself that question before breakfast. Out of pure desperation, I decided it was time for another conversation with Dr. Phil. I settled into Marilyn and closed my eyes.

Robin walked in first; she was stunning as usual. I took a long hard look at my chipped toenail polish and hairy legs. Dr. Phil crouched through the threshold and closed the door behind him. Dispensing with all formality, Dr. Phil shook his big, bald head, put his hands on his hips, and said, "What the bleep are you still doing on that white leather sofa?"

I readied myself to hear him say, "I've been doing this for thirty-five years and have never seen anyone so dedicated to acting like an upturned beetle on a fancy couch."

He didn't say that.

"Damn, girl, you can't make things right even when you try. I am truly sorry you are having such a hard time getting those feet on the ground."

I was enjoying this.

"I don't know what to do," I said, with a heavy dose of vulnerability.

"I don't know what you should do either."

That was a drag, because I was counting on his intel. I admitted I was scared about the trial. What if I said something inaccurate? What if we couldn't prove he did it?

Dr. Phil guffawed at this. "Do you think everything *he* is going to say will be accurate and filled with truth? You need to focus on doing the best you can. The rest is not up to you."

That simplified things tremendously, which is one of his specialties. "But . . ."

"Oh, give me a break, Diana. Why do you use "but" instead of "and" so often? This had been pointed out to me before, so it hit a raw and accurate spot.

"Well . . ."

Before I got another word out, he raised a big furry eyebrow and glared at me.

I primed myself for the next fucking good point he was about to make.

"You have more immediate concerns than that faraway trial. What are you going to do tomorrow? What will get you out of bed in the morning? To what end? You decide."

These were heady questions, especially the one about getting out of bed in the morning. It occurred to me that I was waking up to nothing, other than two clownish cats. There was zilch holding me to Houston, except an apartment I could no longer afford. I suddenly realized that I needed to go back home to my friends and counseling sessions in Austin.

"Look, Diana, right now it is all about doing the *smartest* thing you can at every turn. Forget about trying to see the big picture. Just make one good decision after another, and eventually they will all add up."

Before I could respond, Dr. Phil's cell phone rang. He picked up, waving good-bye. Robin gave me two thumbs up, and they were gone.

CHAPTER THIRTY-THREE

I CALLED BB THAT MORNING.

"Can I stay in your downstairs for a month or so until the trial?"

BB did not miss a beat before she said, "Yes, come—we will help you."

Her offer of assistance revved me up. I began to hatch the plan that would return me to a place that felt much more like home.

Two weeks later, I emptied apartment number eighteen and stuffed Pierre and Spartacus into separate kennels. Five minutes down the road toward Austin, Pierre busted out of his cage and jumped under my feet. I swerved into a parking lot and stopped. I scrambled to catch Pierre, who had decimated the hinge on the kennel door, so I tossed him in with the howling Spartacus. Traveling is not their thing, and believe me, traveling with them is not *my* thing.

Before continuing the trip, I threw the piece-of-junk kennel in a dumpster and rearranged some of the last-minute items in the back of the Dentbucket. Pierre's great escape flustered me when I was already stressed about the move. As I turned the car toward the freeway, a man driving in the next lane honked and pointed to the roof of my car. I pulled off the road and stepped out of the car to find a leaning pile of neatly folded blankets riding in the wind. So much can be said for slowing down and paying attention.

Austin is a place that stirs my heart, despite her trauma and lost dreams. I was happy to be there. My goals were simple: find employment, *any* employment, get help from Stacey, spend time with friends, and practice at the meditation center. It was time to break free from the cycle of my enmeshment with Marilyn and Dr. Phil. I no longer wanted them to be my primary relationships. I needed to branch out, in a big way. Austin was the place for me to do that.

I returned to spring weather, welcoming smiles, broad budding trees, and lively music from East Sixth Street wafting through tall trees. I relaxed, despite concerns, because I sensed a return to home.

In her prior life, BB owned and operated a popular restaurant on East Sixth Street, back when that was the rough part of town. She sweated, cooked, bustled, and dealt with unreliable help and persnickety diners, while raising five kids. Finally, one day for the hundredth time, one of BB's employees stole from her. Upon discovering this, BB untied her apron, washed and dried her hands, and walked up the spiral stairs to the family apartment. BB passed through the kitchen on her way to a hot bath, sharing two words with her kids and Juan: "I quit."

A year later, after indulging in her own version of power lounging, BB took up selling real estate, which is how we met. BB and Juan still live above the former restaurant. The entire space was crammed and scrunched with BB's garage-sale bargains, musty children's stuff that could not possibly be tossed, and the remains of their teenage son's life, in a partitioned porch. He had recently moved to New York, so I took over where their son left off, in the enclosed porch.

I unpacked my kneepads, found a plastic grocery sack full of old

Martini Homes cleaning rags, and got to work. Full of industrious urges, I spent three days on my hands and knees cleaning fifteen hundred square feet of Mexican tile. After that, BB and I moved boxes, vacuumed, cleaned, and rearranged.

A butterfly of an apartment emerged from the cocoon of a teenage boy's sense of hygiene. Once Marilyn, the bed, and my kitchen table found their places, it had some charm. We created a temporary home out of one oblong room, pressed against a jungle-like patio of banana trees and fifty shades of green. It was just right.

BB bought a four-pack of impatiens with vivid magenta flowers, which I scattered throughout the garden in small pots, providing a shock of color against the green. Scrounging through BB's many treasures, I found bamboo window shades and hung them along her fence for privacy. I watered the plants twice daily, and the garden flourished into what BB and I named the Secret Garden. At night, in cooling heat, BB and I would sit in our Adirondack chairs to relax, breathing in humid air spiced with music from Sixth Street.

My first week in Austin, BB and I met with Mary, the state's prosecutor assigned to our case. Mary struck me as kind, accomplished, sympathetic, and encouraging. She never offered platitudes—no "just be thankful you are alive" or "just stay positive!"

It was comforting to spend time with someone who understood the shock of violence and its slimy aftermath. I was with someone who knew better than to tell me it was all going to be fine. I was talking to a realist, not a motivator. She was also going to stick up for me in court, which, in my eyes, placed her on a pedestal.

I also felt comfortable with Mary because she could see me and recognize, without judgment, my awkward pauses and a shy tension in my shoulders. I knew she was not trying to change my perspective. She was not going to make it better, because "it" had already happened. Mary would advocate for me, and for the right of all women to feel safe in their homes. I could not have wished for a better person to do that.

Near the end of our first discussion, Mary asked if I could tell her what kind of impact the experience had on my life. As soon as she asked she backtracked, making it okay for me to answer the question later. The escape from talking pumped a surge of visceral calm through my system. Bored and overwhelmed with the obstacles defining my daily life, I said that perhaps BB could answer the question from an observer's stance. She would be able to provide a more objective voice to Mary's question.

Other than having seen Russell's fleeting facial gesture during his visit, this was the first time I had allowed myself to hear about the ripples of chaos and sadness that reverberated off my messed-up life into the lives of those I loved. As though from a distance, I heard BB describe me as childlike, fearful, isolated, financially devastated, anxious, and unhappy. She said I used to be a cheerful person. *I used to be.* She was right. A sickening wretchedness pooled in my heart, cold and black like stale coffee with a bitter aftertaste. I thought to myself that I did not want to be the person she described. I did not want to add gloom to the world, even though I did.

From listening to BB's assessment and remembering the look on Russell's face, it was apparent I was not cut out for acting. My brave face was not very brave, and the attempts at irony and sardonic stories were not fooling anyone. Damn, I thought, I am faking cheer, and it is not working. We left the courthouse and splurged on buying sandwiches. Both of us were quiet and thoughtful, tired and saturated from the conversation. We felt good about Mary, glad she was the one to handle the case. Mary said that she was extremely confident in the strength of the evidence, yet tightlipped about the specifics. Mary exuded confidence in herself, in me, and the outcome of the case.

BB and I drove home in silence. I went for a swim to wash away all of the words. I was tired of talking, and listening to BB sobered me. She spoke about my miserable facet. There were other facets, which I wanted to think were spunkier, funnier, far more jovial, and full of pleasure. I wanted some sass in my life. Like the woman who wrote the book *Eat, Pray, Love*. Elizabeth Gilbert wrote her bestseller about leaving her husband and abundant lifestyle in a wealthy suburb to travel the world in search of pasta, wisdom, and love. She found fulfillment at every turn.

My comparison mind flew into high gear. How could someone consume all those calories and still manifest exactly what she wanted in life? I felt like the Anti-Pasta of abundance.

CHAPTER THIRTY-FOUR

N MID-APRIL, LIZA AND MARY CALLED TO TELL ME THE TRIAL DATE changed to June 8, 2010. I was not shocked; an April date seemed ambitious in light of the court's packed dockets. Between nauseating bouts of trial anxiety and the desire to call it quits and opt out, I continued to squander hours at the computer, sending résumés into the unknown, never getting anything in return. My school offered a few leads, but nothing came together; legal recruiters were uninterested, due to my lack of law experience.

The housing market crawled to a grinding halt. People were not spending money on any kind of extravagance, nor thinking that anything would sell quickly. I applied for jobs in food services, grocery stores, law firms, government agencies, construction firms—any place that advertised a possible opening. Interviews were sprinkled thin and never panned out. Competition for any type of work was fierce. We lived in a new world.

For millions of us, looking for work became an epic journey through the Internet, full of unresponsive pathways to nowhere. On one of many days, while playing this redundant and aimless game, I followed a link from Monster.com, or Indeed.com, or who-knows-what.com, and ended up on a prominent telephone company's Website. Impressed with the site's organization and the option of attaching my résumé to an application, I hit "Save Profile" and then "Continue."

That led me to the next page, where I regurgitated every item from my résumé into an application. I was satisfied, and in a way mystified, that I completed the task in a mere thirty minutes. As I attached a letter of recommendation, the Web page wobbled, then turned black and disappeared. The home page reappeared. Everything I had tried to send was lost.

I began the process again, worried that whatever I rewrote would not be as good as the first version, the one that I saved before it was lost. Forty minutes later, I clicked the "Save Profile" and "Continue" buttons, with crossed fingers. That took me to the next page, and the next, and finally, the summary. I rechecked everything and then clicked "Submit."

Minutes later, a response from the phone company landed in my inbox. This was refreshing! I received confirmation; my résumé had arrived somewhere. Oh, but wait! The following message read, "Click on this link and add more information, or your application will be incomplete." I studied the directions carefully, almost afraid to touch my laptop. It said there was an edit button next to each section of my profile, with instructions: simply click on the edit button to make changes.

I clicked and ended up in an entirely new section, requesting information about my felony record and number of DUIs. I was up for answering these, so I could get back to the original pages, and felt relief, knowing there was nothing to hide. I thought about The Guy. If he filled out this application, it would not look good. I studied the computer screen—no edit button. I searched—page up, page down, and reread the directions—but found no answers. I finally located and clicked "Submit" on the final screen.

Another email popped to the inbox, with an alert message saying I did not complete the application process. The email included no hints as to how I might complete the freaking moody application, nor what information was missing. At the end of the email, the phone company closed the transaction by clearly stating, in no uncertain terms: Do not write back to us; we are unavailable.

I closed my dry eyes, waving simple massage strokes along my frustrated brow. As I rubbed, I felt an unexpected smile emerge from deep inside. I was at the mercy of the grand world of technology, a cantankerous system that my generation and our brilliant children created. What a mess. I laughed aloud, a gloomy laugh. It still counted as the laugh of the day.

I met regularly with Stacey. Mary and I were ready to move on to the trial, planning for it to occur in the imminent future. I was impatient. Liza and Mary suggested that I observe other trials, to familiarize myself with the proceedings and environment. I took that as the opportunity to go on legal field trips, spending days in the courtroom where the trial would soon occur. After that, I went to Stacey's office. I would go to the safe place and train my heart and mind to remain calm in the face of The Guy.

During the hottest parts of the day, I often sat near the purring air conditioner in the patio apartment. When the sky parched us in waves, I stayed inside and beaded bracelets, enjoying the even, slow hours of stringing copper, black, clear, silver, and turquoise into one long, sleek, spiral. For every bead added to the circle, I thought of a friend, relative, helper, and finally, every person and animal I could think of. I dedicated each bead to the trustworthy ones, the people who refrain from harming others. I dedicated beads to everyone who lives with a kind and gentle heart. With each breath, and each bead, I pulled myself out of mental spam and focused on appreciating the world's honorable people. On a few occasions of mercy, I included a bead for The Guy.

I went minimal for Russell, knowing he was about to start his bicycle trip. I made a narrow three-strand bracelet and asked him to coil it around his handlebars. I wanted a part of me along for the ride. He was going on the trail; I was going to the trial.

As I beaded Russell's bracelet, I thought about his admirable traits. Russell dedicates tremendous personal energy toward growing as a human being. He strives to work with clear intention and integrity. What more could one ask from a friend?

I thought about the voice that gave me specific instructions on how to escape from The Guy. Russell would define that as crazy talk—unempirical, mystical hooey. Despite my respect for Russell, how could I deny that voice existed? The words were real to me. Who, or what, was behind that familiar-sounding voice, which seemed to come from deep inside of me?

On another day, the same question about the voice rose again. I didn't have any answers, so I went outside into the garden to water plants. When I returned, an interview with Lorna Byrne, author of *Angels in My Hair*, was playing on the radio. I had not heard of her or the book, yet the title caught my interest. I sat on Marilyn, away from the beads; Lorna's Irish brogue was thick enough to require my full concentration.

She spoke frankly about her close relationship with angels, beginning in early childhood. I realized it was not that I did not believe in angels. They simply had never been a part of my religious repertoire; the idea of angels felt so Christmassy.

In the interview, Lorna said that at least one angel accompanies every person she has ever met. She went on to depict the angel she saw behind the interviewer. The words Lorna Byrne used were precise, practical, original, and full of detail, right down to the angel's clothing. The conversation, her voice and story, enthralled me. Maybe I could not see angels, but it felt as though I knew a few.

I thought again about the voice I heard. There are plenty of legends about voices, both booming and quiet. I remember remote tidbits of a college class in Greek mythology. I tend to think all that Odyssey stuff was written by men, for men. Volumes of pages about gouged eyes and raped goddesses do nothing for me. However, I did recall some cool stories about Athena, the Greek goddess of protection. She was a fierce warrior who used her wisdom of war and fighting only for the good of her city-state and its people. She was a discerning fighter, unwilling to go to battle for any cause other than civil liberties and protection.

Legend says that Athena whispered words of reason and wisdom into heroes' ears. She implanted thoughts into Odysseus's head during battle. The Goddess of Protection often stood with an owl perched on her shoulder; stories say the owl whispered counsel and wisdom to her.

Maybe what I heard that day during the fight with The Guy was Athena, or her owl relaying direct commands in hushed tones behind my right ear. I decided to pay more attention. Was the owl always there, and I was unaware of her presence? Is Lorna Byrne showing us what we cannot see? Are angels always around, and we are the ones who are blind?

CHAPTER THIRTY-FIVE

I DELIGHTED IN AUSTIN'S BEAUTIFUL MORNING SIGHTS, SOUNDS, AND smells. Life felt familiar. The mantra continued: "I just need a job, I just need a job." I chanted those five words in rhythm to the steps of my early-morning walks.

Returning to Austin felt like moving into Lyle Lovett's living room. Sultry breezes, happy people, and carefree music brought me back to my tribe. We walked within the palms and old oaks like the ones in *Where the Wild Things Are*. I loved the Texas twang, moving at a slower speed than the one in Houston. I reminded myself how grateful I was to live down south, without need for a parka, heavy boots, down comforters, and a fire on bitter winter nights.

My daily life included sunscreen, swimming, music, and grilling hot food in BB's garden. I was broke yet living like a queen, eating fresh avocados and swimming in cool, clean natural spring water. This reality struck me: we do get by in a grand way in this country. Poverty is relative.

Money was a matter of gloom, despite my gratitude. I wondered if

I would ever find work for the rest of my life. In some people's eyes, I was old, and sadly, age discrimination is alive and well in America. One friend suggested asking for food stamps, which had not occurred to me. I applied and several weeks later received two hundred dollars a month for food. When I walked into the H-E-B, those funds turned that place into a grocery store paradise.

I was fortunate to have friends, family, two hundred dollars a month for food, clean water, and shelter in BB's patio. Compared to the Dalit in India, I lived in the realm of the gods. Those day-to-day reminders bolstered my gratitude, moving me gently forward, toward leaning into the lumpy dread of facing The Guy.

That June, a temp agency hired me to drive cars at a car auction. For $32.16 a day after taxes, I did that one day a week, which kept some fuel in the Dentbucket. I worked five hours every Tuesday, and that was the best I could do. Times were tough. Through a force I can only call grace, I continued to live on what felt like nothing, yet in a strange way, I felt sustained and stable.

I made time almost every day for a swim in Barton Springs. The summer heat remained above one hundred degrees for weeks on end. I would wait until my body felt so hot it was about to sizzle and then jump into the pool's vigorous, transforming cold. Swimming below the surface was an otherworldly rush. I loved propelling my body through long sunbeams that formed slanting pillars in a silent underwater world.

I became addicted to fast leaps from the hot sun into the icy shock of the water. I loved the feeling of its pressure against my skin; the contraction seemed to ease the broken zipper in my spine. The initial plunge stunned me into feeling alive, buoyant, and vital. I was gaining strength for the trial, and soon that would be over. I pictured a boulder-size burden rolling down a mountain. Someday I would be able to let go of that rock and watch it tumble away.

Open, unstructured time is one of the few benefits of unemployment. I spent a lot of time at Barton Springs with my friend Greg, a landscaper low on work. He thought only crazy people jumped into icy water, so my daily plunge struck him as fairly ridiculous.

Almost every day Greg and I met up in a specific shady spot underneath a rough, old pecan tree. Our conversations rambled on for hours, strategizing for the future and sharing about the past. No matter where the conversation started, our focus circled back to our mutual concerns about our livelihoods and the current economic upheavals. Our ruminations exhausted us until one of us would groan and, as though rehearsed, we would each pitch our backs down onto damp towels, using crossed wrists to cover our eyes. We could not understand the economy's sudden halt and feared the mysterious, unknowable future.

Greg's disbelief that anyone would choose to jump into cold water was a consistent reaction among Texans. He floated on a long, inflatable raft, savoring the heat and perfecting his tan. His skin could take the sun, which was good because he lived and worked in it. I wore a sun visor and turned my pale back to the sun, as I treaded water and conversed with Greg.

He floated, and I paddled in place as we took pleasure in the ease of play and relaxation. We encouraged and nudged each other forward on our work endeavors. I had not seen but a few paychecks in eighteen months. Greg had sporadic work so kept his expenses low, but he was scared about the decreased demand for his services.

We rarely mentioned the trial, although we both knew it was coming. By then, it was scheduled for July 12, Greg's birthday. We simply continued to float, tread, and talk. It felt like my life was an exercise in treading water. Even at play, I labored in the same spot, not moving forward or aft, expending all my energy to keep my head above water.

No matter how much I exercised, laughed, and prayed, I woke with the same startle reflex in the morning. Waking thoughts began with a headache, straight into money worries. How would I make it financially through another month? I seemed to survive on air. The phenomenal world somehow sustained me through that time.

When swimming, feelings of terror would often subside. At those times, I experienced the present moment as being perfectly fine. I was healthy, nothing was blowing up, and I enjoyed food and water daily. What was the problem? In actuality, all was well with the world. That formed a compelling data set. When I paid attention to what was going on right then—the moisture in the air and the smell of fresh mown grass—everything was perfectly fine. The busyness of my thoughts and beliefs were what blinded me from the moment's beauty.

Focusing on the future made me feel terrible, in contrast to a sense of wholesomeness in the present moment. When I tuned into each moment, each separate film frame instead of the big picture, I found peace and contentment. A welcome vigor coursed through my veins; I felt happy to be alive.

By July 4, they postponed the trial again. The defense said they still needed time to come up with something. It was forever something. I imagine jail is better than going to trial, so they were using every available stall tactic. I was crestfallen. That time Mary was unable to give me a new date, and she suspected it would take at least a few months.

One day while I was treading water I estimated how much time I had spent waiting for the trial. From my point of view, it seemed as though The Guy still had power over me because the delays crushed my patience and good cheer. I felt as if his actions held me at bay. And I allowed my state of mind to sway in response to his actions.

When I continued to hand The Guy the sinking ship's controls, I felt like a victim—of the economy, the justice system, and the jerk who had come into my house with zip ties and a gun. It was and is true: happiness is a decision. In the dark times, I decided that unhappiness is also a decision. Unhappiness is appropriate and human, a natural tip of the scales over to the shadow side of living. Feeling the full catastrophe of life seemed as valid and important as happiness. Allowing all of the flavors to rise to the surface helped me feel honest and real about my predicament.

I was dog-tired of agonizing about the future. It was time to look outside of the box. I admitted to Greg that I was beginning to open my mind about leaving Austin. I was happy there and wanted to stay. However it was time to go wherever I could find work. The worry of unemployment and its twenty-four-hour strategic mission was aging me.

As Greg and I talked about the delay in the trial, a shot of hot anger propelled me into action. I swore that I would not wait another day for The Guy to man up and face his decisions. I despised my role in that dysfunctional relationship with a virtual stranger. Indignation forced me into a new way of thinking. I would leave Austin if necessary and decided to do whatever I needed to rebuild my future.

After my decision, I continued to tread water while Greg rafted. Other times, as he baked in the sun, I submerged my body in the cold springs and practiced looking at life through a different lens. My mess had to have a solution. I was determined to find work, even though my search continued to bear no fruit. My friend Rebecca from Houston mentioned there might be an opening at the law firm where she worked. My friends in Alaska encouraged me to return, telling me about opportunities up there. I mentioned this to Greg and told him that was a door I closed years earlier. I would not move backward. I was going to move forward, away from a freezing place I had consciously left.

Suddenly, BB's father became ill and fell on hard times. He needed a place to live. BB and I talked about it. I knew she was under tremendous stress, and my short stay had gone on too long. BB and Juan offered to help me for a few months until the end of the trial. A few months had then passed. BB and I went to work on the downstairs again and set up the patio apartment for her father. Then we stacked, swept, rearranged, and carved out a far corner on the opposite side of the restaurant for my bed, Marilyn, and a few boxes of clothes.

I literally built a shelter using canvas paint cloths, eighty-four-inch drapes, and blue tarps. I needed to create a space large enough for the bed and a place to sit, so we could cool down the tight quarters with a small air conditioner. It was mid-summer in Texas, and as my earlier writing sample illustrated, A/C is not a luxury in Texas; it is a necessity. I lined up the bed against a wall, with my narrow coffee table wedged between Marilyn and the bed. There was no floor space, just enough room for the furniture crammed together, lengthwise, in a row.

Juan and I rigged a portable air conditioner by running a dryer vent through the only available casement window. We finished off the masterpiece by stuffing insulation, towels, and washcloths around the opening to block out the hot air and retain the cool air. I lived in a tent made of curtains and tarps in a former restaurant. All the signs indicated that I needed to move on.

Juan and BB shared a wonderful tradition of dressing up and going out to dance every Friday night. After we set up the air conditioner, Juan cleaned up so they could go out. BB told me that as the salsa music began, Juan turned to her and started laughing. He said, "It looks like Diana is living in one of Muammar el-Gaddafi's tents! You know, like the one he tried to set up on Donald Trump's property!"

The three of us still refer to that time as the Era of the Gaddafi Tent. Inside the tent, the cats and I stepped across the coffee table to move from Marilyn to the bed. The lifesaving A/C leaked water, which dumped into a plastic dishpan, which then sprayed more water onto a layer of towels. Twice a day I tottered over the bed, across the coffee table, and onto the solid floor as I balanced a floppy dishpan of water.

Again, the world handed me a humorous metaphor for my circumstances. That was quite an interesting place to live. I was close to homelessness, yet far from it due to BB and Juan. I avoided the streets in the folds of their kindness. Marilyn adorned Gaddafi's tent with her exotic beauty. Not everyone gets to live in an air-conditioned tent with a white leather couch fine enough to have a name.

It was time for me to leave; I just didn't know where to go.

CHAPTER THIRTY-SIX

RELUCTANTLY, I CONTEMPLATED GOING BACK UP NORTH TO WORK. Friends in Alaska cast lines my way, offering tempting hooks of work leads. I wanted no part of it; I did not want to move anywhere. All it would take was one job offer, and I could stay.

One sweltering afternoon, I slouched on a beach towel covering Marilyn. Draping my sweaty legs over the coffee table, I rested my feet on the bed as I gazed at the blue tarp on the ceiling. Outside, the pavement melted into puddles. In Gaddafi's tent, the air conditioner whined to keep up with a steady eighty-eight degrees.

I took an honest look at my surroundings. My parents forced (and financed) my college education, so I would not have to live under a blue tarp. I felt a sting as my eyes flushed with shame. My mother and father had gone to the ends of the earth to educate me. Who was I to think I should avoid going to the ends of the earth to support myself? What I *wanted* did not matter all that much. I needed to go to work.

I felt the familiar brand of hesitation. I knew what working up north meant. I had no illusions to support the romantic side of moving to Alaska. "Romantic" applies to a couple of months each year; the rest of the time it is expensive and radically inconvenient. I knew about the dark days, and I was struggling against depression. The idea of moving to a dark and cold place frightened me.

I was hanging on by a thread in Austin's sunshine and joie de vivre. Leaving my temporary, yet safe, sunny home could have destructive consequences. I again looked around Gaddafi's tent. Staying there would be equally counterproductive.

Soon after, Kathi called from Juneau, so we had "a talk." On one hand, she wanted me to stay with her in Juneau as I looked for work. On the other hand, she voiced her concerns about my state of mind and the darkness. It was risky to push more adversity my way. Then again, remaining unemployed in a steaming indoor tent, waiting for a trial that might never happen, sounded like a plan based on magical thinking.

By day, I continued to look for work in Austin. By night, I researched other options. I fantasized about Alaska, however I had yet to *apply* for any kind of work there. I had twenty-five years of experience and knowledge that is rarely valued in other geographical areas. A résumé that describes someone as "versatile, skilled, and proven" in Alaska reads as "spotty, odd, and inconsistent" in the Lower Forty-Eight. In Alaska, employers take less of a risk with a returning Alaskan because they know what to expect. There is a common, crazy thread running through any of us who choose to move that far north. Being an Alaskan is a career decision.

With these ideas churning around, the hit of warm Austin air felt comforting. I refer to the sensation of walking outside and feeling hot air touch my skin and lungs. I get that this is something that many people in temperate climates would have no reason to notice. If you are used to walking outside and squinching your shoulders and fingers from exposure to the cold, you would understand why walking out in Texas air feels blissful.

I interviewed for several paralegal positions in Houston. Of the hundreds of résumés I sent out, I landed two interviews in Austin, both with no offers. I was close to hitting the two-year mark of unemployment. In early July, I logged on and applied for a real estate paralegal position in Fairbanks. It gets cold in Fairbanks, but there are more days with sunshine than in the cloudy coastal regions, so I decided to explore that option.

In late July, I went to an interview in Houston. I arrived at an office that looked much like an art gallery. It was modern, windowed, and slick, filled with underpaid paralegals. They said they would get back to me. I fretted over a move back to the big, steaming cauldron of Houston for such a low-paying post. I was not in a position that left a lot of room for being picky. My unsustainable position was becoming more unsustainable, if that were theoretically possible. Uneasy night anxieties blossomed in direct proportion to my growing deficit.

After the interview in the art gallery, I met my cousin Giggy and her husband Matt for dinner at a restaurant I could not afford. They were continually gracious and kind to me. I wished I could return their generosity, but it was impossible, and they did not expect it. I wished my position on the scales of giving and receiving was not so one-sided.

We sat at the bar, managing to face each other and devour the delicious food at the same time. As we buttered aromatic chunks of bread and savored first sips of cool wine, Giggy's eyes met mine, and then we both closed our eyes in satisfied contentment. The hearty food and companionship eased my body and busy mind, filling me with an unfamiliar contentment.

My cell phone rang. I let it go to voice mail. The saved call nagged me, so I lowered myself from a tall bar stool, asking Giggy for directions to the ladies' room. I hoped the call was for an interview at home, because after one day in Houston, I missed Austin.

The message was from a woman in Fairbanks, requesting a phone interview for the real estate position I had applied for online a week earlier. I leaned against the cool tile wall and stared at the phone, hitting nine for "Save." Panic jumped like lightning from my heart straight into my rushing blood. The thought of moving up there sparked a ferocious funk intermixed with the butterflies of a steady paycheck. "Oh, good grief," I murmured to myself, horrified by how much my life would change if I moved that far away.

The potent flush of trepidation scared me enough that I did not return the phone call, even though it was earlier than five p.m. in Alaska. I edged back onto the king-size barstool and reached for my chilled wine glass. Some things can wait. I returned to the present tense, enjoying every morsel of food and conversation. During the drive back to Austin, there would be plenty of time to dwell on the phone call.

Despite that intention, a troublesome ribbon of thought ran seductively through my mind. Part of my mind jumped up and down for attention. How could I go back to the place I had been so determined to leave? I strained to digest the idea and somehow, intuitively, the situation felt questionable, like the sick compulsion to return to a dysfunctional relationship.

I stopped after one glass of wine, moving on to coffee. The evening light grew pale as I followed my favorite route home through sage green, rolling ranches tinged with rose from the sunset. I passed the gated entrance of a bison ranch and recalled going through that gate, back in the carpet job days—the people, not the bison, had needed a flooring estimate.

I slowed to enjoy the scenery and process that day's new information. Would I accept the position in Houston if they offered it to me? What would I do if I got an offer in Alaska? Would I take it? Could I turn down any offer of employment? These hypothetical questions rolled around and around in circular fashion.

Struck by the landscape and the freedom of the open air, I decided to do the immature, unprofessional thing. I would not return the call from Alaska. I did not want to go back. Five minutes later, I was high on the thought of a paycheck and health insurance. So I postponed making the call for a day, hoping that I would get an interview in Austin within the next sixteen hours.

CHAPTER THIRTY-SEVEN

T HE NEXT DAY, THE FIRM THAT LOOKED LIKE AN ART GALLERY IN Houston offered me a position, with a breathtakingly low hourly wage so described as the "industry standard" and no benefits. Six months earlier, a friend had been hired at the same firm for a higher rate. I asked if there was any possibility of a slightly greater wage, and that insulted her. It is interesting to see how many people want others to settle for thankless, low-paying jobs, so they themselves don't have to do them. I said I needed time to consider the offer.

I hung up and went back to my chore of emptying the leaking A/C water. I carried the dishpan over the bed, balancing carefully. Then I tried to keep the sloshing to a minimum as I wedged in between rows of boxes and plastic tubs, stacked to the ceiling, until I reached the garden. I replaced the empty dishpan on the floor and stood next to the air conditioner as I dialed the number to the woman in Alaska who had called me. When she answered, I turned off the loud air, long enough to arrange an interview two days later at five p.m. my time. It would be two in the afternoon there.

The next morning I called the Houston art gallery and declined. I did not want to go to Alaska, and I did not want to lock myself into a paycheck I could barely live on in Houston. I got back online in further pursuit of an occupation in Austin. I would be more than willing to commit to an income I could barely live on, if it allowed me to stay there.

On the day of the phone interview, I dialed the air conditioner to the lowest setting, so I could hear the broken voices of two women interviewing me from afar. Years earlier, when I worked in Juneau, I had hired many summer employees via phone interviews. Now I was on the other end of the conversation. My hair was still wet from a cold swim. Wearing a thin sundress, I leaned back in the default position on Marilyn, my legs stretched over the coffee table, feet on the bed. It was difficult for me to take the call seriously. Who is hired over the phone after one interview? Why would they hire someone so far away?

I adopted the view that any interview is good practice for the next one, and I wanted to learn more about the specifics of this possibility. The phone call left me with so many questions. The position was in one of the coldest parts in Alaska, close to the Arctic Circle. Only crazy people live that far north.

I thought of a favorite book, *The Future of Ice*, by Gretel Ehrlich. I admire her raw, skillful writing, and often wish I could have a conversation with the only other woman I know of who had fallen in love with Old Man Winter. We both seem to be intoxicated and mesmerized by the cold, white, clean winter life. I thought I had left the old man for good, while she made the noble choice to stay and tough it out, to love him for all of her days.

I stopped by the library for a copy of Ehrlich's book and read through it, late into the night. I stuffed it in my beach bag the next day, as I got ready to meet with Greg, who had a profound, highly romanticized vision of Alaska. Of course he did—he had never been there. He'd read Michener's *Journey* ten times, so he was certain he was made to live in Alaska.

We hugged before I plopped to the ground. Greg was drying off after one of his rafting un-adventures. I applied sunscreen as he sprawled on our grassy spot. Throughout the afternoon, we would reposition automatically, following his sun and my shade across the grass in an unspoken choreography. I opened the book and leaned forward. Greg lay on a damp towel and closed his eyes behind dark sunglasses.

"Okay, are you ready for this?" I adjusted my hat visor.

He nodded. Going to Alaska was his childhood fantasy and his greatest adult dream. I flipped to a scrap of paper tucked in at page eighty-five. I turned toward Greg to preface the reading by saying, "So . . . there are hundreds of microclimates in Alaska. The state is enormous—the size of Texas and California put together." (I do enjoy saying that to Texans; it sets those big, tall hats back into place.)

I continued, "Because it is so large, there are many diverse climates within the state. Each microclimate is cold compared to the rest of the world, but in Alaska, some places are *beyond* cold."

I paused long enough to hear a child squeal and leap into the pool. "The phone interview I did yesterday was for a job in a town called Fairbanks. What I am about to read is the author's description of Fairbanks, even though the story begins with her depiction of the beautiful and bitter cold winters in Wyoming, which is where she lives."

A breeze gave me goose bumps, so I nudged forward into a sunspot and began to read out loud.

"Clouds float, the temperature warms, and four feet of snow on the ground settles to three. It's become fashionable to seek out or retell the worst extremes of weather and travel, as if simply living—wherever we are—isn't juicy enough. I've endured much colder winters than this one. I was in Fairbanks, Alaska, in January 1989 when a Siberian blast dropped the temperature from minus fifty-two degrees Fahrenheit to minus eighty-two degrees along the Tanana River. There were only a few hours of daylight. My breath froze; the town of Fairbanks was encased in a hard fog that crackled like fire. Tires went square, a friend's retina popped out, contact lenses couldn't be worn, a child's tongue became frozen to the school-bus window and had to be cut away from the glass with a scalpel."

I looked at Greg, whose mouth was wide open; his chin leaned down to his suntanned chest. I continued, "Our faces had to be covered at all times. I learned not to cough or laugh outside."

Greg and I both quieted. He turned to me, eyes not quite hidden behind his lenses, and grimaced in my direction, "I sure hope you aren't planning on having much company."

I set the book on my towel. Greg turned his head back to the sun and remained silent; I picked at some grass. Greg was so quiet I figured he had fallen asleep. Leave it to men—most manage to eat and sleep through stress at times when I cannot imagine it. As that thought wiggled in, Greg lifted his sunglasses and turned his head to face me. A pause fell between us until he accentuated one word.

"Wow."

I nodded, my exhale blended with a whispered "Yeah."

After an extended grass inspection, I stood, walked to the side of the water, and faced the sun. I dove into the freezing water, submerging myself in the brisk, liquid elixir of Barton Springs. Below the surface, a bubbling, turquoise world greeted me with silence. A thick sunbeam illuminated a column of water. I swam below the surface like a frog, steering through slippery grass that tickled my legs. The bliss of nature snapped me back to the totality of the present moment, distant from the ongoing mind chatter.

I burst to the surface for more air and went down again, into the otherworld. I could hear laughter echo above as I pressed the water with my hands to go deeper, away from the noise of the world and my head. I touched the bottom of the pool, then pushed off for the surface. On the way up, I shot through distinct layers of water temperature including one patch that was much colder than the others. As I skimmed upward to the heated world above, a strong inner knowing penetrated my cells. Mick Jagger had it right: you can't always get what you want.

I knew I had better get used to feeling cold.

CHAPTER THIRTY-EIGHT

ABOUT A WEEK AFTER THE PHONE INTERVIEW, I RECEIVED A CALL from the company's HR department, with an offer I accepted. I hung up the phone, running through apprehension and joy in the same picture frame. I was feeling like the Queen of Quintessential Ambivalence, behaving in a way Dr. Phil warned me to avoid. He had counseled me that if an answer is not an absolute *yes*, it is a *no*.

When I said *yes* this time, I decided the above rule applied to my personal life; however when it came to supporting myself, an ambivalent *yes* was going to have to do. It was the only viable position offered so far. Desperation is a powerful debater and tremendous motivator.

My thighs were stuck to the coffee table. I pulled my knees up to my chest and dialed my brother. I imagined that if anyone ever got stuck with the burden of supporting me, it would unfortunately fall to him, so I wanted Don to be the first one to know he had been relieved of that duty.

My false cheer and ambivalent delivery of the news left a gap in the conversation.

Cautiously, Don said, "You got a job. That's a good thing, right?"

"Well . . . yes, it is a good thing . . ."

I felt physically weak, kerschlumpy. I rubbed my brow before drop-ping my hand onto Marilyn. Looking up at the blue tarp, I said, "It is just that I know how hard this is going to be."

After our brief conversation, I cracked open a Tecate and eased into my lawn chair in BB's parking lot. Someone rode by on a bicycle with fat tires. I savored the toasty air on my arms and thought of all the people in Texas who never noticed that delicious surge of sultry air when walking out the door. Spartacus and Pierre joined me under the streetlight, form-ing a triangular caucus. They thought moving from Houston to Austin was traumatic. Oh boy, they had no idea what their future held.

My thinking exploded into the realm of logistics, plans, and expenses. The three of us would have to travel forty-two hundred miles to get to a regular paycheck. A decision changes things. It provides a solid path, even when the future is hidden. I finally had a place to go and a direction to move toward, regardless of the fact that it was not my first choice.

I am obligated to say this up front: I know millions of Americans are out of work right now. I know your pain, so please listen carefully: DO NOT move to Alaska without a high-paying job and a substantial wad of cash. Do not read this story and decide that Alaska is for you—you have always wanted to go there, and cold temperatures are not a big deal. Do not believe the stories about gold nuggets pouring downhill from steep places to feed the ferns. Let me repeat. DO NOT move to Alaska without a high-paying job and a substantial wad of cash.

Alaska is a magnificent place that works you to the bone and makes sure you pay the dues to live there. Do not move to Alaska without a good job and lots of money. Do not move to Alaska because you read this book.

I did not follow the above advice. I had future work and insufficient funds to get there. I knew that, yet felt determined to defy logic. I pored over maps and Websites, and made late-night phone calls, researching every shipping and travel option I could find. I needed to find the cheapest way to travel from simmering point A to chilly point B, with two cats and a white leather couch.

If I sold everything and flew to Alaska, how would I get around once I landed? I did not have money to spend on a rental car. What if I got up to Fairbanks and they scheduled a trial in Austin soon after? What would I tell my employer? What if the case never went to trial? The circular thoughts continued; now they just had a broader theme.

Confidence in the Dentbucket was at an all-time low. Driving it out of town was sketchy. A voyage all the way through Canada without an epic hiccup would be miraculous. Taking the chance on buying a different used car in Austin did not seem smart. I could sell the Dentbucket and buy a car in Alaska, but how would I get there with my things and the cats? Shipping anything to Alaska was beyond my means. Buying a car and furniture up there meant limited and far more expensive options.

I thought I had culled through everything I owned, until I perused the tent and my storage unit. I needed to assess the bulk of my belongings with a new measuring stick. Every item I owned, down to a Sharpie pen, would have to pass the test: Is it valuable enough to haul up into the Alaskan wilderness? I refused to pay for storage in Austin. Either I kept an item or it went away, period. If anything were going to Alaska, I would have to drive it there. Shipping was too expensive, renting a small moving truck was unaffordable. Not one agency would rent me a car going one-way to Alaska.

The Dentbucket became my only hope. I measured, probed, calculated, and considered. What could I fit into the back of a Honda wagon? Two cats and enough clothing, bedding, and kitchen supplies to get me started? I reviewed the Craigslist posts for apartments and cars in Alaska. I could afford to pay rent on my future salary, however buying a decent car up there was beyond my abilities, and public transportation was limited.

When the Dentbucket appeared to be my best option, I knew I was in trouble. While my mind churned, there was plenty to do. BB and I held two garage sales. Every day I sold miscellaneous items on Craigslist and gave the rest away. Still, there was more left over than what would fit in the Honda.

Have you ever stood in front of an open refrigerator door, closing it empty handed, yet returning to open the door several times, as if something new and appealing was going to appear? I measured that Honda fifty times, thinking there must be a way to downsize my life to fit into a small station wagon. I had more attachments than I thought; these were difficult decisions. I measured again, drawing everything out on graph paper. I joked that maybe I could tie Marilyn to the top.

The temperature stayed above one hundred degrees, partnered with high humidity. I pushed, shoved, moved, sold, and measured. Yet my life was still too big for the Honda. I needed to start driving. There was no time left to juggle those decisions.

One evening, feverish from another packing effort, I went to the springs and dove into the thrilling cold water. The rush and sense of freedom was intense. I clipped off a few laps to warm up and then slowed my pace to think. I was sick of owning and moving things. I decided to purge and remain free of owning so much stuff. I wanted the rest of my life to feel like an extended camping trip, designed with the bourgeois in mind. I remembered photographs of elaborate tents used on safaris. I wanted to live small and snazzy like that. Aside from owning a car, I decided I would own only enough to fill a small U-Haul truck. The rules felt fair and right, refreshing like the water around me.

Well-intended aspirations aside, I went back to BB's and admitted I could not fit my life into a Honda. That night, I had a dream. I was driving to Alaska, but the view of the road was different, specifically, higher up than the view from the Honda's driver's seat. In the dream, I felt safe, traveling on solid ground, riding up high with a good view of my surroundings.

In the dream, I was driving down a snowy road. The light in the sky was a pastel pink, reflecting a quality of light I have only seen in the arctic on a spring day. As I sat, perched high in the driver's seat, the truck veered to the right in an alarming swerve. It was a heart-stopping instant, filled with fear and alarm. Just as suddenly, the truck reverted to its original course. I felt the tires right themselves into well-packed snow.

In the dream, my intense visual focus scanned up from the road to see the landscape beyond the truck's hood. In the distance, a rosy, craggy, snow-covered mountain range pointed up to an overwhelming powder-blue sky. Still dreaming, I told myself: I had a narrow escape, but the wheels are back on track. This beautiful place is a signal of saved grace. For the first time in two years, it felt like everything might turn out all right.

I woke from the dream, yet still, the pink vision of mountains continued to roll around in my mind. Sitting up high in the dream felt safe and somehow correct. It seemed like the feeling of safety was worth paying attention to—how could I sit up high in a loaded Honda wagon? I knew that a few things in life were impossible, many others improbable. I had qualms about the trip in the Honda because a safe, easy trip bordered on the improbable. Something else did not feel right. I would not be able to sit up high, as in the dream. On impulse, I pressed the speed dial button for my cousin Giggy in Houston.

"Hey, Giggy, I know this is a strange, out of the blue question. A few months ago, in passing you mentioned it was time to sell your Suburban. I was wondering if you would sell it to me?" The suddenness of the request astonished even me. It popped right out of my mouth.

After the words popped, I thought quickly. I could offer Giggy and Matt the proceeds from the sale of the Honda as a down payment and negotiate a payment plan for the rest. Business plus family is tricky, much like baking a soufflé. It is simply amazing when it works out. That said, I needed to ask someone for help, and where else to start but family? The unexpected idea could work. With a steady paycheck, I could make a monthly payment. The Suburban was a ninety-something, so the price might have been affordable.

All of those thoughts rushed through my mind at once, while Giggy digested the unforeseen request. It had astonished me, too.

"Well," she said, "Matt has been bugging me for a long time to stop driving this big thing around the city, especially now that I'm not hauling the kids around. Let me call you back."

I hung up and sat in BB's Adirondack chair. Wait a minute . . . I aspired to decrease my carbon footprint, and I wanted to buy a Suburban? That was one rig I certainly never considered owning. The size, however, was perfect, at a time when size did matter.

As I carried on with sorting and selling, the driving dream with the pink light stayed with me, as dreams occasionally do. That one captivated me. I could not forget the improved vantage point I had experienced. I could sit up high in the Suburban, and I could definitely fit my life into one.

Giggy called me back that afternoon. "So I talked to Matt. We agree: it is time to get a new car. This one is old. It has about 165,000 miles on it, and the A/C doesn't work. We just don't feel like we should sell it to anyone. It isn't really worth anything." I understood. Selling an older car to anyone is a karmic gamble. I was not sure I would want to sell a car to her and watch it drive off into the Alaskan sunset. They would be better off trading it in.

She paused. "But I'll tell you what we can do. Matt and I would like to give you the truck."

CHAPTER THIRTY-NINE

I SAT ON A SUN-SOAKED STONE IN THE GARDEN AND FELT MY HEART jerk. I responded ineptly, absorbing the generous offer with bumbling hyperventilation. "Giggy," I stumbled. My eyes welled, watery and hot. "I didn't call you to ask you to give me your car! I would want to pay you for it. I, no, you don't mean this. I am blown away, well, I am not sure. I mean, ah, can I call you back tomorrow?" I hung up, mortified at my undignified response.

Someone threw me a great big bone, and I did not know how to pick it up gracefully. I was unsure how to respond to such generosity. That truck would solve the puzzle. Salty gratitude poured out of me. This was a solution, a gift, something inconceivable. With money from selling the Dentbucket and the monumental space in the Suburban, I could easily downsize and make it to Alaska with everything I needed.

I called Giggy back and blubbered some more. She and Matt were (and continue to be) understated about this gesture, simply saying the truck was not worth anything, especially without air conditioning. It was worth a great deal to me. A truck without A/C is not worth much in Houston; in Alaska, it would be all about the heater.

I sold the Honda in a couple of days, to someone in Houston. I drove the car there, made the sale, and took a taxi to Giggy's. I sat at the dining room table as Matt signed the title over to me and handed me an organized maintenance file and two sets of keys. At the time, Matt was ill and looked incredibly tired. I did not stay, sensing it was a poor time for company, yet they welcomed me. Clearly, angels were everywhere, in all shapes and sizes.

That night, I drove home, sitting up high, with an improved vantage point. It did feel better. I had three days to pack everything I owned into the new, larger, and decidedly superior rig. Giggy was the original owner, and they had taken good care of it. I felt much safer driving her car.

I rushed furiously the final days, picking through every possession. Greg helped me move furniture to new owners, as he encouraged me to believe I was doing the right thing. I wanted him to drive north with me, but we nixed that idea because there was no room for him. I would be on my own.

I unbolted the third seat in the Suburban and sold it for ten bucks on Craigslist. The empty back seemed massive. My file boxes took up much of the space. I had five boxes of tax returns, closing documents, and bankruptcy files, as well as medical and legal letters regarding The Guy. Those heavy, depressing boxes contained the legacy of my past, and they took up a tremendous amount of space. The boxes went in first, near the center of the truck.

In the remaining space, I packed in layers. There were a few framed paintings, photos, and mirrors, carefully wound in bubble wrap and brown paper. I enveloped my precious She Buddha statue in blankets and set her on top of the framed glass pieces. In the remaining space, I squeezed in my pots and pans, a few books, a tool box, one folding beach chair, a cat box, a box of clean litter, two kennels, my rusted metal life-size armadillo sculpture, ski and camping equipment, meditation cushions, and winter gear. Every inch of the back and the passenger seat area were crammed full.

In an unplanned cosmic joke, the life-size metal armadillo lay on its back, feet straight up in the air against a side window, because that was the only way I could get it to fit. I stuffed rolled placemats and washcloths on top of the armadillo's belly and wrapped its legs with dishtowels for protection. The dishtowels sagged, so the armadillo ended up wearing ballerina warm-up tights, legs toward the heavens, his dented body squished against the window. It was a sight to remember, and turned a few heads on the trip.

I could not downsize to a Honda, yet succeeded to fit everything in the Suburban. It was now serving as the car, home, storage unit, cat residence, and safe-deposit box. Of course, Marilyn finally had to go, a cold, hard fact saved for last. It was not an easy breakup; I continue to miss her more than I care to admit. Once Marilyn and the bed were sold, there would be no turning back.

As I finished my midnight bouts of packing and began to disassemble the Gaddafi tent, BB and I started to avoid each other. An unspoken agreement formed, which left room for only one short, gloomy goodbye.

I prepared for the drive north as Russell rode his bicycle south. We would cross the same latitude at a point which neither of us would be able to identify. I knew his bicycle would be wearing the light copper bracelet, which made me smile. Later that year, Russell would ride into El Paso, Texas, and lock up his bike. He would walk into a store to buy two pair of Levi's and a few shirts. Looping the bags on the back, he rode his bike to the bus station and caught a Greyhound to Philly. Most people would be popping champagne, tweeting thousands of friends to brag about the end of an epic journey. Not Russell. He just went to Sears.

PART THREE

The Armadillo

CHAPTER FORTY

A T SIX O'CLOCK IN THE MORNING ON SEPTEMBER 8, 2010, EVERY article that survived the final cut was squeezed into the truck, except for the cats. As I lugged Spartacus in the cheesy plastic kennel out to the Suburban, I passed one last item left behind on the floor, my three-inch-foam sleeping pad. I thought of the day I scrubbed the squares of tile beneath the vacant-looking pad.

To save my back I dragged rather than carried the kennel across the tile and over rough pavement to the truck. The loud scratching rudely interrupted an otherwise placid hour: dark, moist air rippling with the sound of crickets. Spartacus wanted no part of his place in the Suburban. I lodged his carrier behind the front passenger seat and next to the rear window. There was barely enough room to close the door. I wedged pillows and blankets on the kennel's roof. Nothing was going to move.

I nestled Pierre's kennel in the passenger seat, on top of flattened layers of meditation cushions, bath towels, and blankets. I made four or five clumsy attempts to strap the seatbelt across and through the kennel openings before a solid click held that precious cargo in tight. I opened the windows enough so they both had air and pulled myself up onto the front seat.

The cats had a lot to say about this. I am generally sympathetic to their needs, but right then the incessant howling was hacking away at my patience. I drew in a gulp of air and slid the key into the ignition. Before turning the key, I rested my forehead on the steering wheel. I missed Greg and BB, and everything about Austin, before I had even started the truck. I could stop this madness right now, I told myself. I could choose not to turn the key, thereby avoiding eight days on the road with distraught cats as my only company. I thought of BB upstairs, asleep for a few more hours. My eyes tingled and stung. I cranked the key forward and released the parking brake. I reached for the headlight dial and turned it to the right, so I could see thirteen feet into my future while everything else remained a secret.

I turned left on Sixth Street, followed by a right onto I-35 North. The cats moaned and squealed, undeterred by the pet tranquilizers I had forced down their throats. As I pushed the accelerator to flow with freeway speeds, the truck felt cumbersome and sluggish. Of course it did. I had loaded my entire life of belongings (baggage, so to speak) on two sets of axles. What else should I expect? The gas tank was full, and the gauges held steady. I needed to do the same—hold steady and take everything thirteen feet at a time.

As I reached the high spot on an overpass, I noted the light of dawn seeping above the horizon, pale hints of seeing further ahead. A tanker truck roared and rumbled by in the passing lane. This added to the melodrama for Spartacus and Pierre, who were quickly regaining my attention and sympathy. I did feel bad for them. This was frightening and uncomfortable. I too wanted someone to scratch the right spot behind my ears and assure me that everything was going to be all right.

I suspected that Giggy and Matt had spent a good deal of money to repair the air conditioning before giving the Suburban to me. The A/C cooled for a few days and suddenly transitioned to spewing hot air through every vent. Soon after the sun rose, heat gathered in still spots, so I kept the windows open for the rest of the day, listening to the loud, rotating hiss of tires on the highway. The wind whipped through the cab in constant thunder, while our cargo layers shifted. I began to psyche myself up for the drive through Dallas. I resisted a cry because I was too scared about navigating through the next big city to allow for that sort of indulgence. I was the one who had turned the key that morning, so we were on a mission. The cats' distress signals were forlorn, relentless, and inconsolable, singing the blues for all three of us.

Our journey teemed with the unknown. A force of fate pushed the truck along, as I swallowed my doubts and aching sense of loss. I knew that Alaska circled the earth several orbits away from where I wanted to be. I was on my way to life inside of a walk-in freezer. In one giant, reluctant push, I forged ahead for the one thing I could not find in Austin, the elusive paycheck.

The promise of a regular bank deposit and benefits pulled me like a magnet. Austin disappeared in the rearview mirror. I looked down at my tanned legs and suspected it would be years before I ever saw color on my limbs again. Arbitrary thoughts like that pricked my eyes with sudden shots of emotion. Loss is painful; however, at the end of the long drive, I would gain something of unquestionable value, employment in my new field. That was something to celebrate, to hold in gratitude, so it was a mixed bag.

As we rolled along buffeting winds and heat, I digested the reality of my situation: the winds of fate were moving north, despite my fomentations. I have heard my meditation teachers suggest that the winds of fate are perfect. All I have to do is to accept whatever is actually happening as perfect. It all sounded tranquil and wise, so easy. Nothing about the journey felt easy or perfect. The cannonball in my gut said something different; it felt heavy, blue, defeated, unfinished, joy cut short. I was slow on the uptake to believe in this perfection. Later, Russell captured it best: "Well, maybe you just haven't *caught up* with the perfection yet."

Loaded down with the weight of my life, the Suburban purred along through Dallas, north to Oklahoma City, on to Salina, Kansas. It was muggy and loud inside the truck, hot with a dry wind roaring through half-open windows, my cobalt-blue glass dinner plates rattling in their boxes. The cats bawled in confusion and insult. They were used to getting exactly what they wanted at all times. I was tired of their wails, tired of feeling bad for *them*. I was the one driving. It was a good thing I loved them.

Spartacus released another world-class poop. Even with the windows open, long-term exposure was out of the question. I pulled over onto a wide gravel shoulder on a straightaway. Moving the crate, opening the door without losing the cat, and clearing out the mess was not a simple 1-2-3 task.

I pulled off a few pillows and turned the crate out enough to open the door. Wearing rubber gloves, I managed to pull the disgusting pad out from under Spartacus, who cowered in the back of the kennel. Shoving, wrangling, rearranging, I deposited the pad in a plastic grocery bag, secured the kennel door, and set everything back in place. As I patted down the last pillow, my right clog slipped on the shiny, slick with *Armor All* threshold of the door. I twisted, toes pointing toward the sky. My tailbone landed on the truck step before bouncing off and onto the grimy, roadside pebbles.

Both cats wailed in unison as I sucked in two or three groaning breaths. The truck jiggled and swayed as cars sped past us. I knelt to relieve pressure on the tailbone, shocked from the direct hit. One can be certain that bouts of expletives followed. I don't remember which ones exactly, or in which order. My already sore back had a new partner in crime—a pulsating ball of fire attached to the sitting part of my body. After a few minutes, I urged my shaken body up from the roadside. Grabbing two pillows from above the big kennel, I padded my seat, preparing as best I could for the possible torture ahead.

In the hotel room that night, I eased into the bathtub and moaned, allowing myself to feel a bit beaten down. It was a choice I could always make: happy or sad. I chose sad, sore, knocked down, disheartened. In the morning, I turned around at the full-length mirror, to see a tattoo of a humongous purple plum, centered perfectly at the base of my spine.

I tried out a few different pillow arrangements to pad the pain throughout the following days. We drove northeast on 81 to 83, passing through McCook, Nebraska, North Platte, and Valentine, on to Pierre, South Dakota. As planned, we spent the night in Pierre. Comical that the name of a town would influence the route I chose to take, but it did. I bagged cubes from the dreary motel's ice machine and lay flat on my stomach, ice on the plum, hating to admit to such a heavy level of deflation. I skipped eating dinner, remaining face down on the clean sheets as the cats ate and played deliriously in their freedom outside of the kennels.

By day three, the cats began to understand the routine and go along with it, to a quieter degree. They figured out that if they slept all day in the crates, they could eat and poop and play all night long. They discovered the joys of two beds in one room, and the fun of bounding from one bed to the other all night long. It was a blast! They were tired all day, snuggling into the sleep mode of a teenager the night after a slumber party. I was dazed with sleep deprivation as they became rested and relaxed about the road trip. The northern temperatures cooled the air, so I could keep the windows closed. The roar of the road receded.

The broad space of the Midwest became cooler, more remote through the winding ribbons of North Dakota. Fresh into an ambitious early-morning start, I fiddled with the radio until it tuned into a station playing "Follow Your Bliss," by the B-52s. My heart soared. I felt suddenly happy and free, buoyed by the joy of the morning light and one of my favorite songs. I enjoyed sitting up high in the seat as the heavy truck rolled over a lumpy hill. At the crest, the vista opened up to a view of endless fields of sunflowers. As far as I could see, I was driving through a van Gogh painting.

The sunflowers blasted pure exuberance and vitality into the air. I pulled over, shut off the engine, and sat still. The moment stopped in time. I was in awe of the morning, the flowers, the peace, the magnanimous elegance. A red-winged blackbird landed on a nearby fence. This was heart-stopping beauty.

With a goal of six hundred miles that day, I went back on the winding road, dazzled by hundreds of straight, even rows of sunny faces turned toward the sky. Even the cats took note and stretched to sit up and wonder what I was so excited about. Soon the van Gogh fields stopped in an instant cut, as though abruptly shaven down to stubble of dry, brown earth.

I took 52 northwest to the Canadian border, where I hooked up with 39 to Moose Jaw, then on to Medicine Hat in Alberta. The next day, with another early start, it felt as though the Suburban and I purred together. My morning cup of coffee was still steaming out of the hole on the plastic lid when Spartacus evacuated something. He yowled in what sounded like a mix of mortified and disgusted, then launched into a frantic attempt to break through the kennel door. By that point in the trip, Pierre did not even lift his head; this was our morning routine with Spartacus.

I pulled into a vacant, eerily rusted-out 1950s filling station. Trying to hold the back door as close to me as possible, I reached in to wriggle open the kennel and pull out the offending pad. In a frenzy to get away from his mess, Spartacus leapt toward my face. I ducked, and he dashed out through the open door. I turned to see him disappear behind the ghost-town gas station. Sunrise spread a wan, dreary tint on the corroded fuel pump. The station's windows were made of more air and plywood than cracked glass.

Fighting the desire to chase a cat is akin to the willpower it takes for a smoker to refuse a Marlboro. I held still, wanting to chase, and knowing better. Weary, weepy, on the edge of falling over the cliff of useless worry, the thought of driving west without Spartacus whining in his kennel was more than I could bear.

I left the dusty white Suburban's back doors open in an effort to air things out and lowered myself down on the rusty gas pump's platform. Leaning forward to avoid the plum, I gazed in the opposite direction, as if I could care less that he ran away someplace behind me. It was early, about six a.m. No one seemed to be awake or moving in the desolate, wayside highway town. It was quiet in a mournful way, as though ghosts were still there to open the filling station and make a first pot of harsh coffee. Two semis drifted by along the highway's scratched surface, leaving a silent loneliness in their wake as they disappeared around the corner.

In serious lack of hope, I imagined my life without Spartacus. I thought about his thick black coat, his larger-than-it-should-be body. Holding Spartacus was like holding a big, wild cat. I would never find another one like him. What if he was gone, forever? How could I find a way to accept that loss right now? Those thoughts pinged and swirled through my exhausted, frenzied mind. I was spinning around in my own highly developed version of neurosis. Staring at the ground, I used a stick to pick at delicate, oily plates of rust by my feet. I strained to be optimistic, but I was unable to come up with a positive spin. My inner dialog morphed into a stubborn handshake with the darker side of life. I wiped some grit out of my eyes and tapped the dirty stick farther into brittle layers of rust.

Ten minutes later, Spartacus returned, looking sheepish, apparently not so sure about living behind the old ghost station. He slinked back to my hands on the ground, allowing me to scoop him up in a death grip, kissing his big, soft head as I stuffed him back into the safety of his kennel. From then on, Spartacus never tried to escape from my arms.

On day six of the drive, I planned a stop in Edmonton to gas up and have the oil changed. Twenty miles south of Edmonton, the sky flipped from blue to dark, deep gray in a minute, resulting in hours of thick rain. I decided to stop early and find a hotel room.

Each night I hauled in cat crates, the litter box, ten pounds of cat litter, the small broom and dustpan, two food bowls, one water bowl, the food, and my cosmetics case. It was a twenty-minute ritual. The entire time the cats believed they were being tortured, as I hauled all that stuff around.

Right after dinner, I turned on the television and immediately dropped into a heavy sleep, gaining a wide span of relief. In that delicious glimpse of grace, I also forgot the delicate wire-rim glasses around my eyes. I woke in the morning wearing the imprint of a pair of smashed glasses. I bent them back into relative shape and removed the left bow, which dangled helplessly.

At eight a.m., I adjusted my glasses and held down the left lens with my pinkie as I turned left toward Fort Nelson, six hundred and forty-one miles ahead. Thirteen hours later, we pulled onto the main drag through Fort Nelson. I filled the gas tank (at one hundred seventy-five dollars Canadian per fill), checked the oil, and cleaned the windshield, noticing the formation of a shell of mud around the Suburban. I stopped next door and found a decent salad and a piece of pizza. I eased under the covers of old soft sheets as the cats settled into the new smells and spring tensions of both beds, secure in their anticipation of a wild night in a dingy motel.

Early the next day, I aimed for and reached Whitehorse, Yukon Territory, almost eight hundred miles closer to Fairbanks. Hotel rooms were difficult to come by, so it took several hours to find a room. After I finished hauling everything through a narrow back door and down a flight of stairs, I fell into a short-lived yet thorough sleep. It was easy to ignore the incoming bombs of hyper cats. I was simply too fatigued to care. I slept for nine hours and then leapt out of bed at first waking blink, intent on an early start. I wrestled the crated cats and supplies up the stairs, out the propped-open back door, and back into the crammed Suburban. The next step involved hot coffee in a paper cup.

The twilight of the morning sang, chilled and clear, rough and magical, diamond like. I stopped by Tim Horton's to pick up a donut and a cup of road coffee. The cats were sleeping, by then seasoned road trippers. I accelerated the truck on the black, silent highway, advancing west and north on the last day of my migration. By making a right turn toward the North Pole, I was defying the birds' wisdom, as the sand cranes flowed south. If all went according to plan, we would be in Fairbanks that night.

CHAPTER FORTY-ONE

E ACH TIME I CROSS THE BORDER INTO ALASKA, IT CONJURES UP A page in a small coffee-table book I read years ago, called *Children's Letters to God*. In one note to God, a curious five-year-old asked God how he decided where to draw the borders around states and countries. I thought that was a great question because I have noticed that sometimes these borderlines make sense, as though the people deciding on that line could feel the difference in, for lack of a better word, vibration. In Alaska, crossing the line from Canada opens the gate to a world of automatic awe. Canada is earthly beauty; Alaska is heaven. Maybe I feel that way because most of us feel that way about returning home.

Pink morning light pulled red from the rocks that lay exposed on snow-speckled mountains. The sky was clear, and the autumn leaves were hatching bright colors. As the sun rose higher, overflowing brush-strokes of yellow and orange ran through evergreen forests. Rivers and lakes sparkled as they reflected snowy peaks. Confectioners'-sugar snow dusted lower elevations, the early snow affectionately referred to as "termination dust." Most seasonal work in Alaska ends at the first sight of these powdered mountains. I use the term "lower elevations" because Mt. McKinley's head and shoulders, heavily clad with snow and free from a typical cloud cover, loomed in the distance.

I know it is a fact that we cannot attend our own funeral, but it is fun to think about. I definitely want a party, not a sappy, weepy affair. I hope my loved ones will set up a state-of-the-art sound system, and ask everyone to stand up and dance to at least three songs: "Girls Just Want to Have Fun" by Cyndi Lauper and "Follow Your Bliss" and "Roam" by the B-52s. I pulled out one of the six CDs I had refused to sell in a garage sale, including the B52s.

Looking straight down the road toward the massive peak of Denali, once called Mt. McKinley, I rode and rocked into the wilderness playing "Roam" five times in a row, a shameless act I would only do alone on a road trip. By the third round, I felt a strong tinge of bliss, and I forgot about my worries for a while. A faint trickle of hope emerged as a surprise to my heart. I was almost there and less than a week away from going back to work. Denali's exalted, snowy face welcomed me home, laughing at the folly of my ways, as though I could ever be anything but an Alaskan Woman. It felt natural to be the prodigal daughter returning home.

I stopped at a pullout next to the Tanana River, near the infinitesimal town of Salcha. We were so close, only forty miles south of Fairbanks. The plum and the broken zipper competed for my attention. It was time for a good stretch. My posture felt permanently crinkled. I stooped cave-woman style. My right foot barely knew what to do without a gas pedal.

I scanned the horizon. Every turn introduced a new form of magnificence. It was a National Geographic day in Alaska. I noticed that the Suburban's left rear taillight cover was close to dangling off. I opened the back door, fearing an avalanche of shoes and miscellaneous household goods. Everything held, so I reached around and found a couple of loose screws. I used my Leatherman to tighten them and returned the tool to the console between the front seats. Maneuvering carefully into my position behind the steering wheel—I had developed a professional feel for perfect pillow placement on the seat—and cranked the engine for the last push.

Five minutes later, I banked into a large arc on the road. A last round of the curve exposed an enormous, freshly hit moose laid out in the middle of both lanes. A few people stood next to two trucks parked to the side. The moose was dead, and the first truck was well-twisted. I slowed yet kept driving, flashing my lights to two oncoming cars, warning them of the obstacle ahead. When I see a dead animal on the road, I usually sink into a sense that we are not doing such a great job of taking care of those who came before us. Road kills are not on the list of humanity's crowning glory.

I could see the people standing on the side of the highway were uninjured, so I continued, shaken and reminded of the dangers on the road. If not for the wobbly taillight repair, I would have been driving around that corner a few minutes earlier. I wondered if Athena's owl was riding on the baggage rack, with a vantage point much greater than my own. Or perhaps it was simple, random luck, because life was about to get a whole lot easier.

On September 15 around four in the afternoon, I rolled out of the Suburban and stood on the pavement of The Final Destination, purging a sigh of pent-up worry. I had made it to Fairbanks. I slipped my fingers through the belt loops of my wrinkled pants and bent back in an attempt to stand tall. Looking toward the sky, my tailbone radiated fire shaped like the sun.

I lugged the cats and a bag of clean clothes into a motel room on Airport Way. Of course, Pierre and Spartacus had no way to know that this was our final destination, but I sure did. I took a shower and threw my gray carpet-job T-shirt and a pair of stained, baggy pants into the trash. I wore them the entire trip, so I would not have to unpack anything other than underwear. That was part of the plan, a symbolic gesture of dumping my old, difficult life. This was a new chapter. It was time to open my bag and pull out some clean clothes. I sent emails to let people know I made it and walked stiffly next door to the northernmost Denny's in the world.

I gingerly worked around the plum and managed to insert myself on an unmercifully hard seat at a booth. I missed my pillows and wondered how sitting in a desk chair was going to feel. I decided to order an omelet from the seniors' menu, available to anyone over fifty-five. The server disappointed me, offering not even a glimpse of suspicion that I was scamming her. To this day I regret ordering from the seniors' menu, wishing I had ordered a burger from the kids' menu instead.

I was ten years away from retirement age, starting all over again at the bottom of the food chain. I was headed to a low-paying administrative position and felt lucky to have it. Thirty-two years prior, I had landed in northern Alaska with youthful exuberance and a sense of adventure. That night in Denny's, I was back to financial square one, forced to reinvent a life I had spent thirty years building. Rebuilding a livelihood on the shoulders of an armed robbery, bankruptcy, a plum, a broken zipper, and aging skin should never start out with a Denny's senior citizen meal.

When I returned to the room, the cats had front-row seats on the windowsill, looking out through the leaves of a small birch tree. I had parked the Suburban where I could see the upside-down rusted armadillo pressed against the side window. Back inside, I sat near a cheap motel coffee table near the window and counted my money. There was not much left, enough to stay in the hotel for less than a week. I stood to lean against the windowsill to pet the cats. High clouds set a dreary tone in the sky. The breeze tickled the birch leaves, so they sounded like a waterfall. A twisted twinge of the past, tenderness and melancholy, surfaced as I inhaled the evening air. For the first time in my life, I realized that I could actually smell the cold. It was both possible and easy—winter was already flirting with the air.

In Alaska, magic is everywhere, except for the strip malls, one of which I looked at out the window. The road trip was over. I took stock of the truth that the bossy winds of existence plunked me down on that particular spot on Earth, because I would not have picked it myself. The currents of change were immune to my wishes, my reluctance and feeling of loss. The trajectory called fate slapped me down on the ground in a location I would never have chosen of my own volition. I suspected that whatever happened would not be easy. Alaska is not an effortless place.

Wally Hickel, former governor of Alaska, once described his first sea voyage to Alaska. When he crossed the line into the land of awe and looked up to vast, intimidating walls of snow and stone, he said, "Alaska, you be good to me, and I will be good to you." I had made a similar vow the first time I arrived, and I repeated it that evening. I would find a way to thrive. I drew the stiff motel curtains closed. It was time to sleep.

Arriving a few days early provided time for rest and a refresher course on the town. I had lived in Fairbanks for about a year during my early days in Alaska in the late 1970s. I left the cats at the Motel 8 and found a car wash to remove crusted layers of road dirt off the all-successful, almighty truck that made the trip without incident. I wanted to pat the vehicle and tell it "thank you" before setting out on the first drive through Fairbanks. Brilliant yellow birch leaves rustled on gleaming white stalks, shocking against the cornflower-blue sky. Life along the quiet roads seemed remarkably slow compared to the rest of America. It felt remote and somewhat barren. No matter how it felt, it was going to be home, so I had better adjust.

Although I was relieved to make it to town in time to start work, arriving early meant spending money for a motel, so I was nervous. During our phone interview back in August, I understood that my new employer would help me find housing for the first couple of weeks after I arrived. The day after I drove into town, I called and left messages for my new supervisor. She returned my call on Thursday afternoon. I mentioned our discussion about help with finding a temporary place to stay. She seemed puzzled and quite put out that I would bring that up. She suggested that I contact the housing department and wished me luck. Stunned, I wrote down the phone number and called it. A woman politely explained that one of the dorms was closed for repairs, so they had a long, urgent wait list of students.

I hung up the phone and immediately questioned my reality. Of course I had asked about temporary housing during the interview. I had also requested a relocation allowance over the phone, which was declined, according to my HR contact, Joan. I based my decision to move on the understanding that I would pay for the move, and they would help me with a place to stay for a week or two, until I could settle in. I based that assumption on words something like "We can help you out for a week or two, in a dorm or something." Besides, that was a common arrangement for people moving up north. People in Alaska take newcomers in and help them get settled. At least that had been my experience.

I reviewed all of our conversations in my mind, realizing that my new supervisor, the person who had offered those words, had never directly communicated with me after I accepted the position. I spoke to her only once after the interview, so Joan was my point of contact. Come to think of it, Joan spoke in sound bites whenever I mentioned needing help with a place to stay.

I was suspicious. This felt like a blatant disregard for a promise made to me on the phone. I soon figured it out: Joan was stuck in the middle of a "she said, she said" conversation about temporary housing, and she knew my supervisor had made no effort to help with the arrangements. I called Joan, speaking as diplomatically as possible, "Apparently, our housing conversation did not work out as expected. Do you have any suggestions?"

I could tell she was uneasy. Joan offered to send out a mass email to all department members, asking if anyone had a place for me (and two cats) to stay for a week or so. In typical Alaskan fashion, she received almost fifty replies in one day. Experience told me that people in Alaska step up to the plate, which was why I was so puzzled and anxious about that particular lack of follow-through.

By the end of Friday, I had met Karl, my first new friend. He offered me the use of an almost new, cozy studio until I found a rental. I backed into his driveway and left most everything in the Suburban, moving in only the cats and the basics. I could still only see thirteen feet ahead; if I lowered the left lens of my glasses, everything seemed to be leaning in the right direction when I met Karl.

I sprawled on the futon bed in the studio, trying to bend my spine in the opposite direction of the Hunchback-of-Notre-Dame look. I marveled at my safe landing into Karl's orderly and generous world. After a minute of relaxation, my stomach flipped in queasy, nervous jitters. I tasted a nasty feeling about my new employer. She said one thing then did another. I wondered if there was yet one more demon I needed to meet.

I had been in that position before, where I set myself up to rely on unreliable people. I *knew* we talked about housing. I would never move up there without having that conversation, and it felt as though her attitude was that I made it up. I called Christie and lined out the events, nervously admitting that I had a fishy feeling about the situation. Christie did too. She remembered our phone call when I relayed the housing comment during the interview.

The cats and I stayed with Karl, his son Alexander, five cats, and fourteen chickens for over two weeks. The apartment and house had running water and bathtubs, uncommon luxuries when living that far north. Karl and Alexander made it easy to be friends, so we bonded hard and fast. If angels show up wearing spectacles and rubber boots, they can also grow beards and hang knives from their belts.

Over the weekend before work, I slept more than I had in weeks, and gained a sense of strength and excitement about starting on Monday, September 20, 2010. The plum and the broken zipper were raw and sore. I ached from my scalp to the tip of my tailbone. On Sunday night, I showered, smoothed out a few wrinkles from a set of clothes in my duffle bag, twisted and messed with my contorted eyeglasses, and tried to sleep. I wanted to be rested and clear for the next morning; sadly, sleep felt impossible.

That night, after the first day of work, I relaxed with a kitty in each arm, flat on Karl's futon, with a towel rolled under the small of my back. The Suburban had successfully moved us from Austin to Fairbanks. My tired eyes watered, thinking of Giggy and Matt. As always, BB and Greg also were in my thoughts. I marveled at Karl's salt-of-the-earth generosity, and my good fortune to have his help. A hopeful resolve settled in my bones. Only three weeks to go before a paycheck.

Innocent of what lay ahead, I believed in a three-week wait for salvation. I was in blind territory, unprepared for my first fall into the arms of the next devil along my path. After a mere two days on the job, I figured out that instead of wearing Prada, my devil wore Uggs.

My initial concerns were on target. To say I was not working with a team player is a glorious understatement. As I drove north, I was concerned about the cold, which ended up being a slight annoyance compared to the hothead I was paired up with in the office. Within two days, I recognized the dynamic. This time around, my new boss was the porcupine; again, I was the balloon. This was far different from my relationship with Kathi in Juneau. Kathi is a kind porcupine, and she loves me. At work, I found myself in the ring with a professional, and I knew it. I spoke harshly to my imagined angels: I simply wanted to make a living. I did not want to wrestle a feisty rodent. The impact of her sharp, attentive quills and mean, glistening eyes transformed my earlier assessment of Kathi. Meeting up with that porcupine turned Kathi into a cute stuffed animal.

Unfortunately, my return to Alaska started out with ambivalence, yet quickly turned to misery. I had a hard time feeling any commitment to my situation, and spent most of my time wishing I could leave. Seeking free entertainment, I drove to the library. Libraries are one of my favorite free things, right up there with fresh mountain air. On my first of many passes through the local public library, I slipped through pages and pages of the biggest dictionary I could find. I wanted a word, one word, to describe the porcupine. I needed to put words to the experience, thinking that would help make sense of such an immediate and unexpectedly painful situation. I found a word within minutes, not too far back, in the *B*s: *bumptious*, which means "aggressive, forward, obtrusive, insolent, pushy, arrogant, over-bearing, brazen." It was helpful to find the word, and deeply discouraging at the same time.

I went to work every day to face a one hundred and fifty-pound porcupine, waddling on her hind legs, wearing fluorescent green "look at me!" spectacles. She squeezed a red legal file folder in the crook of her left arm and pointed her sharp index-finger claw at my stupidity. I was expected to know how to fulfill a list of tasks without any clear training. Porcupine was one of those people wired and skilled for eating people alive, dedicated to making sure that no one gets what he or she wants or needs. They devour us sensitive let's-all-just-get-alongers in protracted, snarling gulps, waiting in ambush for the next bite, complaining about our lack of flavor.

CHAPTER FORTY-TWO

I RENTED A SMALL LOG CABIN WITH SOUTH-FACING WINDOWS, FIVE miles from work. The sixteen-by-sixteen-foot floor plan included an upper loft, creating almost five hundred square feet of useable living space. After Gaddafi's tent and the Suburban, it was a leap into spaciousness. I borrowed money from Kathi and my friend Maggio, in Skagway, Alaska, to cover the deposit and first month's rent.

Spartacus, Pierre, and I settled in. With my first paycheck, I bought two twin-size foam pads, nesting them upstairs, side by side as a bed. I unpacked the truck over the span of two evenings after work. I bought a few staples at the grocery store and prepared for the long winter ahead. Ceremoniously unfolding my fluorescent green beach chair from Galveston, I placed it in the middle of the room, facing the largest window. I used my toolbox as an ottoman and wrapped myself in a fleece blanket. The cats jumped onboard.

The cabin did not have a phone line, TV, or Internet; nevertheless it was new, with electricity and the most treasured luxury of all: running water. Fairbanks has a unique set of challenges when it comes to construction, resulting in rental units referred to as "dry cabins." This is the polite way of saying you have an outhouse instead of a powder room.

The term "running water" means you have a finite tank of water, which requires replenishment on a regular basis. Replenishing means calling the water company for a truck delivery, carrying it in five-gallon plastic jugs, or various creative solutions in between. In my case, an insulated room big enough for a three hundred-gallon water tank was attached to the square cabin. The tank was not built to accommodate water truck delivery, thus requiring a far more manual and labor-intensive process than dialing the phone. For the cabin's system, I needed to carry water from a water-filling station in town, (much like a gas station, only for water) and load it into the large tank at home. Flexible hoses carried water from the tank to a kitchen sink and upstairs to a small shower. Both sink and shower drained out as "gray water" through a black waste pipe that simply ended four feet from the cabin.

Having lived in Fairbanks before, I knew I was signing up for water inconveniences, which was one of many reasons I had felt so meh about returning. I needed to purchase the gear required for the transfer of water over time. Karl let me borrow his one hundred-gallon tank on the days he was not pumping water into his underground water tank. The portable tank he used to carry the water from point A to point B fit perfectly in the back of the Suburban, as though I planned it that way. By November, I had one hundred and fifty dollars to buy a pump and another one hundred dollars for hoses and fittings, so I could pump the water from his one hundred-gallon tank into my three hundred-gallon storage tank at the cabin.

Winter was on her way. In addition to buying a water system, I needed to "winterize" the truck. This describes the installation of a battery blanket, oil pan, and transmission-fluid heater, and an engine block heater, all connected to a heavy-duty electrical plug mounted on the vehicle's front grill. When the temperature hits zero and below, we connect an arctic-grade extension cord to the plug. Once turned on, the heater toasts all of the important parts and fluids, in preparation for starting the engine. Customarily, cars require at least two hours of applied heat before starting, which means mounting electric bills throughout the winter.

I was not getting ahead. Every dollar I made went right out of my account. The cabin owner had left about seventy-five gallons of heating fuel in the tank, so heating oil was at the top of the shopping list.

Kathi loaned me more money to "winterize." My debts continued to stack up, even as I collected paychecks. I thought constantly about work and how to manage the tension there. For two years, I grappled with my feelings about The Guy and his bizarre, fateful decisions. Now I faced another layer of human negativity.

I wondered aloud to Christie: Why do people decide to bully? Why do some people commit violent, brutal crimes against their fellow man/woman/child? Why did I have to run up against so many mean people? Why do many show profound capacity for empathy and caring, while others care only for themselves? I came around to remembering the futility of "why" questions.

In a storybook, or an advice column in Cosmo magazine, a healthy choice would involve eliminating people like the porcupine from my life. That sounded great, yet in that particular situation I did not consider that an option. I needed to find a way to work with her. How I handled the malevolent behavior was the point. How could I respond without confronting the over-armed porcupine head on? Would it come to that? I just wanted to exchange honest work for a paycheck, not another challenging growth opportunity.

The bully and the criminal are not all that interesting, yet they sure seem to gain a great deal of attention in the news, in the courtroom, or the work environment. I was beginning to figure out that they are practiced and skilled manipulators of people and situations. People like the porcupine and The Guy were mean people who wouldn't admit they were mean. They refused to admit their actions and fought to the end to protect their rights to be the way they were.

I know that people who abuse power are not one hundred percent bad, but they do manage to get their way by tipping other people off balance with their nitpicking, making-wrong, and belittling behaviors. They have perfected their own versions of nasty, controlling strategies by controlling situations with their tempers, tones, and moods.

It does not take a Jungian therapist to see that being the target of another's aggressive, overpowering, manipulative behavior might strike a chord in me. I felt weary from fighting off invasive people. The Guy overpowered me physically, and the porcupine did everything she could to overpower me psychologically and emotionally.

Because the porcupine's behavior colored my experience with bold, broad, and messy strokes, it is tempting to write anecdote upon anecdote, oily sardines crammed into a smelly can, to justify my feelings. That would serve no purpose, except to shine attention on the person who most wants it.

Many people say that heaven and hell happen after we die. I suspect that heaven and hell are states of mind, right here, each moment. How could I deal with the moments that felt like hell?

I was fragile. In 2007, I had felt the first tugs of financial strangulation. In 2008, a stranger held me captive with his gun. Then, in 2010, I was controlled by a paycheck and a spiky porcupine who got high from stirring up trouble. I did not know how to overcome feeling like a victim.

At work, my intuition told me that people knew what was going on yet turned the other way. It was easier for them. Understandably, people wanted to remain on the porcupine's "good side." As friendly as all of the employees were, I noticed that no one asked me how I liked my job.

On the bright side, the porcupine taught me how I do not want to act. I watched how easy it was to blame and to make someone wrong. As Perry Mason said, one can make a case for anything. Porcupines master the art of making everyone wrong so they can feel right. It takes work to help people succeed, and it takes a few words to tear them down. I was learning fast.

I realized that my responsibility was not about changing the porcupine, rather how to change my position within our cramped space. Some people are worth confronting, and I reckon that others are not. I wanted to choose my battles carefully. I missed my friends, and Marilyn, and Dr. Phil.

I drove to work with trepidation squeezing hard on my esophagus. I knew I was out of this rodent's league. Why was everyone pretending this was not happening? I hated myself for taking on the role of a cowering puppy, in hiding. The porcupine loved an audience and enjoyed every opportunity for "expert" talk. As I sat in my nearby office, listening to her voice felt worse than filing my teeth with an emery board.

There were questions pinging from all directions. Why did I leave Austin? What in the world had I signed up for?

After one of my stops at the library, I went home and sat on the beach chair, strategically placed by the stove, so I could read Andre Agassi's book, *Open*. Describing his early years of playing competitive tennis, Agassi discovered the profound distinction between not losing and winning. Early in his career, he worked dog hard on the court to make sure he did not lose. It was not about winning. Once he figured that out and reframed his intentions toward winning, the game changed for him.

After reading that, I realized that I walked into the office every day filled with thoughts of how not to lose. I was angry with myself for being in such a double bind. I felt bogged down in a no-win situation.

Sadly, winning had not occurred to me. If I said, "That notebook is black," she would assure me that it was, in fact, institutional green. I watched her play the same games with other people, so I had some reassurance that the "maybe *I* am the crazy one" thoughts were harebrained. When I watched the porcupine entrap coworkers in her double binds, they usually shook their heads and walked away, sometimes griping about her, and returned to their respective desks *away from her*. Therein lay the distinction: I did not have the ability to get away from her. I was her primary target as she created knots upon knots of double binds.

My theory is that mean people know exactly what they are doing. These people know what they do and continue to do it because it works.

With time, people within the company opened up about her history. Four people had already quit the job I had before I drove up from Texas. Everyone in town probably knew better than to apply for that. I often recalled the voice mail message I listened to in the cool bathroom of the fancy Houston restaurant. My first response had been, "Do not call them back."

So much for listening to my instincts.

The days grew grayer and colder. My prized Austin suntan flaked off in a dusty mass of the past. I scraped money together from paycheck to paycheck to prepare for the winter. My wire-rim eyeglasses were still broken from the night in Edmonton. I could not afford to buy a new pair, so I got used to the lopsided look and feel.

Karl would often visit me in the file room, also known as my office. It felt as though he was my only friend in Fairbanks, so I began to call him My Only Friend Karl. As we talked, I would see him look down at the holes in the soles of my black leather boots, and I could tell the holes bothered him. I was not happy about the gaps either, but I had come to accept them as a part of life until I could pay off a few more things.

Even worse were my crooked glasses that listed to the right side of my face. I am sure that was an irritating sight to a detail guy who likes to polish the finer points. That all added to my confusion and lack of confidence.

Finally, he suggested that I bring my glasses over to his wood shop after work. I met him there and handed them over with no apprehension; I trusted his skill and judgment completely. He tried using narrow, sharp drills to make a crisp, new hole. Despite his persistence, the lens was impenetrable. So he used an *X* of copper wire to lash the old temple onto the frames. The repair worked, though it left a troublesome dark spot that looked like a fly. Karl would look at me and say, "Doesn't that bother you?"

I learned to ignore it, as I continued to train myself to avoid unpleasant thoughts and irritants. The repair felt like an improvement to me and served as a reminder that I had a resourceful and caring friend.

At home, I coveted the heating fuel, choosing thicker socks over nudging the thermostat up on the Toyostove. I leaned back in the fluorescent green beach chair and looked around the empty, unfurnished cabin. I had left Austin and my friends behind. I did that for this unhappy set of conditions and circumstances.

Dr. Phil describes integrity as holding ourselves to a high standard when we are alone and no one is watching. I contemplated the situation, eventually asking myself: How do I handle myself around the porcupine, so in the end (Oh please, God, there will be an end to this, right?) I will know that I made every effort to act with integrity, causing no harm?

As usual, I had more questions than answers. I rarely spoke about the porcupine, and only to friends who did not work at my office. I decided to stop talking, because it constantly brought unsatisfactory advice. "Just kill her with kindness" was among the top three tips. Being inauthentic and sweet to an abuser did not feel like integrity. Being mean and spiteful did not feel like integrity either. I was in the classic entanglement of the double bind.

I concentrated on defusing the situation, reacting as little as possible. That made everything simple, in principle. I was responsible for my behavior, no one else's. Some days, patience and forgiveness came easily, other days not at all. I feared the loss of my ability to forgive and forget. I wanted to be above it all, yet my capacity was limited.

I was still waiting for the trial and wondering about my ability to forgive The Guy. Though I hated my position within my work relationship, she did not have a gun to my head. However, she was messing with my mind. I was allowing her to mess with my mind.

My "blessed second chance at life" felt miserable, which added guilt to my mental mix. Our days grew in gulps of darkness, with short dots of bright light and extended days of below-freezing temperatures. Sitting in the beach chair, I checked in with myself. I still loved my life, right? I wanted to feel grateful for this second chance, even if that included physical pain and financial loss, right?

In the same troubled breath, I was already tired from the second chance. Why was I blowing this supposedly great opportunity? I lifted my feet off the chilled cabin floor and rested my calves on the toolbox. Drafts of squeaky clean, below-zero air snuck through small cracks in the cabin walls, around the windows, and under the door. Dog teams down the street barked back and forth to each other beneath the white-frosted moon. I felt beaten and degraded in my second chance at life. I fiddled with the same familiar psychological Rubik's Cube. How could I stop feeling like a victim when I was feeling like a victim?

CHAPTER FORTY-THREE

T HE WEEK OF MY FIRST THANKSGIVING IN FAIRBANKS, WEATHER patterns brought a rainy, cold storm, leaving roads impassable; we all slid around on a giant ice-skating rink. Most businesses sent employees home. I tried to get to work, but on the drive up a slight hill to the main road, the Suburban ended up spinning in spirals, almost slipping over the edge of the road into some birch trees. Humbled, I inched the truck back around toward the house, where I stayed holed up for four days. I read library books. I balanced my checkbook and figured out how to pay for a table and some shelves. Everything remained in cardboard boxes lined against the cabin walls.

I had a television, but it took a month or so to figure out that I could pick up a few local channels without cable or satellite. That misperception steered me toward using library videos and books, which is usually more enjoyable anyway. I did not own a radio and could not connect to a local channel on my computer, so I had a lot of time on my hands. I had no desire to make friends, because all I wanted to do was leave. I also struggled with the question of how much I wanted to share about the previous few years of my life.

The details felt personal and private, so I hid them. There were things I wanted to omit, and those omissions left out much of who I was. Other than talking with My Only Friend Karl, I kept to myself and dedicated social time to phone calls with Christie, other friends, and family. There were too many things I did not want to explain to someone I barely knew—the headaches, the broken zipper, the porcupine, the upcoming trial. It was easier to be quiet and alone than out trying to make new friends in a place I wanted to escape.

That included Thanksgiving Day. I stayed home, roasted a chicken, and talked on my cell phone. The weather outside was unseasonably warm, in the mid-twenties, so I took a walk around noon while there was daylight. The next day, the air chilled by forty degrees, and the cold of winter officially started. Every outside surface instantly glazed over, bearing slick layers of ice.

By Monday, the road crews cleared and graveled the streets, so it was time to go back to work. At the office I found myself moving through space with a wincing deflection. I did everything I could to avoid interactions, to get through the day without incident. I saw myself turn into the dog with her tail between her shaking legs. I hated that about myself, so I was at a loss.

In early December, Kathi flew up from Juneau to visit me. She was my first brave friend, one of the few who chose to venture that far north to see me. Greg had been right—I did not expect a plethora of visitors. I put money down at a rent-to-buy store for a small wooden table and four stools, so I would have a place for both of us to sit. I have strict policies with the cats in terms of staying off the dining room table; however that rule quickly went out the door. Any self-respecting human or animal is going to get as far away from a cold floor as possible, so thinking they were going to stay off that table was delusional. Rules sometimes have to change.

Preparing for my first visitor, I cleaned the table multiple times while I prepared stews, baked pies, and bought a small bottle of Knob Creek Kentucky Straight, which does warm the soul, no matter what anyone says. I piled down comforters and blankets over my meager foam pads so we each had a place to sleep. I had saved all of my winter clothing and bedding from my prior life in Alaska, so I had enough protection from the blistering cold of that first winter.

If I'd had to buy all of the clothing required for a subarctic winter, in addition to heating fuel and winterizing the truck, it would have been impossible to make ends meet. The boots I had were stiff climbing boots leftover from my days of working on glaciers in southeast Alaska. They were clunky and unstylish, well insulated, so they kept my feet comfortable and dry. I had sufficient winter gear to fight off the cold, and enough blankets and sleeping bags to maintain a reasonable temperature for the two of us in the cabin. Fighting off the elements is expensive.

I had to swallow my pride and admit that I still could not afford snow tires. Kathi has lived half of her life in Alaska, so she knows the reasons it is insane to go without them. She stepped up to the plate once again and bought me snow tires. She also filled the Suburban's gas tank, which was the first time the tank had been full since I arrived in Fairbanks. Beyond the expensive tires, the full tank gave me a leg-up for the winter; keeping the gas tank full helps to prevent water condensation in the tank and lines, moisture that quickly turns into problematic ice in the fuel system. Confident with our new set of Blizzak tires, we ventured out of town. I wanted Kathi to see what Karl and I referred to as "the favorite place."

We stopped at a lone filling station in an area you could easily describe as the middle of nowhere. After pumping the gas, Kathi and I walked into a sizable convenience store connected to a well-stocked liquor shop.

The smell of hot dogs from one of those rolling grills was an affront to the senses, considering the fresh, early-morning clarity outside. There is nothing like the aroma of scorched coffee, overpowered by the smell of grilling nitrates. Teasingly, Kathi offered me a pint of Häagen-Dazs for breakfast. I declined, so we walked to the counter to pay. An attractive woman processed Kathi's credit card as I scanned the room.

I checked out the array of cigarette packs on a wall rack behind the cashier. It still amazes me that we allow public sales of cancer in a stick while people sit in jail for growing pot. Just above a colorful row of cigarettes, I noticed a prominent wooden sign with a distinct and accurate carving of a revolver. I looked above the gun illustration to read a message, dug deep into the varnished wood in large, bold letters: We Don't Call 911.

I leaned in close to nudge Kathi's side as she folded her receipt and motioned with my eyes for her to look up at the sign. I started for the front door as Kathi zipped her purse and checked out the sign. We squelched our laughter until the door closed behind us. Shuffling through accumulating snow, we each bent forward to wipe away freezing tears. Every time we looked at each other, we relapsed into giggling.

Kathi removed her hat to shake off the snow. She reached for a Kleenex and shook her head, saying, "Only in Alaska."

We agreed that the message was clear: do not mess with those people.

The Suburban's new tires gripped the icy road leading to the favorite place. The surroundings were black, except those thirteen feet ahead of us. I had become used to that; however, not knowing what lay ahead was easier with a dear friend by my side. We poured tea from a thermos and cruised through the day, which looked like night. I drove cautiously, steering my way through harsh country, where people make no apologies for saying, "Do not mess with me."

Kathi left for Juneau, which made the cabin feel too quiet. I pulled out my television and some rabbit ears. If I situated the antennae in the right spot by the eastern window, I could catch a few channels. Public television is deeply valued in Alaska, and Fairbanks was no exception, offering four different channels of programs. I had free TV and didn't even know it until I tried.

I downloaded an app on my phone, so I could tether it to my laptop for an excessively slow Internet connection. That served as another link to the outside world. I was relieved to establish those connections before winter solstice because I know that cabin fever is the real deal.

Winter solstice is a significant benchmark near the Arctic Circle. Depending on subtleties in the calendar year, on one day right around December 21 the sun climbs above the inky horizon for the shortest span of daylight all year, less than four hours. It is called the shortest day of the year, yet I always consider it the longest day. At least there is a built-in silver lining to that day, because daylight will grow from that point forward.

I sat by the window and watched a low band of washed-out yellow smothered under a dense, blue-gray sky, moving swiftly to shut the lid on the last pale flash of light. Once the light goes out, stars, puffs of gray sky, white snow, and black trees led me to believe I was living inside a black-and-white photograph. Around the solstice, the morning sun rises at eleven a.m. and sets at about two p.m. The sun barely lifts above the horizon, hovering at an altitude of two degrees. It takes discipline to get dressed and drive to and from work in the dark. Many days, getting to work with a smile on my face felt like a tremendous accomplishment. According to the calendar, winter had only begun, so I had plenty of time to practice faking it.

CHAPTER FORTY-FOUR

CHRISTMAS, ESPECIALLY WHEN I AM AWAY FROM FAMILY, IS NOT my favorite time of year. Not wanting to be all Grinch and Scrooge, I wanted to do something festive and memorable.

Since that first paycheck in October, I had squirreled away some cash for a couch. I knew there would never be another Marilyn, but many fish were in the sea. The furniture selection in town was skimpy, yet I found a couch I liked and could afford. We set up a delivery date of December 23. The cashier restated the company's policy: no deliveries when the temperature was colder than thirty-five below zero.

That seemed more than reasonable to me. On the 23rd, the temperature fluttered between thirty-three and thirty-eight below. We left work early for Christmas break, so I sat in the beach chair, expecting a cancellation call. At the appointed time, a big truck backed down the long driveway, and a pair of cheerful men emerged carrying the sofa wrapped in blankets. I tipped them what I had in my wallet, which was probably not much, and wished them a happy holiday. Movers have it tough in the first place, but at thirty-five below?

As soon as the truck pulled away, I knew our new piece of furniture was the right choice. She was made of soft, tawny leather, with smooth, crescent-shaped arms, and hips wide enough for a perfect settle—and it was *on sale*. After lunch, I strung zigzagging lines of white Christmas lights inside the cabin, delicate, sparkly, festive, and cheap. By three p.m., the sky displayed a frigid, solemn steel-gray, so I plugged in the lights and lit a few candles on the table. Spartacus and Pierre were busy smelling and testing out the couch. I parted the sea of cat fur to the side and climbed aboard with a fluffy fleece blanket. We were fully furnished.

Instantly the cats assumed position, and we settled in. While the cats curled in restless dreams of summer mice, I snuggled in to enjoy some long-awaited comfort. The couch was not Marilyn, however a superb substitute. Anything that comfortable deserved a name. Our new Italian leather lady of the north needed a name.

Karl and I met for an Italian dinner later that day. We share a penchant for delicious food and sick humor. Interspersed within our conversation, one of us would insert a new idea on our list of names for the new Marilyn. We shared a piece of turtle cheesecake then drove to the university, where he parked in his truck on a hill. We wanted to see the lunar eclipse at around eleven that night.

He kept the truck running and blasted interior heat as we listened to a Pink CD. An eclipse is a special cosmic occasion, and we admired the glorious night, so silent, peaceful, and unforgettable. Even within that undisturbed beauty, I was the ultimate party pooper. I wanted to go home to the new couch. Karl understood my impatience and was probably tired of listening to me reminisce about Marilyn, so we agreed to leave. Karl shifted the truck into reverse, stopped, and turned to me with mischief in his eyes. He did his funny eyebrow wiggle and uttered two words: Sofa Loren.

He won. Sofa Loren she was. By the time I got home Spartacus was nestled into a blanket stretched out long, legs and belly up in the air, chubby and confident. Pierre's front legs hung over each side of Sofa Loren's back, chin flat down against a blanket. He appeared to be under anesthesia. The depth of their relaxation was remarkable; I was envious. I imagined it would be a while before I could hang like that, yet Sofa Loren was a step toward ease. As I reclined onto her curves, I decided that life without a bathtub is difficult, but life without a couch is a sin.

I had a paid week off from work, which was the best Christmas present ever. I listened to a few Christmas CDs while I whisked chocolate pudding in a shiny copper pot. Warm, verging-on-hot pudding is the Number One Comfort Food in my book. I think of it as love in a box for less than a buck. I listened to Christmas music on library CDs, and danced to the song *No money, no honey. No hot toddy, no warm body.*

I am in the deep with the people I love. I am also fond of alone time. The idea of spending holidays alone horrifies some people. Fortunately, I am not one of those people. I could not wait to spend time away from work. The simplicity of home time with a few pieces of furniture felt like a holiday. I read books under lamplight, looking up to the twilight on the other side of the big window, finding sweet solace in the snowflake's rain of blessings.

My Only Friend Karl invited me to join his family for their traditional Yule celebration at his house. Karl's mother Hanne lived in Denmark until she was in her twenties, so each year she cooked up a Danish feast of crispy-crusted pork roast with potatoes, beets, and a creamy rice pudding with dark cherry sauce. Satiated and nurtured by his family and their traditions were enough celebrating for me. I drove home and dove onto Sofa Loren, wiggling in between firm, territorial kitties and a disorganized stack of library books on site—plenty to make the first Christmas back in Alaska memorable and special.

I missed Austin and my family in the northeast, but I was glad to be away from the center of America, to live on society's fringes. I was positioned to look in from the outside at shopping malls, traffic jams, and last-minute runs to the store for one more material item. I did not have to do that; I didn't even have to watch someone I knew do it. I was able to relax and feel a twinge of liberation. Daily existence felt fine, as long as I did not think of work.

It appears to me that Christmas Day is highly overrated, and everyday life is highly underrated. I sometimes feel that I am missing out when I spend a holiday without my family. I have noticed that feeling goes away the next day when I get multiple calls from friends who *did* spend time with family and promptly needed to vent.

I spent the rest of Christmas break writing cover letters and sending résumés out for different work. I considered moving to another town in Alaska, if necessary. I was in a good place with food, heating oil, a water pump, health insurance, and an income, so it was tough to think about moving. I would not quit or give in before finding a different work situation, if I could.

I was unsettled by the porcupine's behavior the day prior to our holiday break. Most of the staff and both of our supervisors were gone. She stood outside my door, theatrically dropping heavy clumps of files to the floor, sighing repeatedly to ensure her upset resonated down the hall. Normally, I would offer help to someone who was clearly having a bad day. I was not in the mood to invite an attack. I made up my mind to fight the battle in my own way.

Before leaving work for the holiday, I stapled together the sides of a blue file folder, and wedged it into the back of my drawer. Every time the porcupine crossed the line, I made a note of the event, date, time, and any witness information. I already had a few handwritten nasty-grams from her, so I slipped those into the folder too.

I meditated, and contemplated ways to find equanimity and grace around the porcupine, worries about the future, and the impending trial. I was in a constant state of waiting for the other shoe to drop, living on tenterhooks again. How could I end up feeling so trapped, one more time?

I could not come up with easy or profound solutions, so I went back to the basics and decided on baby steps. Every morning, I would walk into work with a smile on my face, committed to adding cheer to people's day. It sounded like baby steps, and still a tall order.

Perhaps this is the nature of spiritual practice: the meeting of absolute ideals and the direct experience of the rough stuff life throws at us. It seemed that my reactions held more importance and personal responsibility than the obstacles surrounding me. I wanted my own actions to align with the ideal to avoid harming others, not about me being on top. This did not mean I liked being on the bottom of the food chain, nonetheless I saw what it looks like when people build themselves up by putting others down. I vowed to resist the temptation to behave badly just because the porcupine chose to do so.

I rested on Sofa Loren, watching the cats fight in a spinning pile of black and white fur. Ardent about hissing, biting, chasing, and tail swishing, it all ends up being a show in the game of playing fair. What a concept—tangling, fighting without any collateral damage. I guess some humans do this by playing fair in sports. I wondered what it would be like to live in a world where people played fair in the arenas of love, money, and politics.

CHAPTER FORTY-FIVE

O N New Year's Eve, the black sky glowed with a sprinkle of stars. Even at night different versions of luminosity filtered every hour in watercolor glazes. It felt as though we lived in an exquisite painting, albeit a cold painting. I decided that living in Fairbanks was like living inside a commercial freezer and gazing at a new painting each hour. It was the first time in a month that the temperature moved above zero. Most disconcerting was the fact that it felt balmy outside. This had everything to do with the theory of relativity. Living here and feeling warm at zero teaches a person that everything is relative.

The broken zipper and headaches still plagued me, yet the irritation diminished as I began to accept them as an unavoidable part of my existence. One of the killers about chronic pain is the nagging thought that it could continue for the rest of your life. I decided to adopt the attitude that the infirmities would stay with me, so I stopped thinking they would go away. I was still uncomfortable, yet happier when I stopped resisting and began accepting.

I decided to ignore the pain and strap on my old cross-country skis. Fresh air and snow are reliable remedies. I love the first day of the ski season and the rituals involved with getting out the gear. Unzipping my ski bag every year feels like a holiday. I cleaned a thin layer of dust off my goggles, rifled through a tangle of hats, scarves, and heavy socks, found a bar of ski wax in a dirty baggie, gloves, mittens, a travel Scrabble game, and a roll of TP. I certainly had all of the bases covered. Selecting the right gear for the weather, I began the ritual of dressing to ski.

I laced up my old leather boots and pulled my skis out of their bag. My skis are sacred objects, cherished tools of travel—intimate friends who carried me through untouched fields of snow countless times. In smooth silence, those skis shimmied between tight trees, slid through wide white meadows, and trudged up hills, for the ultimate grace of turning the skis back down the slope.

It is no mystery why the Inuit have dozens of words to describe snow. Every time I go outside to ski, the snow conditions vary, much like the sky, in endless cycles of nuanced change.

Up north, the snow is usually light and fluffy. Skiers call it "champagne powder;" it is feather-light and sugary, easy to shovel, and a soft turf for a pair of skis. Often I did not have to shovel the new snow at all; I could use my broom to sweep the snow off the porch and steps. In contrast, the snow in southeast Alaska is often damp and heavy. Skiers call that snow "crud," though I imagine the Eskimos have developed a far superior and more precise description.

Layered in clothing, I marveled again at my fate. There I was, back outside in the freezing cold, despite every effort to move to a sunny temperate climate. As I leaned forward to click my boot into the binding, the action felt familiar, exhilarating, and fundamental to the core of my being—like coming home. So much for making plans to leave a place or a relationship before its time has come. I wondered how much free will I actually had.

The first day of a ski season is typically a test run. My right binding shifted loose, swiveling back and forth in a lateral direction. I slipped off my left ski and clomped up the porch steps to retrieve a screwdriver in a kitchen drawer. Bulked up in winter clothing, a scarf around my face and goggles strapped on tight, I burst through the front door in a loud crash of boots, rustling snow pants, and creaking door hinges.

Pierre was curled up on Sofa Loren, in a deep sleep until I lurched into the room. His eyes snapped open into full moons. Every strand of fur stood at attention as he rocket-launched straight toward the ceiling and then flew up the stairs. I walked over to examine myself in the mirror and laughed as the moisture fogged the scratched yellow lenses of my beloved old goggles.

To Pierre the Texan, who had never seen a skier, I was an abominable beast of noisy fabric, with a covered face and bug eyes, who suddenly invaded his territory. Spartacus remained on Sofa Loren, unfazed. In Oregon, he used to ski with us around open fields, so all of the noisy clothing was familiar. Scampering, leaping, and running wild, Spartacus would join our ski parties as though he belonged on a ski trail.

The first day of skiing inspired me to continue skiing most every day. On days when the temperature hissed around twenty-five below, I skied in short spurts, close to the cabin. As soon as my fingers burned from the cold, I turned around and quickly returned to the cabin. I skied past a yellow half-moon as it skimmed the horizon, behind short, spindly statues of trees. The New Year's moon glowed in a buttery-yellow light, like a melon floating in the night's blue-gray sky.

That far north, the air is so dry and cold, any smell or sense of aroma is rare. The arctic air is a vacuum of non-smell, compared to the summer's air with subtle hints of taste. As I skied, no smell could overpower the aroma of snow and silence. I pushed one ski forward, then another, across a glowing surface of the earth. Lit with moonlight, the terrain I glided through looked like the face of the moon.

Peaceful holidays inevitably led to Sunday night thoughts about the next day's work, which did not sound so peaceful. On Monday morning, hungry kitties coaxed me out of bed. It was minus thirty-two degrees, clear, and starry. I peeked out the window to a world that appeared to be uninhabited—more like uninhabitable.

I wrapped myself in fleece blankets for my morning meditation. I sat looking out the dark upstairs window and watched the sky. I noticed the small pleasure and reassurances of detecting my neighbor's lights flicker on in the morning, knowing that an hour later his car would pull out of the driveway at the same time I left for work. As his cabin lamps formed small squares outside on the snow, I could hear excited dog teams barking on the trail.

Some mornings I could spot the lone headlight of a musher bouncing off the trees along the dark dog sled trail. Other mornings, my sole neighbor's cabin remained dark, and the dog teams slept. I sat in wonder, breathing evenly and watching moon shadows form zebra stripes against the glowing, white ground. The view was vast, yet shielded by a massive, dead spruce standing directly in my line of sight. Enormous trees are rare that far north, and that spruce somehow survived for decades before dying and turning into a brushy visual obstacle.

I understand that my morning walks to the outhouse might sound terrible and inconvenient. Getting dressed in my down jacket and winter boots was a pain if I was in a hurry. However, once dressed, my first step outside in the still, dark landscape was breathtaking and tranquil. Every morning brought a new star, a rearranged moon, a strong mist of clouds, or slow snowflakes rocking side to side toward the frozen ground.

Those breathtaking morning walks nourished me with a sense of inexpressible gratitude and wealth. I was the only one standing in a quiet treasure of white tranquility and silence, feeling alive and privileged. On a somewhat ironic note, those trips to the outhouse were often the highlight of my day, a glaring indication of the misery factor at work. I loved the morning's brisk wakeup call and silent, still reverence for the natural world. How often did I feel that sense of reverence when I lived with central plumbing?

One dark, moonless morning, as I walked back to the cabin from the outhouse, I could see two large objects moving toward me in the driveway. In the interest of seeing the morning stars, I had turned off the porch light, and I was not wearing my glasses. Stepping up my pace, I rushed inside the cabin, found my glasses, flipped on the porch light, and poked my head out the door.

I came face to face with two moose standing at the bottom of the steps as though waiting to come inside. Sniffing cautiously, they extended their long necks toward me. I fought the impulse to brush off icy snow caked on the muzzle of the smaller, younger moose. I wanted to relieve him of the discomfort, reminding myself that they were wild animals no matter how cute and vulnerable they looked, so I kept my hands off.

I moved my foot on noisy Styrofoam snow in a loud, scratching noise that pierced the morning silence. Both moose skittered away toward the Suburban. A few yards away, they stopped and eyed me suspiciously. Another moose emerged from behind the truck, whereby all three plodded off in clumsy, wobbly, steps into a dark grove of trees. At thirty-five below, it was hard not to feel pity for those critters.

I quickly opened and closed the front door behind me to dissuade the cold from entering. I pressed my nose against the front window, next to the cats that were doing the same. Creamy light from the cabin beamed through the window, out and onto the frigid black morning. I felt spoiled to have secure shelter and food.

CHAPTER FORTY-SIX

I N CONTRAST TO THE LULL OFFERED FROM MOTHER NATURE OUT-side, work in the office felt crazy. Still in my six-month probationary period, I was afraid of losing my job. I knew the porcupine had nothing positive to say about me, and I watched her cause trouble wherever she could. This was an outrageous position to be in. I had enjoyed years of success in school and work, and now someone had decided it would be in her best interests to undermine my reputation.

After months of hand-wringing, I approached several supervisors to discuss my struggles. Those conversations resulted in no further discussions, just a passive "sorry you feel that way; we don't want to lose you" approach. I heard promises of having a meeting about it the following week; nothing ever got on the calendar, so the weeks came and went. I watched the porcupine walk around, carting a backpack full of pesticides. One person has the capacity to poison the world.

Dr. Phil would have come in handy. I sensed that he had done his part and moved on, trusting me to make good decisions. Besides, he was too smart to travel to the arctic, where springtime in Alaska is forty below. There is not enough fur in the world for a Texan to come up here in the middle of winter. Times had changed; I needed to find a new ally.

I wanted to feel as though I had physical boundaries from the porcupine's quills. One night, lying on Sofa Loren, I wondered how I might pretend to have physical boundaries. I thought about the badger, and how that had helped me fight The Guy. Maybe I could play a game again and find a funny way to protect myself?

Mid-thought, the teakettle frothed at the spout, spitting a reminder to get up and turn off the burner. As I stood, my eyes fell on the rusty, recycled metal armadillo that somehow made the cut in Austin. He was standing proud on top of the heater, looking whimsical and goofy. Armadillos might look foolish, such unlikely warriors, yet they survive because of their tough, funny-looking, and impenetrable shell. I wanted a shield like that.

While the tea was brewing, I contemplated the hard shell idea. If I wanted to maintain my soft interior, I needed an armadillo-like exterior. I remembered that I found a way to put someone in a metal box, talk to Dr. Phil, and climb a statue of the Buddha. In a similar vein, I should be able to learn how to grow a hard shell.

I turned the volume up on Lyle Lovett and inspected the armadillo up close, under lamplight. Christie and I picked out this particular armadillo amongst dozens of them because he had the biggest smile. We bought him in Wimberley, Texas, at a store that had at least one hundred different creatures made out of recycled metal, each one formed and scaled true to life. The artist creates motley sculptures of birds, pigs, dinosaurs, saber-toothed tigers, armadillos, and a brood of longhorn cattle. The artist is, after all, a Texan.

The particular armadillo we chose sports a barrel-shaped torso made of rusty corrugated metal and ears of corroded sheet metal. His smiling, wooden face has a long snout, and four goofy legs and paws stick straight out from his barrel body. I walked around to admire the armadillo in my living room. Christie and I had made a good choice; he had a great grin. I wiped a cobweb and a few black cat hairs from the armadillo's back, examining his hard, crusty exterior.

I love making costumes. One year for Halloween, a friend and I made twenty Dalmatian costumes, and found the right candidate to play Cruella De Vil. We lived in a small Alaskan town, so finding one hundred and one participants was out of the question. Twenty of us stormed the town, wearing black and white spots, barking through restaurants, sniffing people's plates, and begging for food. At one bar, where there were more Dalmatians than people, we were shooting pool, sitting at the bar sipping wine, and of course, some of the guys felt compelled to lift their legs on people sitting in chairs. People in town talked about the night the dogs outnumbered the people for years, and they never found out who those dogs were.

I thought about making an armadillo costume. I could wear it to work. No, that was a seriously stupid idea. I was in enough trouble showing up at the office wearing my best pair of shoes. The vision kept popping of me wearing a rusted barrel and floppy ears to work. If I could be a badger, why not pretend to be an impenetrable armadillo?

I rushed into my horizontal position on Sofa Loren and closed my eyes. I gently pushed the cats off our favorite mint-green blanket and nestled in for a good thinking session. I got right down to the details reminding myself to keep the design simple, clear, and effective, like a Martini Home. I pictured what it would feel like to wriggle into the barrel, moving like a stiff robot waddling over to a full-length mirror and securing two floppy ears to my head. I manipulated the left ear to poke out in a droopy angle to the right, like the armadillo in the living room. From there, it was easy to envision my life inside the barrel.

I imagined walking into my windowless office at work wearing a barrel around my torso, with holes on each side for my arms to stick out in hapless angles. Nothing in the world could look as inane as I felt just then. On the other hand, it also seemed as though no one could touch me. The armored shell felt oddly real.

I even pretended that mean words would simply roll off my body like water drops on a well-oiled cast iron skillet. The armadillo had powerful and healthy boundaries that made clear what to accept and what to reject in every situation. There would be no moments of regret for hours after a conversation with the porcupine. No need to palm my forehead and wish I had come up with a snappy rebuttal.

Despite a willful attitude and solid rationale, my efforts lacked elbow grease. It seemed wasteful to expend so much energy resisting the porcupine. That much effort seemed better spent at a spinning class or learning how to open myself to a lover under soft twisted sheets. I began to resent my need to be an armadillo when my true goal in life was to become more open and soft.

I realized that I did know how to have firm boundaries in every situation. I had cultivated many trustworthy and loving relationships in my life, and I had learned to steer clear of the porcupines. This was different; *this* porcupine had total power over my livelihood, and she enjoyed it.

CHAPTER FORTY-SEVEN

———————————

By March the porcupine was still in power, yet the days were longer, with spacious hours of welcomed illumination. Everything outside took on a rosy hue. I savored the light; it nourished me.

Suddenly, on March 6th I got a call telling me to get to Juneau as soon as I could. My mother-in-love, Stella Mae, was dying from pancreatic cancer.

Kathi picked me up at the airport around midnight. I waited until morning, then took Kathi to work and drove her car to Stella's house. I'd already called Stella's husband, Tim, so he was expecting me. If you have ever been an ex-anything, you know how clumsy that status can be at the best of times. Despite my ex status, the family made a point of including me, and I love them for it. Stella and I were close, so they encouraged me to be there. Her family wanted what she wanted.

I knocked softly on the front door and let myself in. Then I removed my boots and lined my pair up with about six others. A wonderful sense of home and Stella washed over me. The house was silent. I tiptoed into the living room to see the loves of Stella's life: Tim, her two sons, and two grandsons, kneeling and sitting around her hospital bed.

Her bed stood in the middle of the room, next to gloriously high prow-front windows facing Auk Lake. It was a rare sunny day in Juneau, with no sign of clouds or rain, only raw spring sun ripening winter's snow. It would be a challenge to find a more beautiful place to die. I thought, "Good for you Stella—a perfect day."

Stella's back was turned away from her favorite windows that faced the outside world, so I knew it would be soon. She had turned away from the view she loved. Tim stood to hug me and whispered that it had been a tough night. I knelt with my back to the spectacular view and pulled the hair back from my face before I leaned over to whisper in her ear.

"Don't you worry, Stella. I have your back, and I always will. You are so loved." I took my place behind her, lightly stroking her thighs and resting my head on the bed.

Stella was the most organized and prepared dying person I knew. We spoke on the phone often during her last months, and her courage astounded me. She took death on as an adventure, confident in the continuation of her journey. She finished her memoir, completed her will, and planned an after-life party in the time it takes most of us do our taxes.

The one thing she admitted to me that she could not prepare for was leaving Tim behind. That was easy to understand. Stella and Tim were one of those couples who made you feel happy just to know that two people loved each other that much. They cherished each other, and it showed. My friend Ana wisely pointed out that a successful relationship needs both an anchor and a set of wings. Tim and Stella had the anchor and the wings part down.

Two months earlier, Stella decided she would have a nerve block for the pain, but she would not fight the cancer. We all wanted Tim and Stella's marriage to go on forever, because their devotion deserved it. The collision of life with cancer changes plans; staying together forever was replaced with ensuring that Stella no longer suffered.

Stella's breath was even and shallow. Tim sat by her head, holding her hands as she lay on her side. For a while I sat next to my stepson Chase, both of us softly touching her limbs. Her other grandson, Isaac, stood next to Tim, watching Stella's face as she began to breathe unevenly. Tim spoke in undertones to Stella, telling her it was all right if she was ready to go. He would be okay. I thought my heart would turn inside out. Why does this happen to the people who love each other the most? Then I remembered that "Why?" is a waste of time. Stella was leaving; the reason did not matter.

Her breath slowed significantly by noon that day. Tim went to the kitchen to stretch, standing above the kitchen counter to eat a sandwich his best friend, Frank, had made for him. Moisture seeped at the corner of my eyes. It was moving to watch a man take such loving care of his friend. Frank quietly tended to the house, food, and company, so Tim could take care of Stella.

Chase leaned his head and shoulders into the kitchen to alert Tim that Stella needed him. Tim hurried to his chair and sat on its edge, leaning over to hold Stella's hands. We leaned toward her, touching shoulders as we silently passed around a box of Kleenex. In a few short minutes, Stella slowed her breath down to a whisper; then the whisper paused. Tim bowed his head and uttered a thud of grief. Stella returned the resonance of his ache with a desperate draw of air. We held still. Tim collected himself, setting his emotions aside, and cooed into Stella's ear: "Lovey, it is okay—you can go now. I will be fine."

My heart blasted open, a big bang, and the essence of Stella shifted.

We all held a collective breath and waited for another sigh. Tall pillars of sunlight had been warming the room, but now clouds chilled the air. Everything stilled. Stella exhaled without taking in another breath, and Tim could finally cry.

CHAPTER FORTY-EIGHT

I LEFT THE HOUSE SOON AFTER, SO MORE FAMILY COULD VISIT. WE were all raw and tenderized by Stella's last hours. I was proud of her stellar bravery, as I ached for Tim's loss. It is hard to know what to do immediately after touching the intimacies of birth and death. Everything truly does pale in comparison to those milestone events.

I stepped outside of the house to melting snow and the promise of summer; without Stella, the world felt revised in mysterious ways. I still had an hour before it was time to pick up Kathi, so I decided to drive to the Mendenhall Glacier, a few miles down the road. The gift of nature serves to ground me, and that particular glacier reflected a large part of my life, and of Stella's. Crying makes my eyes mega-puffy and tired. Stella deserved mega-puffy. She was a champion. I parked the car and walked through a white mist patch that momentarily obscured big chunks of the glacier. The view was limited, yet the understanding clear: my mother-in-love would remain inside of me as my anchor and my wings.

The next day, I flew back to Fairbanks on "the milk run," which includes at least five stops between Seattle and Anchorage. In common weather, that means five possibilities of places to get stuck in for a couple of days. The weather goes down, and there is nothing to do except wait it out. Since I boarded in Juneau, my flight included three of the five stops. Maybe Stella ordered another clear day, maybe it was the way the cookie crumbled. Heat radiated from the stronger sun through a clear sky. The jet flew over miles of untouched beaches rippling up the coastline toward Yakutat, where Stella had lived for years. I leaned my forehead against the window on the right side of the almost empty jet, studying the beaches where Stella and her boys had loved to walk.

I went back to work, feeling unprocessed yet unwilling to talk about my life with anyone there. When I had trustworthy relationships with people like my Juneau family, why bother with the treacherous ones? Not everyone was watching my back, and I knew it.

I plodded through workdays, feeling blue, trying to hide it. I continued to put on my imaginary armadillo suit every morning. I knew Stella would approve of the humor. On the short drive to work, I visualized the porcupine as Phyllis Diller, wearing fuzzy slippers and a muumuu. My friend Donna in Florida suggested the Phyllis Diller idea, as well as picturing everyone else in their underwear. The techniques worked well, especially if I could stay with that vision all day long, unmistakable mischief in my eyes, while the porcupine criticized every move I made.

I finally mastered enough tasks to work independently some of the time. I enjoyed getting lost in spreadsheets, absorbed in solving problems, or finding better ways to provide information. On one of those blessedly independent days, my cell phone buzzed, caller ID indicating a call from Austin. I closed my office door and answered, hoping it was about an interview somewhere else. I was certain that cleaning floors in Austin would be better than what I was currently doing.

I heard Liza, from the DA's office, say hello, and I flushed with relief that the door was closed. My heart thumped in-out-in-out as I figured out that Mary was also on the call. I sat erect in my chair, happy and nervous to hear from them. Getting right down to business, Liza told me a trial date had been set for May 1, 2011.

May Day.

Mary said she thought the date was going to stick this time, and Liza gave me contact information for a woman in their office who would secure my travel arrangements. I ended the call and gawked at the wall calendar, counting out five weeks to May Day.

My heart jammed against my sternum, and I felt my mind flying in a dissociative blur. The room felt remote, cloudy, and unimportant. I felt shaky inside, and my heart raced. I swirled in confusion, aware that my mind was hovering near the ceiling, rather than in my body, where it needed to be. That was PTS—not a decision, not a disorder, just a fast hit, like a lightning strike. My internal file folders dumped messy sheets of paper across the floor. I wanted to go somewhere that felt safe, which was not my office.

I dashed up the stairs to My Only Friend Karl's office and shut the door. He gestured toward the door and opened his eyes wide, joking, "What is that about?" I moved a couple of rolled-up blueprints from a chair and sat, hoping that would keep me from running out of breath. Karl waited for me to gather myself before I told him about the trial date. He knew how long I had been waiting.

I spent the rest of the afternoon trying to hide from everyone. I drifted back down to my office in a stupor, where I do not recall any sense of touching the ground. Relief (it was finally going to happen), mixed with equal amounts of consternation and panic, kept my mind on everything but work. Confounded and distracted, I made the fatal mistake of sending the pink copy of a form to the accounts payable department.

The next morning, I sheepishly confessed my mistake to everyone. When I phoned the woman who ultimately received the white, pink, and yellow documents instead of only the white and yellow copies, she said, "Not a big deal, I will send the pink copies back with the yellow ones." I was under the impression that would solve the problem. However, this unspeakable, stupid act would never be forgiven, and certainly not forgotten. If the porcupine could have plopped a dunce cap on my head and sent me to a far corner for a flogging, she would have. The porcupine's nostrils flared, and her chubby cheeks blushed the color of those pink forms. It seemed the harder I tried, the more I bungled things up.

A few days later, I sat in the porcupine's office to explain what happened on the day of the pink paper mistake. I told her about the subpoena and the nature of the crime, in detail. I wanted her to appreciate my situation and stop thinking I was a big, fat idiot. I had no super-size fantasies about her changing. I was just hoping to see a slice of the porcupine's soft side. Besides, I had to tell her, because I needed her approval for the time off. If it had not been for that, I would not relinquish such detailed information about my life.

From that day on, it was business as usual, and she avoided any reference to our conversation. I was fine with that, thinking the less said the better. I did everything possible to become invisible in the office. My goal was simple: live through the day without landing in the crossfire of her battles. I was too overwhelmed, preparing to face the other demon.

Against all of my strict financial rules, I pumped enough gas to go home every day for lunch. This gave me one whole hour away from work in the middle of the day. Each day while I drove home, noontime sun glazed on white snow. The outside world knew how to dazzle my senses. At home, I would open the curtains, feeling spring light and powder snow cheer up the cabin's insides. I sat at the front window, the day's brilliance mesmerizing. I borrowed bulky, ponderous volumes of *New*

Yorker cartoon collections from the library, free fun. I read a minimum of three pages per day. With each reading a hearty and spontaneous laugh provided a delightful window of relief in otherwise dismal days.

The daylight in Fairbanks blushed and bloated in five-minute bursts each day. The sun remained above the horizon forty-seven minutes longer each week. Everything perked up. The birds began to sing, testing out their extra energy. Thirty-two degrees felt almost hot when the sun was out. We all had made it through another winter into the time of year when seasoned northern Alaskans wear light sweatshirts and rave about the fabulous weather.

Every day in the office, I walked on eggshells to avoid attention. On one successful escape for lunch, as I drove up to the cabin, I noticed a beam of shimmering light penetrating a stand of white birch. The sun's rays reached down in long, sunny stretches to the melting snow and ice. Within the stand of trees, on snow and musty leaves, lay a female moose, curled in a cozy knot inside a broad beam of light. She held her bulky head high, wiggling her nose up to the sun, swaddled in this new hint of spring.

I crept up the steps to the porch, watching her watch me. She stayed in her sunny spot until after I left to go back to work. That one peaceful lunch hour, in the company of the cats, a contented moose, and a book of clever funnies, was worth the expense of those few additional gallons I burned to escape my life on tenterhooks.

On another March day, I headed home for lunch and the *New Yorker*. Thin frost shavings reflected colors from a prism over the ground in front of me. It was late in the month, and a stronger tinge of rose infused further depth into winter's cool citron light. I was driving south on our unplowed road, skimming through fresh, light powder, feeling high from the radiating sun, celebrating the need to wear sunglasses. In a hurry for food and comics, I sped up, joyful in my thinking: yes, almost home.

Suddenly, a few yards ahead and to my left, a white pickup truck shot into the road from a hidden driveway. I swerved to the right. As our truck mirrors came within inches of each other, the other driver and I locked startled eyes. We both yanked our steering wheels in opposite directions, sliding forward like two slithering fish, our tails swerving, managing to sweep away from a collision at the last second.

With an overzealous grip on the wheel, I wheezed and sputtered a few "*whews*, OMGs, that was close." I lifted my eyes off the road once I knew my tires were back on the right track. The truck's momentum steamed ahead, away from a narrow escape. As my gaze moved up toward the sky, I was startled by the rosy view directly ahead of me.

My heart stayed out in a double-thump, and I realized I had already seen this place. This was the white road and pinkish sky with a sharp veer to the right—like the dream I'd had in Austin, about a narrow escape in a car, where I was sitting up high. The dream that had prompted my call to Giggy.

I had dreamed about the road before I lived there, but I did not recognize it until that sharp, startling swerve to the right. I walked into the cabin, soaked with wonder. My sense of space and time warped instantly and permanently. I had dreamed about that exact experience before it had happened. I had dreamed that pink, mountainous future while still in Texas.

I did not try to tell anyone about the near miss, because it sounded improbable and mystical. But deep inside, the magic stayed with me. Life had its challenges, but I began to feel steadier on my feet. With each paycheck, my breath and frail system relaxed by one degree. Much of the time, I thought about the trial yet somehow trusted everything would be fine. I tried not to obsess about remembering the details. Stacey warned me about that. I spent two years straining to forget the details, yet a time would come when it would be important to remember them again.

Fortunately, I was busy at work. The flow of concentration and spreadsheets served as absorbing distractions. The porcupine was not around much, so there were relaxing breaks between waves of walking on eggshells.

By April, the day stretched its luxurious, long, and lovely hours into pliable, temperate evenings. Mud began to soften in the midday sun. After work, immersed in pastel light, I slogged my old skis through thick, mashed-potato snow, burning off worry and carving out room for untroubled sleep.

All the logistical pieces for the trial were in place by early April. My time off had been approved; the hotel and flight reservations were set. My brother Don and sister-in-law Sue booked tickets from Syracuse to Austin. Christie would fly from Seattle to meet me a few days early. I needed to arrive ahead of time for trial prep and wanted to spend time with BB.

The weekend before court, Christie would treat us to a weekend at our favorite spa. It could not get any better than that. Giggy planned to drive over from Houston. It helped to have all of that to look forward to, as I searched for a precarious balance between funk and excitement.

As I skied after work, I thought about the trial and gave myself pep talks, setting a strong pace and tone for the stance I wanted to take. I decided to go into the courtroom and tell the truth as succinctly as I could. I wanted to look The Guy straight in the eye, acknowledge him, and then let go of him, no matter the trial's outcome. I wanted to tell my version as clearly as possible, and then forget him.

Justice would be up to the jury. I wanted to set myself free from The Guy's haunting. Whatever happened to The Guy would fall to the hands of God. I needed to accept any outcome, because that part was beyond my control.

By mid-April, I had worked myself into a heated-up ball of nervous energy. I wanted to go to trial right then so it would be over. I wanted to see the trial as a past event, not a staggering figure roaming madly through my thoughts of the future. I was so jumpy that each time the porcupine roared into my office in a tizzy about someone's infringement, I thought my heart would jump out of my chest. I spoke to my doctor about this, and he reassured me that was "normal" for someone with PTSD. My response to alarm was spring-loaded, and her high-octane entrances triggered sudden panic in my system. I was recovering from one of those episodes when my cell phone rang, showing a 512 number. I was in my office, so I shut the door, preparing for an update from Mary and Liza.

Mary began with her classic warning: Well, there is good news, and there is bad news. I felt my heart bracing for disappointment and setback. My immediate reaction was screw it, enough of these games. I thought about quitting everything—the fight in the courtroom and the mess at work. I doodled on the margin of a spreadsheet as Mary continued. A shift in her voice put me on notice. The Guy decided to plead guilty and waive his right to a jury trial.

My pen continued drawing small pink circles inside of blue squares, as I fought to anchor my mind in the conversation. Absorbed in the mental wrestling match, I strained to stay in the chair and listen to Mary.

Mary had often speculated that he would plead guilty after the defense ran out of stall tactics. She explained that I would still testify. Instead of sitting in front of a jury, the prosecution and defense would present the case to a judge, who would then determine the sentence. Mary warned me that a guilty plea often leads to decreased sentence time.

It was a leap for me to believe he was going to admit to the crime after two and a half years of denial. Mary continued, "Now we avoid the risk of ending this with a hung jury or mistrial . . . he is admitting to the charges. We just don't know how the judge will respond." This news should have given me hope, but I was crestfallen at the thought of another delay. My life revolved around getting through May Day. Now I had to extend those hopes to a later date, still to be determined.

By May Day, the date for the hearing had been set for June 20, the summer solstice. All of us changed our airline and hotel reservations again. I had re-psyched my mind four times for a trial, and now I faced the fifth effort. It felt as though our legal process went to great lengths to protect his rights, which certainly got in the way of my sense of right. I sat in my office, once again wishing I could go home for the day, to sit in silence and prepare myself mentally, one more time. I strained to avoid another pink-form mistake and reminded myself that it was not going to be over until it was over. What will be, will be.

My nervous system began to wilt. My post-work ski sessions were more like trudging through peanut butter again. My being had no sense of glide. The porcupine was around a lot more those days, looking at the fiscal year-end reports and spreadsheets. I lived in fear of the next thing that would set her off.

The first week of June, I created endless spreadsheets, calculating future rents, charges, and termination dates. Nervously, I would place the documents on her desk in the evening, and the next day they returned to my desk, miraculously approved.

I was pleased and amazed. Maybe I was getting the hang of this after all. For this particular project I had collected all of the approved spread-sheets, combined all of the information, and turned it in as the final draft. By then I was feeling confident; the porcupine had approved every-thing so far. The next morning I walked into my office and turned on the lights. The final draft rested front and center on my desk with a big, fat *X* across the page and INCORRECT printed in loopy, bold, uppercase ink.

Who does that! A big *X* would have been sufficient. No need to rein-force the message. She caught me in another double bind, approving the numbers only to disapprove them later. Having supervised many

employees myself, I could not imagine writing INCORRECT on anyone's work and feeling good about that. I sucked in my breath and my
pride. I did not like this situation, but I could not blow this opportunity.
I knew if I got fired, my future prospects were doomed.

On my way home that day, I pulled up behind a rusty Subaru with
a clean bumper sticker that said, "Mean People Suck," and heard myself
mutter, "Amen." I knew I was allowing the porcupine and The Guy to
drain me. I could feel my body dumping internal power when I pictured
their faces. That was not easy to admit. I wanted to be the impenetrable
armadillo who never granted that kind of permission to someone else;
nonetheless I let them get under my skin.

I contemplated forgiveness. What does that word mean? I wanted
to find an answer that reached far beyond a canned speech or self-help
theory. What does it *really* mean to forgive? How does it feel? Is it an
event, a one-shot thing, a linear process, or a multidimensional layer cake
of complexities?

I felt thrashed. Every time I stood to walk forward, my demons
pushed me back onto the bloody oak floor. I read books and articles that
said forgiveness eliminates potent charges of emotion from the equation.
The Guy did what he did. The porcupine does what she does because
somehow it makes her feel better. I've never understood the payoff, it
must be worth it. I wanted to fizzle the rage and fear in my body and
tried to imagine what it would feel like to wear a buoyant life ring of forgiveness. When my anger foamed up, forgiveness hid in dormant folds,
eons away from kindness. I wanted that freedom, but I was not there yet.

I reasoned further. If forgiveness meant a decrease in the electrical
charge in my system, how could I make that happen, when the porcupine and The Guy were acting as though they were the victims? I felt
isolated and doubtful. I wanted to forgive, even more than that; I wanted
to get away from them. I wanted to escape, again.

I made valiant attempts at humor, sending IMs to my friends in the Lower 48: "Just trying to ignore the corn cob growing in the office. lol," with a smiley frog jumping up and down. I read cartoons, prayed for help, and set my sights on the end of June, assuring myself that after the trial ended, I would find a new work scene. I was much better at visualizing escape, compared to forgiveness.

My résumés were only trickling out. My work search was halfhearted because I was distracted by my upcoming trip to Austin. I could not allow the porcupine to injure my financial position and professional reputation. She was in for the kill. I had a strong and healthy intuition that she was waiting in ambush for her chance to jump me at my most vulnerable, lowest point.

I felt paranoid and cheerless about having such a strong flavor of doubt and suspicion toward someone. Then again, nothing indicated anything trustworthy about my situation. Literally, not figuratively, I began to experience a stabbing sensation in the left side of my back, between my shoulder blades. I trusted the hint. There was no reason to give the porcupine any benefit of the doubt.

Late May and June brought sunny summer days to the cabin. I draped mosquito netting across the doorway, gauzy, white fabric that almost looked fancy. It kept the bugs out while letting in fresh air and allowing new freedom for the cats to run in and out. I luxuriated on my chaise lounge, basking in the sun, thinking that if I could sit in Lucy's psychiatry booth for a day, I would tell people, "Not a good idea to buy one lawn chair." One chair has a terribly lonely feel to it. Most days all I needed was one, however it would have helped to feel like someone else might be joining me. I had spent a lot of time alone in my life without feeling cut off, but loneliness plagued me as I waited for the hearing, and the day I would get fired.

On a sunny June weekend, I dragged out the solitary chaise lounge from beneath the cabin, brushed off the dirt-colored cushions, applied sunscreen, and opened a novel. Summer had arrived for a brief visit, and I was not about to miss it.

Pierre and Spartacus lounged in the long marathon of sunlight, sprawling on their stretched backs, feet facing the sky, tolerating slow and sharp mosquitoes. They exemplified contentment, absorbed in the lazy living of felines, catching mice and chasing rabbits. We were worlds away from winter's bipolar months, during which frozen gusts of snow burped in fast from the open door and sent the cats scrambling upstairs to get away.

Two pages into my new novel, I set it down and gazed up, admiring variegated shades of green against a cerulean blue sky. Reading was not serving as a distraction, so I circled back to the idea of forgiveness. I wanted to feel the feeling, and clearly wanting was not enough. I speculated that forgiveness would not feel like one event. It might be more of a continuous, moment-to-moment decision. I understood why forgiveness might be impossible for some people, but I did not want to spend the rest of my life drowning in a vast pit of despair.

People endure horrible atrocities, unspeakable violence, wretched conditions, and I understood why they could not forgive. I thought of Holocaust survivors and women who live through rapes and torture yet manage to survive and thrive with loving hearts. If they could move on and forgive, then I could too.

Distracting ruminations on remembering, forgetting, and forgiving churned harder as the weeks wore on, until finally, it was time to pack my duffle bag for Austin.

CHAPTER FORTY-NINE

I CHECKED MY BAG AT THE AIRPORT AND HAND-CARRIED MY NEWLY dry-cleaned dress onto the jet. It was the same black dress I visualized wearing each time I practiced walking to the witness stand in Stacey's office. Two years earlier, it took several appointments with Stacey and numerous "comfort vs. style" conversations with Christie before I could decide on the best outfit. The ridiculous amount of attention on the "what to wear" question was funny, even to me, and often kindled the laugh of the day. However, the thorough query paid off, because once made, I never wavered on my decision.

I left on the one a.m. jet, feeling organized and prepared. My Only Friend Karl offered to take care of the cats and water the plants, so I knew they would be fine. I logged off from work-mind mode and headed south toward my other set of "growth opportunities." At six a.m., I fueled up with a breakfast croissant in Seattle. Several hours later, I flew on to San Jose for a long layover, and finally landed in Austin around eleven p.m.

When you live in Fairbanks, there is no such thing as a quick trip anywhere, except for Anchorage.

Karl sent me twenty-two "IP" texts that day, our private code for Inner Peace. I thought of Russell riding his bike through British Columbia, with the copper-beaded bracelet on his handlebars. The level to which I missed my friends and family was unspeakable. I was so excited to see them in Austin and feel like a part of something again. I was a fish out of water in Fairbanks, yet felt immediately at home in Austin.

After a lengthy cab ride through a construction zone, I made it to the hotel. Flushed with relief and the thrill of a bathtub, I spoke to the front desk clerk, who informed me that I did not have a reservation. Five nervous minutes later, we figured out that my reservation was at another Marriott, closer to downtown. I was too tired to flog myself for the mistake, so I called another cab and stood outside to enjoy the naturally heated and notably humid evening air on my skin.

Another IP from Karl pinged through my phone. I tapped out a reply text: "IP IP IP IP. Made it to Austin! IP" and hit send. I thought better of this, because of my vow about not lying, so I sent a second, more honest text: "Well, maybe not exactly IP, but I did make it."

The correct hotel was unbelievably close to my former east Austin neighborhood. I had no memory of the hotel. I knew I was in rough shape if I did not even read the address of the hotel on my itinerary. My file folders were definitely out of whack, because logistics are something I usually manage well. I leaned against a post as I waited for another cab, while humid, silky air eased my pores open to the contentment of unmanufactured heat.

Once inside the second hotel lobby, I checked in, reaching down to lift my duffle bag and grab my dre . . . where was my little black dress? Right arm in midair, I paused and told myself not to cry. The cab was gone. The night auditor noticed my mouth-dropped pause, surely used to watching disheveled, confused travelers realize they had lost something important.

He phoned Marriott #1, where the night auditor confirmed that my dress was hanging on her front counter. I would go there the next day to retrieve the dress. I have no memory of that night, if I slept, or if I did not. I do remember the bathtub. I was up early the next day, my stomach sending tight and queasy signals.

Once I signed and initialed multiple layers of dot-matrix forms in approximately one hundred different places, I managed to get the keys to a generic rental car. I drove to the other hotel to retrieve the (so far) unwrinkled dress, and then turned back toward east Austin to meet BB for lunch.

BB is one of those friends who I might not see for a year, yet once we sit down to visit, we pick up right where we left off the previous time. There is no blip in the screen, nothing to re-familiarize—a familiar return to the groove of humor and friendship. The eggs and coffee at Cisco's were mediocre as always, such a comfort. An hour later, I dropped BB off at her house and drove to the courthouse to see Mary and Liza.

The search for an afternoon parking spot near the courthouse removed any worries over low blood pressure problems. Once parked, four blocks away, I passed through lines of x-rays and security wands into the bustling courthouse, whispering to my heart, "Could you please pound softer?" There was no tone of command in my voice; it was more of a plea than an expectation.

I knew the drill. After the security checkpoints, I entered the DA's office and signed in to see Liza and Mary. I slid the clipboard for the sign-in sheet under a bulletproof glass window and began pacing the room, staring at artwork I knew I would not remember.

Liza gave me a hug and walked me to a narrow conference room with floor-to-ceiling windows. She was excited. "You've got to see this!" she said, smiling as she pointed to the north side of the room. About twenty-four inches outside of the glass, a pigeon settled in her nest, resting in a long patch of shade. Directly above the bird, a squirrel hung his chubby legs casually out of his tree hole, almost touching the bird. The squirrel was sleepy, his eyes shut, stretched out, paws relaxed and limp, resting his listless chin on the tree's rough bark. Liza said the two of them napped together every afternoon, so people in the office called it the Tree of Life.

The sight of the bird and squirrel napping as friends made me smile. Liza, Mary, and Mary's assistant spent the afternoon reviewing elements of testimony, asking me to regurgitate the details I worked so hard to camouflage. I continued to rehearse seeing The Guy outside of his steel box. The bird and squirrel pulled my attention in a good way, adding a sip of sweetness to an otherwise unsavory and stressful afternoon.

Adding to the cheer from the Tree of Life, I looked forward to a weekend with Christie. It was not easy to stay present with the conversation at the courthouse, but I managed. Mary promised me the date would not change this time, so I focused on her questions, telling myself I would be hanging with Christie in a few hours.

I swung into the arrivals lane at the Austin airport, just as Christie walked outside with her carry-on. After a quick hug, we rolled down the windows and laughed about our destination, a resort we called the "land of doing nothing." I told her about the Tree of Life and gave her a brief overview of the questions Mary had asked me. Christie understood that the best part was that I did not have to listen to a recording of the 911 call. For some reason, that was something I did not want to hear. Christie had listened to me process this on multiple occasions, so she knew it was a touchy subject. I still don't know why that was so important—I still recoiled at the thought of listening to Jackie's frantic call to dispatch.

On our way out of town, we passed the prison where I suspected The Guy was incarcerated. Showing tons of compassion and maturity, I rolled down the window, calling out to him through rushing highway air: "Eat your heart out, sucker! We are on way to Margaritaville."

I felt lucky, liberated, lighthearted, and melancholy. The glow of the fading Texas sun reminded me to return to the present moment. Christie was leaning back in her seat, wearing big sunglasses and a Cheshire Cat grin. I was cruising with my best friend to the land of forgetfulness and escape. He, I imagined, was not. The melancholy stayed put, as I wished for the millionth time that Danny Lott had made different choices on that beautiful Saturday afternoon in 2008.

When Christie and I travel together, our habit is to do absolutely nothing and brag about it. Thanks to past experience, we knew exactly where we wanted to lounge by the turquoise pool that faced open fields of stout trees shaped like broccoli stalks. Each visit, when we sat by that particular pool, we noticed a solitary white duck drifting lazily on a nearby pond. It never changed. Every year, one duck (we assumed the same duck) floated around, alone. We enjoyed projecting our stories onto that solitary duck. On that trip, we decided the lone bird appeared to be quite content—a happy, single woman of the duck world.

I smeared on SPF 50 and sat in the shade while Christie defied all dermatological recommendations. We have a ritual of trading novels on trips, so we each dove into a fresh book. I was not concentrating and finally in a position where it was fine to allow my mind to wander. There were no pink forms to worry about, and I did not have to think about anything until the hearing on Monday morning.

I watched Christie read, engrossed in her book. I remembered the last time we read books by the same pool. Christie was fully engrossed by a novel I had given to her about an elephant. As she read the book, she kept looking over at me and exclaiming how much she loved the elephant. The more times she said that, the worse I felt, because I knew the elephant was going to die. I reminded her about the elephant, and we melted into hilarity.

We ordered a cocktail and appetizer from the restaurant, so we could sit in the sun as long as possible. Such is the life of sun worshipers from Seattle and Alaska. I folded my hat brim low and relished a taste of carefree happiness. As we waited for our order, we speculated on the cuteness factor of the young male server. Turns out, he was extremely cute, and very young.

Christie reeled him into a conversation with skill, so he sprang into an enthusiastic discussion about the newest plans he and his girlfriend were forming for a future trip to India. Christie had traveled there several times, so she mentioned some worthwhile stops. He said that he wanted to go along with whatever itinerary his girlfriend planned, not because he was that interested in India, but because *she* was.

He got a big tip for that statement, as well as accolades. The waiter turned to leave as we tapped our glasses together and winked, whispering a toast to all men who know how to put their women first. Nothing could be sexier.

Therefore, we continued to put ourselves first. I should say, Christie continued to put me first. After all, she was financing the luxury; I was the lucky recipient. Soon the sunset left a few neon streaks across a dark dome of sky. We hoisted ourselves up from the horizontal bliss of sun-baked chaise lounges, moving onto a breezy patio for dinner. When we ordered drinks, the young woman serving us asked to see our IDs. We quizzed her if that was required. Did she have to check everyone's ID? She told us that management instructed her to check anyone who may even possibly look underage. We liked her, and the poor lighting, so she got a good tip too. In twilight air, sipping tropical drinks and eating delicious food with my best friend, I realized that the present moment did not get any better. I hit send on another IP to Karl. That time the message felt sincere.

On Saturday morning, Christie maintained a steady calm with her book and tanning efforts. I stayed in the shade by the pool and tried to fake calm, cool, and collected. I gave up trying to concentrate on a book or magazine or on anything except staring at the sky and watching the white duck. I knew that alcohol was a headache waiting to happen. Even the effort of a walk did not sound inviting. We quipped that exercise was against our policy.

I sat, shifted positions, lay, stood, went swimming, stewed, ate a few bites of food, fretted, and shifted. The broken zipper of my spine ached, as expected; the sensation never totally went away. I reminded myself that the jagged tear and pinch had dissolved, serving as a pleasant reminder that sometimes things did get easier. However, a constant ache remained. My head always hurt to some degree, and I learned to live with that too. Moments like the one I was enjoying erased the gray days. That Saturday, clinging to our last minutes at our sacred oasis, we put off leaving the pool until the last second. By the time we arrived at the hotel in Austin that night, Don and Sue were there.

We all took showers and drove to town for dinner. Christie had never met Don and Sue, although they had heard about each other for years. I loved remembering how it felt to be around people who knew and cared about me. I had been getting used to feeling like the dunce, which did nothing for my self-confidence.

The next morning, I got up early to go to the regular Sunday morning mediation I used to attend each week. The resounding strike of the familiar gong and the peace of sitting quietly with others moved me to wet emotion. Instead of meditating, I wiped drop after droplet from my cheek and prayed for bravery. My fellow mediators sat quietly and allowed me to have my experience.

While I found solace in silence, Don and Sue explored the capital, and Christie went for a stifling walk near the hotel, which turned out to be in the local cemetery. I called her cell when I returned to the hotel and joined her for a sweaty walk through scorched and weathered tombstones.

It was Father's Day, so we took Don to a gospel brunch in a dark, sticky, beery bar. Nothing could have been further from his typical New England Father's Day dinner, yet the contrast seemed to amuse him. We spent the rest of the day wandering through the heat and humidity. Each of us felt our own version of anticipation and wanted to rest, reserving our energies for the next day.

Giggy arrived from Houston late Sunday afternoon. By then I was so uptight I had to work to keep breathing. We enjoyed an early evening on South Congress with some margaritas and tacos. I smiled at another IP from Karl. Athena's owl tightened her grip on my shoulder and whispered, "Tomorrow will happen in its own time. Stay here, in this moment. Latch onto this delicious intermission with the people you love."

By the end of dinner, I could do neither small nor big talk. Everyone understood, so there was no pressure to be anything other than what I was: nervous. We formulated a morning plan to meet in the lobby, pick up a cup of coffee or muffin, and find a parking spot close to the courthouse.

As we wished each other pleasant dreams, I warned them that I might not feel like talking in the morning either. We all seemed to be on tenterhooks, so everyone simply nodded. Silence seemed right.

After a bubble bath, I got into the second double bed, closest to the window. Before turning out the lamp, I observed Christie in a deep, still, even sleep. I used her easy breathing as a reference point. The entire world was not spinning; it was my mind that ran in frenetic circles. I reclined in the dark and watched a noisy Autobahn of thoughts speeding, revving-up, faster and faster around the next turn.

Bob Marley's rendition of "Sitting Here in Limbo" played in repeated tracks along one layer of my mind. On another level, I wondered how in the world people live through highly publicized trials. How did Casey Anthony's parents make it through the nights before her trial? How did Amanda Knox survive the tension?

Minutes dragged by in slight clicks of the digital clock. My feet cramped in tight strands of tendon and nerve. I tried squeezing my arches and straightening my toes, which remained hard and unmoving. For hours, the air conditioner buzzed as I ran through every possible state of mind, from excruciating impatience, to prayer, then nausea, fear, heart-clapping memories, and dread. I did not want to go into the courtroom. I wanted to run away. I yearned for the sweet solace of my cabin. I wanted to be anywhere except inside that courtroom.

I knew that it was too late for escape. I wanted to reframe and find good reasons to stay on course. I recalled the words of wise teachers who say that we humans are much happier when thinking of others, as opposed to caring so much about ourselves. So I decided to focus my frenetic thoughts on all of the people who cared about me and expected me to stand up to the ones who hurt me. I stared at the dimly lit ceiling, creating a mental list of every person I could think of who radiated love, as opposed to harm. Hundreds of smiling images percolated in front of my eyes, each wearing the face of patient love.

I thought about the possibility of The Guy hurting any of those faces. How I would feel if he put a gun to Christie's head, or against my niece's temple, perhaps behind my stepson's ear? Those images fired waves of rage through every cell in my body. Of course I would do anything it took to prevent the ones I loved from harm. Of course I should do the same for myself. Remembering and loving all of those people erased any lingering specks of victimhood. We owe it to society to speak up when we see a devil. I had people to protect.

A quiet calm seeped in warm rushes along my tense muscles, flowing through my veins. I looked at the clock and hoped seven in the morning would happen soon. I was ready.

CHAPTER FIFTY

I DO REMEMBER RIDING THE ELEVATOR UP TO THE EIGHTH FLOOR OF the courthouse. Beyond that, there are noticeable blanks in my memory files. I have no recall of moving from point A to point B. I felt Don next to me, paying attention to everything as I walked in tunnel vision. Mary met us in the hallway before we reached the courtroom. The unhardened twinkle in her eyes served to delight and soften me. We hugged, and I felt lucky to have her as the champion of my cause.

After introductions, Mary pulled me aside. I remember thinking, "If she tells me there is another delay, I will implode." I grabbed a lung full of air and readied myself.

"Here we go. This is it," she said with a nervous smile.

This is it—finally. I exhaled, cleared my head, and straightened my shoulders; this was no time to slump. I sealed my gaze in single-pointed focus on Mary's strong blue eyes. The tension of the moment had blurred her exact words forever, but she said something about the judge invoking "the rule." I remembered that term from the flashcard days in Houston.

It is a procedural and evidentiary rule that excludes witnesses from the courtroom when another witness is testifying. Mary said the rule applied to everyone subpoenaed, except for me, because I was the key witness.

She went on to explain why the judge invoked the rule. The defense subpoenaed The Guy's son, who was about nine years old, to speak as a character witness for his father. My stomach dropped to the floor. They asked a child to testify on his father's behalf, after the father committed a felony? What kind of man would put his son through that? I guessed I knew the answer. Mary seemed stunned by the decision as well.

She said the defense attorney told her that he did not plan to cross-examine my testimony. That was incredible news. The years dedicated to worrying about a cross-examination melted away. I had less to prove since he was pleading guilty. Mary did not share the details yet often reassured me that the evidence was compelling. She was confident in the case, so I followed her lead.

I emulated Mary's steps into the courtroom. I set my gaze to the carpet six feet in front of me, telling myself, "I am breathing, in-out-in-out, the floor is here, stay with the floor." We all sat in the front row, behind Mary. Liza sat next to Christie, who was on my left. Don sat on my right, then Sue, with Giggy far right. As we waited for the judge to arrive, my breathing probably sounded like a room packed with husbands and wives practicing Lamaze.

Christie leaned over and asked me if I had looked to the left to see The Guy's family sitting in the courtroom. I shook my head, so she leaned in again and said, "There is a shitload of people sitting over there, at least ten." She was the only person in the world who could have made me laugh right then. I cracked a smile, then thought about having his family as an audience. All of my planning and practice had not accounted for that.

The room began to rotate, so I grabbed onto the bench in front of me. Don leaned over, conspiratorially, and whispered, "This is where having played sports helps, doesn't it?" Leave it to the seasoned athlete to say that. He was right—it takes practice to live under pressure. Eyes pinned to a scuff mark on my black shoes, I nodded with a mini dip, enough to avoid rocking the seasickness in my belly.

The judge entered the chamber, and we all stood.

Two deputies accompanied The Guy into the room and to the defense table. I peeked, enough to see the back of his striped polo shirt. It looked as though he had lost weight, and his shoulders slumped forward in an exaggerated curve. Leg shackles restricted his gait, the indisputable trappings that cooled my apprehension over his release from the big metal box. I *had* to glance at his face and decided to make a furtive move when he turned to look at his attorney.

A swift shift of the eyes confirmed his identity. Yes, it was the same man who haunted me, only this one was childlike and pathetic, not the cocksure, polished dude I remembered. As the court clerk read the charges—aggravated robbery, kidnapping, and burglary—The Guy did a class-B acting job of trying to play the part of a confused and innocent man, who had no idea why he faced such puzzling accusations.

BB and I walked to the bench and stood beside each other to take our oaths. She then left the courtroom because of the rule. I was the first to testify. Instead of wearing my glasses, I carried them. I wanted everything in the courtroom, especially his face, to be blurry. I focused on Mary's eyes, allowing myself no peripheral view.

Mary asked me if I recognized the man in the room whom I accused of this crime. Trying not to fiddle and shake, I put my glasses on, and turned my head slightly, steering my eyes to his impassive face. I held my gaze long enough to know that he and I were both uncomfortable. I identified Danny Lott as the man who committed the crime.

I turned away, removed my glasses, and began to answer Mary's questions. I watched only her eyes and lips, in a state of intense concentration.

Nothing else was important. I was one hundred percent involved in the process. I listened closely to her questions, using her voice to anchor me to the room. Mary had a grasp on my line and a sword at my back. It is a precious opportunity to have someone like Mary sticking up for you. I was not going to let her down.

For some reason, blurring my vision of everything except Mary's face helped. I was not up to multitasking, so all I had to do was pay attention to Mary. At one point in the testimony, Mary asked me if I turned to the right or the left. I stopped to think about her question and faltered, noticing my brother grinning behind her. I knew he was making fun of me because one of my recent driving instructions involved a left, when it should have been a right. I darted my focus away from his smirk.

Reverting to my six-year-old inner child, I strained to resist the standing urge toward immaturity. I wanted to punch his arm as hard as I could and yell something smart like "You are such a gooberhead!" Swallowing a laugh, I bit down on the inside of my lips and locked my eyes back on Mary, trying to tune Don out, secure in the knowledge that paybacks can be a lot of fun.

Mary's questions covered a precise chronological order of the day of the crime. She worked through slides of the First Martini, Jackie's house, pieces of duct tape on my old front deck. I went into auto drive as I looked at the photographs, working my way through, word by word. The images were concurrently real and surreal. I traveled back into a deafening, strong, forced, unnatural heartbeat. Mary showed a slide of blood on the oak floor, and my heart beat louder.

I gagged internally at the photograph of the zip ties, but I willed myself to remain steady, staid, tearless, grounded. Although I use them occasionally, I still gag at the sight of white zip ties. Right then, I wanted to be a warrior, not a weeping willow, so I held myself in grave attention. I was safe in the simplicity of having nothing to embellish, and it was easy to refrain from looking over at The Guy again.

In my mind, the first morning in the courtroom remains a string of snapshots, projected on a screen in a strange jumble of nonlinear precision. I don't know what we ate for lunch during the break. I remember walking down a set of steps back to the courthouse after consuming something at an archaic basement cafeteria in the old Guadalupe Courthouse.

It was a relief from the heat to return to the courtroom, which was simple, cool, and elegant in a modern, gray institutional way. The room had high ceilings, and it was spacious, more streamlined than older, ornate Texan courthouses. Although I did not look at her while I was on the stand, from our perspective looking toward the bench, the judge struck me as a smart, strong, beautiful woman. I wondered how many flashcards it took her to become a judge. I considered all of the flashcards it would take me to get through law school, then pulled my mind back in, amazed at myself for being such a goofball.

Turning my attention back to the judge, I decided that I liked her, and I could trust and accept her decision regarding his sentence. That set me free.

The Guy's wife testified, but she did not do the "stand by your man" thing. During her testimony, she appeared to be horrified and repulsed that her husband could behave so brutally. I believed her. I recognized her weary heart; it had the earmarks of mine. As she answered questions, the varied layers of the story became both more defined and more confusing.

In October 2008, she and The Guy were married, with two children, living a happy, middle-class life in Abilene, Texas. He owned a pallet business, and she had a successful tanning salon and smoothie business. The Guy got in trouble with the law, and in trouble with his wife, one would assume. He faced federal felony charges for five counts of child pornography and several fraud charges. She and The Guy borrowed fifty thousand dollars from her grandmother for an attorney to represent him in court.

On or around October 9, 2008, a month prior to his court date for sentencing on the child pornography charges, The Guy was still a free man. He told his wife he needed to go on a spiritual pilgrimage, in search of his soul and a way to make amends for his mistakes. Several days later, he returned to Abilene to see his family. In a matter of hours, he absconded with her grandmother's savings, stole his wife's business information, including smoothie recipes from her shop, borrowed his father's Lincoln Town Car, and promptly disappeared, minutes before the U.S. Marshals showed up at his front door with a warrant for his arrest.

As we knew, he was on the run for six weeks. According to his wife's testimony, he had no contact with his family from the time he dashed out of Abilene until his arrest near Dallas, on November 26, 2008.

The Guy's wife testified that they were divorced by then, and she had custody of their two children. She looked wrecked when she talked about it. I tried to imagine what his disappearance must have felt like to her and their son and daughter.

The Guy stared at the floor, impassive, as his former wife spoke. She left the stand looking drained. We share similar physical qualities, both blond, almost the same size. I thought about his rage toward me, what I might have represented to him. Did he stalk me, or was the event random?

On her way out of the courtroom, his ex-wife stopped and turned back to the judge and then to me, saying, "May I say something?" Before the judge could speak, she wiped her eyes and faced me.

"I am so sorry for what happened." Her eyes were tired and bereft. I bowed my head and lifted my hands to my forehead in a brief acknowledgement. She was a kindred sister, another torn-up kite twisted in the branches of The Guy's games.

I am unsure what the defense was trying to do, because the more testimony they provided to beef up The Guy's righteous Christian character,
the less credible he seemed. I cringed as his teenage stepdaughter sobbed
on the stand, describing her devotion to him as her father. In distraught
sound clips mixed with tears and frantic attempts at eye contact with
him, her sincerity and affection sharply contrasted his self-serving, nar-
cissistic behavior.

His son's testimony was brief: "Yes, my Dad was our baseball
coach. Yes, he is a good father. He buys me things." It was awkward
and heartbreaking. All of us were disturbed to see his son in such a
terrible position.

The Guy's mother testified that he was a good Christian boy who
loved to sing and play the guitar at church. She pled for mercy for her
son and assured the judge that he was a good boy.

Cousin Larry got up on the stand. The Guy had a business in Abilene
and hired Cousin Larry when he was on hard times, a favor he would
never forget. As far as Larry was concerned, The Guy always showed
himself to be a fine citizen and a good family man. It was hard for Larry
to imagine his cousin's involvement in the crime. He had all of the finest
things to say about his cousin.

As he thought she was finished, Mary shot a zinger his way: "Is it
true that the defendant's brother is a registered sex offender?" After an
electrified squirm, Cousin Larry hiccupped, looked at the judge, and
said, "Ah, do I need to answer that?" The public defender stood and
objected. The judge sustained, but Mary's question still hung in the air,
like a bold banner flapping in the wind behind a slow, single-engine
airplane.

After a break, Mary continued her questioning. Both of the officers
who first arrived on the scene testified. Jackie was next on the stand. Don
mentioned to me that he had spoken to her earlier in the courthouse

hallway; I had not seen her yet. She flicked a wave to me from the stand as she sat.

Jackie testified that when she first heard the screams from inside my house, she could not tell where they came from. She thought it might have been a child screaming in playful glee, or it could have been someone in trouble. The sound was too muffled and far away to make a clear distinction. She answered questions and after leaving the stand, she passed a note to me, saying that she had another appointment, and to please call. I never got in touch with her while I was in Austin. I wanted to see her, yet I have a difficult time doing so.

I never fail to cry when I see Jackie, because everything feels so complex when I look into her face. I think these emotional eruptions happen because she represents the moment I knew I was going to live. I remember her tiptoeing behind her house, waving for me to follow, and I still see her transparent wings. She saved me, yet I avoid the very person who helped me. Liza and Stacey assure me that this is normal, a common pattern for people after trauma. Nothing about that seemed normal to me.

Mary called the next witness. Brad was my former neighbor, who lived in an adjacent lot behind the First Martini. We lived that close and never met, a sign of the times, I guess. Mary asked him what he remembered from the afternoon of October 11. He said he heard a woman screaming but could not tell where the yells were coming from. Then he noticed that the sounds stopped for ten or fifteen minutes, until he heard me shouting for help as I ran down the driveway. He described the screams as blood curdling. I had not thought of it that way; it curdled me to hear him say it, and to remember those strange, desperate shrieks coming out of my throat.

Brad is a musician and happened to be working at home that Saturday in October 2008. His studio is located on the side of the house The

Guy ran past after scaling my rickety backyard fence. Naturally attuned to sound, Brad was able to provide a credible, succinct account of the sounds the defendant made while he was running and jumping over several high, newly constructed fences in Brad's yard. Brad testified that he got up from his desk and rushed to open the front door of his house in time to come face to face with The Guy as he jumped the final fence. Mary asked Brad if he could identify the man in the courtroom who was in his yard that day. Brad pointed at The Guy.

Mary asked him what happened next. Brad said The Guy was out of breath as he mumbled something like, "What's the best way to get out of here?" Brad, wisely, pointed that way (as in away from here) and watched The Guy walk coolly down the street, then head east one block, and duck into a back alley. Not only did we have an eyewitness, we also had someone who paid close enough attention to remember details of The Guy's appearance and clothing, which all matched my description. I realized how lucky we were to have an articulate musician, gifted with sensitive hearing and keen attention to noises outside, as an eyewitness. Brad's neighbor on the other end of the duplex was watching television at the time and did not hear a thing.

Next to take the stand was a neighbor who lived several blocks away from my house. He testified that he was pulling out of his driveway around two p.m. on October 11, when he saw what looked like a man with hairy legs and a five o'clock shadow wearing a skirt walking toward him, pushing a dilapidated baby stroller down the block. The green scarf draped over the guy's head and chin failed to hide his size ten men's tennis shoes and one hundred eighty-pound frame. The witness said he stopped his car to ask if The Guy needed help. Pushing the scarf close to his mouth, he said, "No thanks." My neighbor, scratching his head, drove off in the opposite direction of the man pushing an old, wobbly baby carriage.

After Mary's interrogatory, the defense attorney asked the witness a few questions. Christie leaned over and whispered something derogatory and utterly clever about the defense attorney's ill-fitting suit. I adore her cutting edge.

The attorney asked the man, "South Austin is a pretty liberal place. If you had seen a man dressed in woman's clothing down on South Congress, would you have been surprised?"

"No," said the man, "I would not be surprised at all on South Congress, but up here on my quiet street, we do not see that often."

The woman who had owned that skirt and scarf took the stand next. When she and her husband returned from a weekend trip on Sunday afternoon, they discovered a broken cellar window. Mary showed slides of the shattered glass and of a large basement filled to the gills with women's clothing and an array of fascinating piles of stuff.

My neighbors called the police about the burglary. While investigating the break-in, police found a pair of men's shorts stuffed tightly into a far corner, behind some old pieces of furniture. They were khaki cargo shorts, marked with splats of dried blood.

A TAG Heuer watch was in one of the pockets.

The watch led the detectives to The Guy. They looked up the serial number of the watch and tracked down the store where it was purchased, linking up to The Guy's credit card. That, in turn, connected him to the basement break-in and to my bloodstains. The facts churned into place in my mind. The discovery of the watch led to the photo lineup.

The case adjourned until nine the next morning. The five of us finally had a chance to talk and process all of the day's details. It felt as though we had exited a virtual reality tank. Giggy, Sue, and Don rounded one side of a private booth in Bessie's Kitchen as Christie and I slid into the other side. We were beginning to see a pattern—everywhere we ate, at least one server teased Don about his four dates and asked if he was the new Bachelor. After that lively discussion, we started with margaritas, followed by food and debrief, ripe with disbelief.

We passed ideas around the table. He pushed a stroller down the street wearing a skirt? Moreover, how about that question from the public defender about men dressed as women on South Congress? We all agreed that definitely blew up in his attorney's face.

I asked Don and Sue if The Guy ever showed emotion. They said he remained stoic and impassive through everything, except for a bit of a shake-up during his stepdaughter's weeping. That might have moved him. Other than that, they detected no visible emotion.

Giggy decided to stay another night. The hotel was out of rooms, so she took over Christie's bed, and Christie shared mine. We turned the lights off around ten thirty, and I spent about ten minutes in bed before I got up and started to pace. My feet were cramping. By then I knew to drink quinine water and walk out the spasms. On top of muscle cramps, I kept thinking about Giggy's last words before going to bed. She checked the mattress for bed bugs and reminded us about the current levels of national infestation.

Bed bugs? Oh my, I did not want to think about those nasty hexapods. They were out in force that summer, making it big on the evening news. Between foot cramps, the ordeal in general, and the mention of swarming, bustling bugs, I was destined to stay awake.

Christie woke while I was roaming around in the dark, and she cracked up, "What in the world are you doing?" I was stuck in a stiff hobble, lurching forward like a creepy, aged ghost in a dark hotel room. I whispered, "I'm fine—just walking out a foot cramp." She rolled over and turned the sleep switch right back on. I was so jealous.

Hours later, I lowered myself down, arranging pillows beneath my knees, trying to relax my arms, feeling fully agitated by my hypervigilant mind. I closed my eyes and pretended I was driving through the sunflower fields of North Dakota. My vivid memories exceeded the quality of any photograph I could have taken of those flowering fields. I felt grateful then for that road trip to Alaska and remembered that gratitude is the best way to go. I thought of the voices, faces, hands, and paws, of everyone and everything I loved, as I faced my biggest demons.

CHAPTER FIFTY-ONE

O
N TUESDAY MORNING I WAS NERVOUS, BUT NOTHING CLOSE TO
the first day's meter reading. We sat on the shiny wooden bench, waiting
for the judge and the next witness, wondering what to expect.

A court-appointed DNA specialist sputtered lengthy, impressive statistical answers to Mary's questions about the blood found on the khaki shorts matching Diana Martin's DNA. No shocker, the chance of that blood belonging to me was high, though I do not remember the particulars.

Next on the stand was a U.S. Marshal. We listened to his description of the arrest and subsequent discovery of The Guy's new life in Dallas. According to the marshal, sometime in November 2008, The Guy moved to Dallas, changed his name to Calvin Jones, and rented a townhouse with one other man. In The Guy's area of the home, he set up an office furnished with a new desk, computer, big-screen TV, sofa, and bed. The receipts for those items amounted to over twenty thousand dollars.

On the wall above his desk, The Guy taped up street maps of Dallas and Greater Texas, placing pushpins in specific parts of town, later discovered as locations of existing tanning salons. They found documents supporting a plan to open another tanning and smoothie business, using the smoothie recipes he stole from his wife. I squirmed uncomfortably, considering the ramifications of a man involved in pornography running a tanning salon. Not to mention the concept of stealing from your wife and using her grandmother's money to finance these purchases.

The marshals found an assortment of homemade documents and how-to books on changing one's identity and starting a new business. They found a completed change-of-name application, copies of cover letters and résumés for Calvin Jones. Calvin Jones also had cleverly printed glowing Gold Star Certificates of Appreciation for participating as a Valuable Leader for various youth organizations. According to his mother's earlier testimony, The Guy had served as a youth pastor and football coach in Abilene.

The agents found paperwork for a truck loan and title in the name of Calvin Jones. He told the marshals that he bought the truck for his former employee who was named Calvin Jones. They uncovered a receipt for twenty-five hundred dollars, a written record of a down payment to a plastic surgeon in Dallas.

Then, Mary played a recording of a phone call between The Guy and his wife, taped by the U.S. Marshals while he was in custody. In federal cases, phone calls from prison may be recorded and used in a court of law, something I did not previously know.

During the call, The Guy's wife asked him specific questions about what happened in Austin. In sobs and secretions on the phone, he professed his love for her and said he was going through all of these hoops and changes for her. He said he ran from Abilene with her grandmother's money so he could build a better life for all of them, in a new town. He planned to move the family to Dallas and build a brand new start for the family because he realized his past mistakes.

Later in the call, Lott's wife asked him about his watch—how did he lose it? He said he was not feeling well on the Saturday he was in Austin, so he rolled down his truck windows and eased back in his seat to take a nap. He woke to the sound of a homeless man grabbing his duffle bag, with his watch in it, right out of the front seat. The Guy said he got out of the truck to chase the thief and couldn't catch him.

His wife asked him about the story of a woman he hurt in Austin. He assured her that was crazy talk, and simply not true. He would never do a thing like that, he said in incredulous tones. She asked him about the receipt from a plastic surgeon in Dallas.

He sobbed, "Baby, that was for you. You know I always wanted to change my face for you. Baby, all of this—moving to Dallas, looking better—it was all for you."

She asked about the money and the receipts for his new furniture and electronics. He moaned over the phone, "Baby, I was building a new life for you, and for us, away from Abilene."

As Mary stopped the recording, I felt embarrassed to be listening in on a deeply personal conversation between two people I did not know. I looked over to see if he showed any reaction and wondered to myself why he kept the incongruous charade going. He sat passively, the shackled buffoon, allowing this story to spiral deeper into the quicksand of the ridiculous. Why didn't he man up and say, "You know what, I did all of this. I apologize for hurting each of you, and for wasting so much time and money to run my BS story. It does not make sense to do this any longer. I did it. My defense is terrible. Let's get on with the fact I did it. I am ready to take my punishment." Instead, he sat silently slumped with poor-me shoulders, acting like a sullen boy looking down at the floor to avoid taking responsibility.

The defense called their expert witness, a professor from a college in Appalachia, touted as a specialist on psychological drug reactions.

The doctor was portly and bespectacled, with a Hollywood silver-gray Freudian beard. I could tell he was an expert in "Doctor-speak." I've dated doctors, so I am fine-tuned to the charm and posture of The Expert. Eventually, these wizards blow up in smoke, although in the meantime, they work the authority advantage to the bone.

Since the defendant waived his right to testify, it ended up being the expert's role to tell The Guy's side of the story. The doctor reached his conclusions based on conversations he had with The Guy and his own research. He said The Guy told him he attended a party the night before entering my home. The doctor explained that the defendant appeared to be very naïve about drugs; he did not know the names of any street drugs or their uses. The defendant told him it was the first time he had ever taken drugs.

The Guy told the doctor that he ended up at a hot-tub party with people he met that day. He took some sort of drug that caused a violent, sickening reaction, and claimed he did not know where he was or what was going on. The Guy had no memory of the rest of the night or the next day.

The doctor said that scenario was quite possible. He explained that there are documented reports of hapless folks consuming mixtures of drugs and alcohol, who then do unusual things such as dancing around a room wearing a lampshade on their head, yet are unable to remember a single thing about it the next day.

The lampshade testimony was too good to pass up; Christie and I both suppressed smiles. I remembered thinking that someday I could write a book about this guano, which was way better than fiction. I placed my attention back on the doctor because I did not want to miss a thing he said.

The doctor claimed the drug The Guy thinks he took (but remember, he didn't know names) was Ativan, and he mixed it with alcohol. Christie elbowed me; that is one of America's favorite combinations.

The first medication the ER doctor gave me was Ativan. From my experience, the prescription drug does not crank people up; it slows most people down.

Wouldn't you think if The Guy did not know names, maybe they could have come up with something more exotic than Ativan and a drink? I was willing to bet that a handful of people in that courtroom had taken Ativan without feeling the urge to take someone down with a gun and zip ties. The first thing I noticed when The Guy came into my home was his egotistical cool. He was not hyped up on drugs or alcohol. On that day, he was chill, clear, and fully confident. Scrubbed clean, he did not fit the description of someone who had been up all night, drugged out. There was also the matter of scaling fences—not bad for the day after a drug-enhanced drink at a hot-tub party.

The expert driveled on about studies indicating how many people take Ativan and subsequently do things they cannot remember. He cited another example of people on Ativan who do things like eating the second half of a chocolate pie and not remembering it the next day. A bailiff sitting behind the defendant leaned back in his chair, bulky arms crossed, watching the expression on my face. He sat still, holding neutral countenance, until the end of the drug reaction testimony. Then he rolled his pupils up a centimeter and slightly shook his head.

Mary called me to the witness stand again and asked me to describe the impact of the day The Guy claims not to remember. His actions altered the acceleration and direction of my existence; however finding a way to articulate those changes was another thing. I again focused on Mary's face and tried to describe my life before October 11, 2008.

I explained that I was already under financial stress because of the recession. I talked about *Martini Homes* and the difficult decisions I was facing in terms of cutting my losses. My family had loaned me money to move into the Second Martini's garage. I was trying to unload a house or

two, so I could save at least one property through the downturn. After
the robbery everything changed, and those plans fell apart.

She asked me questions, again in chronological order. I talked about
taking out a student loan to go to school in Houston. I told her about
selling my car and inventory, the losses on the last two Martinis, about
finding and losing work, being unemployed for two years. I answered
questions about my current life in Alaska. We covered my medical history of back pain, chipped teeth, headaches, and PTSD.

She asked me about the end result of the financial implications, the
bankruptcy, and loss of livelihood. I did not know how to express the
enormity of that one life-force change because it was impossible to catalog or quantify.

I thought of a word I liked, *nunima*, the immeasurable, but did not
use it then. If I could have measured and reported, I would have said that
my anxiety was the hardest burden to bear. I had the advantage of meditation training, precise steps for how to work with my mind and habitual
thoughts. Even with the advantage of counseling and meditation, anxiety
drained me during the day and forced me to wrestle in worried sheets at
night. The demons of disquiet created my life on tenterhooks. The immeasurable elements easily hid themselves behind the physical and financial.

When Mary finished her questioning, the defense attorney stood,
expressed his condolences for my loss, and requested no further testimony as to the consequences of the crime. Sweet. Dodged that one. The
judge concurred, so there was no need to call BB to the stand. Mary
covered enough territory for people to get the point.

On we moved to closing arguments. Mary asked for a long sentence,
up to life. His attorney asked for mercy. The judge said she would return
with a decision in half an hour.

CHAPTER FIFTY-TWO

I DON'T REMEMBER MUCH ABOUT THAT HALF-HOUR. I COULD TASTE
the tension, once again waiting for the other shoe to drop. I was ready
for the answer, knowing that no court decision or apology from The
Guy would soothe the prickle of alarm that ran through my spine. No
matter how hard I tried to let go, I worried about every aspect of my life.
Each time I opened the door to the cabin, a car, the office, or an elevator,
I began to ready my weapons. When I walked to the truck, I grasped
my hearty Suburban key firmly between middle and index fingers, sharp
end out, ready to go for the eyes. I keep a nasty fencing tool and a
baseball bat by the front door. A long, heavy metallic blue flashlight
sits under the front seat of the Suburban, year round. The batteries die
in October and I leave them in to corrode; it is heavier that way, good
as a weapon, not a tool. The wiring in my body runs in constant channels of urgent, electrical charges compared to my innate wiring before
the brown-out. I am one hundred percent mentally prepared for battle

one hundred percent of the time, just in case. That was the new me, the newly wired me.

Was the change in my system all bad? I doubt it. I am much more realistic, and my radar is fine-tuned. I spend more time thinking and talking about "violence," what that means, how pervasive it is. What would happen if we all talked about this more, and fought together against human cruelty? Millions of people around the world live in violent relationships, both domestic and on the streets, in the workplace, in their homes. Many live inside someone's shadow of terror for years.

It disappoints me that the majority of the world's perpetrators are men. I love men and appreciate the evidence that millions of decent men inhabit the world, yet many abuse their size and power. Some men choose violence as a means to get what they want. Some women do, too, but the statistics are clear that males commit the majority of crimes. The price of violence seems so high.

I wanted to avoid the temptation and pitfalls of "poor me." Yet acknowledging The Guy's dominance over me, his abuse of power and self-serving intentions, was important. The dust of evil still percolated in my bone marrow. How much sorrow and loss could I rightfully blame on him? How much on the winds of fate, and how much on my own actions? I was, and continue to be, incapable of quantifying, nor do I want to. It is simple: things happen—be prepared. Do the best I can.

Be prepared for anything, from winning the lottery to fret, depression, and betrayal. I learned the hard way that paying attention to discomfort has the capacity to flip on my present-moment-reminder switch. The present moment pulls back the Wizard of Oz's curtain, to expose my weak illusions.

Thinking about the now, the present moment, shot me back to it, and I remembered I was sitting on a bench in the courtroom. My mind flew off again, and I wondered, what can justice mean when the victim, the perpetrator, and their families have already lost so much? Incarceration is clearly not a solution to this polluted swamp of sorrow. Then again, slapping someone like The Guy on the wrists and sending him back out on the streets would not be intelligent or just either.

Again, relief washed through me: this was not my decision. I said that in my mind, knowing that if they let him go, I would be enraged. I was too close to find objectivity.

As a result of The Guy's decisions, my life changed in broad, uncontrolled strokes. On a molecular level, my path and The Guy's actions are inextricably bound in a tight knot of karma far beyond my understanding. The past will not change. It is a matter of radical acceptance. My fate brushed up against his; whether we were meant to collide or not, we did.

I would find a way out of the dark hole. I was determined to move on emotionally and financially. Danny Lott might not get to move on in the same way; he probably won't. He will watch his family suffer for his actions in terrible ways. Allowing The Guy to poison the rest of my days could only happen with my permission. I was on track to pick up the pieces and build again. As I said before, he picked the wrong girl.

He also got the wrong judge. After fifteen minutes of deliberation, the judged returned to the courtroom. She sat with a slight flourish and began speaking. Her message was short as she handed The Guy three concurrent sentences: thirty-five years for aggravated robbery, thirty-five years for aggravated kidnapping, and ten years for the residential burglary. In a feminine tough/sharp/scary school-principal way, the judge cut through it all by saying she thought The Guy's actions were premeditated and decisive. She went on to say if I had not been so strong and so clear-headed, she was convinced we would have tried a different case that day. Then she leaned forward, gestured her reading glasses toward The Guy, and told him how shocking she found his lack of remorse not only for the crime but also for the ordeal he put his family through.

When the judge finished, I stood to hug Mary. Several members of The Guy's family hurried toward us, pleading with me to forgive him. That was a sizeable request, and I was feeling rushed. The Guy sat in the same room with me for two days, blankly denying his egregious acts, and they wanted my swift forgiveness. The pressure to forgive felt a bit premature.

A bailiff gently herded us away from The Guy's family, through the courtroom's back door, and down a hall to an elevator. Eight of us packed into the elevator. It jerked down toward the first floor, forcing a long, bumpy sigh from my lips. Air locked in my lungs for two and a half years spilled out in a primal, guttural release. Everyone in the elevator remained quiet, a respectful pause, allowing time to assimilate. I heard myself say, in a hushed tone, "Thank God. It is finally over."

Minutes later, we convened in the hallway near Mary's office. Liza, Mary, the U.S. Marshals, and our band of five cheered in the hallway. It was fun to see how excited the marshals were about the success of their hard work. As we chatted, Mary walked up to hand me a folded sticky note, whispering that it was from The Guy's sister. I glanced at her scribbled plea for forgiveness, squeezed the adhesive on the paper together, and handed it to Christie. It was not the time to think about my social and moral obligations to The Guy. Don asked me what the note said. "Forget it," I said. "It's time to celebrate and read the note later."

Giggy left for Houston in the car she had bought to replace the Suburban. It meant so much to have her there; it was hard to watch her drive away. Back at the hotel, Christie and I headed for the bar. Don and Sue joined us an hour later, and we drove to South Congress for another delightful dinner. Don only had three dates that night.

I remember a big blue bowl of steamed mussels, Italian food, and two mighty fine martinis. There is a story out there that suggests I hugged our waiter. Sue says he didn't appear to mind, as he exclaimed that this was his first thirty-five-year sentence party.

Back at the hotel, Christie and I said goodbye to Sue and Don, who had an early flight out the next morning. Our hugs, exuberant and strong, had victory in their core. Christie and I flopped on our respective beds. No more worries about a wrinkled dress. No more worries. We were too tired to speak. I reminded Christie of the words on a greeting card she sent me: "If cats could talk, they wouldn't." There was so much joy in our laughter.

I sent an IP—35 years—IP to Karl and tossed a lump of Calgon into the tub.

CHAPTER FIFTY-THREE

MY CAB DRIVER TALKED THE ENTIRE TWENTY-MINUTE DRIVE home from the Fairbanks airport. He was pontificating on gardening and the impossible task of wintering-over roses in northern Alaska. I thought fondly of the lavender rose bush thriving on my front porch for the second year and kept my mouth shut, allowing him to be the pro.

I craved time alone to stretch, digest a few emotions, and peace out with the kitties. I was not in the mood for garden talk. It was midnight, a few days after the longest day of the year. The sky was luminous and radiant, translucent with an almost-morning light. As the taxi pulled up to the cabin, both cats sat on the front windowsill, two expectant triangles. I carried my bag to the front door where a five-gallon bucket overflowed with scarlet begonias. Standing within the blaze of flowers stood two visitors—pink flamingos wearing Groucho Marx noses and eyebrows, sure signs of My Only Friend Karl.

I was bone weary but could not sleep because of the sun and the buzz of the trip. As planned, Karl pulled into the driveway five hours later. We jumped into a fierce and protracted bear hug. I felt first tears erupting. It felt miraculous to have someone hold me tight. After a few minutes, we agreed that crying could come back later; right then we were headed to the favorite place. I threw a small duffle bag into the back of his truck, and I strapped into the front seat. We bounced down the road toward our beloved destination. I felt drugged and drunk with relief, as some of the tenterhooks oozed out of my body. My Only Friend Karl's steady presence soothed and organized the day. As usual, I smiled when we passed the store with the sign of a big revolver, remembering how hard Kathi and I had laughed about the sign that says: We Don't Call 911.

After a few hours, my thoughts congealed, and I was able to talk to Karl about the hearing in Austin. I had no idea how cathartic it would be to participate in a hearing, to officially, procedurally be heard. People listened. The hearing and the sentencing freed me in a way I could not have predicted.

Over the next few days, some people commented, "Now you can have closure." I suspected the experience of closure would probably happen after forgiveness, if there is an actual order to these things. Perhaps what I felt was not closure, but a heavy load of cargo lifted from my shoulders. I never expected the shift of weight and balance to be so immediate and effortless.

I took the weekend off from chores to regroup and revel in a new and unfamiliar sense of contentment. I loved seeing the cats, yet it felt lonely in the cabin. I missed BB, my family, Christie, Austin, and the unbending support I received from Liza, Mary, and Judge Sage. I had no illusions; everything would be status quo at work, so I wanted to enjoy the weekend and live in denial about Monday's realities. I knew we had only four days to complete the fiscal year when I returned to the office.

On Monday I drove to work, giddy with relief. I was on easy street now, with a few predictable, albeit dreaded, work dynamics—nothing compared to the list of dreads I had burned back in Austin. I said hello to some friendly faces at the front desk. They all knew I had a week off but did not know why I went to Texas. I had remained quiet at work about my personal life. It was too complicated. Still, I was happy to see everyone at the front desk.

As I turned left around the corner to my office, my stomach plunged with a vague feeling of being the kid in trouble. I turned the key to my door, raising the switch for the fluorescents, which illuminated a stack of papers on my desk. Before the lights stopped flickering, and before my heavy book bag hit the floor, I lifted the first sheet and felt my euphoria and new energy drain away.

A bold, blue circle of ink highlighted a mistake on my email vacation responder. In my haste and spaced departure, I entered the wrong out-of-office dates on my Google email account. This meant that wrong dates were included on all of my email responses for the time I was away. The porcupine noticed and pointed out my mistake after the fact. She didn't take the fifteen seconds required to send me a text or leave a message on my cell. Would it have hurt to say, "Hey, Nervous Nellie" or "Stupid" or whatever she wanted to call me, "Change the dates on your vacation responder"?

I know lots of bosses and coworkers who have made the same mistake. I know how easy it is to watch someone's back. Simply reminding a coworker to change the dates in Google is not a catastrophic event. If someone, including my not-so-favorite person, had to go to court over summer vacation, I hope I would help, not shame them. Rage popped to the surface. I was hurt down deep, close to the place where anger flowed.

I looked at her pompous ink circle and felt every one of my rested and nourished cells plummet back into a state of toxicity. I had mistakenly expected someone else to look at the world and behave as I did. In foolish, automatic gear, I dove straight down into the feeling of being stung by a queen bee. The mean blue circle sent my morale from confident and victorious to flustered and hurt. I was too fragile to combat all the passive-aggressive energy in that one blue circle. I slipped another corrected paper into my secret file folder, cleared my desk, strapped on my armadillo suit, cleaned my glasses, ruffled my hair, applied bright lipstick, and gained composure.

I did not bring up the offending loops of blue ink and spoke of my trip in sound bites. I was not one to invite a fight. I had just had the big warrior talk with myself in the courtroom, and I was already retreating. I did everything I could to avoid her, using an "avoid and do not conquer strategy." I was guilty of trying not to lose, having given up on winning. I wanted to celebrate the end of The Guy, and there I was, too upset with work, and with myself, for allowing anyone's behavior to affect me so viciously.

I wrote on scraps of paper and shoved them in the secret file folder, simply looking for a way to vent. On the back of torn paper, I scrawled, "Any time the first sentence in your business email starts out with 'Pursuant,' you have probably lost your audience." She sure got away with playing tough with our clients.

I amused myself by thinking that if someone could get paid for that kind of outrageous behavior, it meant I could have guaranteed job security. The joke did not ring true; I felt my livelihood was in jeopardy. I sensed the porcupine's nose tipped up a tad higher. Smugness flamed from her nostrils, and disdain bled from her beady eyes. I could feel and smell our mutual distaste.

One morning, two weeks later, the porcupine danced into work all dressed up. She wore a classy pair of sandals instead of her usual cheesy flip-flops. She also wore a flattering tunic over a pair of uncharacteristically formal pants. Her hair was clean and carefully coifed, and her makeup was above the normal porcupine standard. I eyed her walking by and calculated the amount of time that went into all of that.

Something was up. She avoided my eyes, while conversing in mega-cheerful tones with other people in the office, a neon warning. My first thought was that maybe she had an interview, which was immediately followed by a prayer for divine intervention: Please, God, Gods, Angels, Whoever you are, whatever you are, with all due respect and devotion, please find her a fabulous job somewhere, anywhere . . . else.

I talk big about not asking outer forces to grant my wishes, thus living life on life's terms. By that time, I was ready to fold on that principle and pray fervently for the porcupine to move on out of my life.

By the next day, pieces began to fit into the puzzle's curves. I sat in my office, waiting for the porcupine to approach me, because I sure wasn't jumping up to track her down. She swooshed into my file room/office with a swift fluster of hello. I could see her paws shaking as she stood above me, but I remained seated and folded my hands. With a creased forehead, she said, "Frankly, there are some performance issues here. It would be unfair for me to do a formal performance evaluation right now." Those were not her words; someone coached her to say that. She continued, "We need to sit down and discuss the issues, as I see them."

As *she* sees them. I'd been down that one-way road many times before. The porcupine was going to inform me of the issues; it was not going to be a discussion of the issues.

I knew from the performance evaluation comment that she was preparing to write me up. I figured she had dressed up the day earlier for a meeting with human resources to complain about my performance. Five days earlier, we had finished the fiscal year on time, and it had been two weeks since the hearing. I had never missed a deadline.

It was not a case of personal paranoia. I felt the tension and saw the signs of the porcupine's warpath. Panicked, I confided in a few friends at the company, and someone confirmed my suspicions: the porcupine indeed had met with HR to report problems with me. I drove home in a state of shock.

I was no spring chicken. I had worked more years than all the years she had lived on this planet. In every one of those situations, including the ill-timed layoff in Houston, I earned high recommendations and excellent performance reviews. Now, a porcupine with fluorescent green glasses was threatening my hard-won career.

I leaned back on Sofa Loren and stared out the window. My poor performance under her stern style humiliated me. Then arose a familiar feeling of being cornered, dominated, disrespected, and underestimated. I did not require a performance evaluation to know how poorly I satisfied her mercurial demands. I was tentative, feeling unsure and miserable.

I was sick of it. An urgent *No More!* bubbled out of my throat. "Girlfriend, are you ready for this? Because honey, it's time to take this one down."

I repeated the phrase "it's time to take this one down" three or four times before my head began to nod in sync with the rhythm of the words. I got up from Sofa Loren and flicked some white cat hair off my Levi's. The nod continued as I stretched my legs and back before stepping toward the big front window. Folding my arms across my torso, I began to grasp the importance of those words. It was time to take her down.

On Thursday, close to five o'clock, I extracted the Porcupine Papers from my drawer and slid the folder into my book bag, shut off the lights, and locked the door behind me. On the way out, I stopped in to see Joan, the one who found me a place to stay with Karl, who also knew about the work problems.

My tone was flat and committed as I said, "It's time for me to file a formal complaint."

She turned to me with gentleness and regret in her eyes, "This is not going to be easy. You know that, right?"

I nodded, and we hugged.

CHAPTER FIFTY-FOUR

I WENT HOME AND CALLED DON AND SUE. THEY PROBABLY GULPED and wondered if my life would ever stabilize; so much for that stupendous sense of victory in Austin. I was headed for battle again. I lost six pounds the week after returning from Austin. Christie warned me not to tell Sue about my weight, because she had commented more than once during the trip that I "was way too skinny." I find it odd that saying such a thing would be considered socially acceptable, when saying, "you are way too fat" is considered rude.

Obviously, I was touchy about people trying to take control of my life, so I tried to keep my sensitivities to myself. However, in my work life, it was time to open up and speak out. The old, familiar anxiety and anticipation of a fight flooded my emotional center. I felt beat up, psychically and psychologically. I resented going to war when all I wanted to do was celebrate.

I reviewed the process of filing a formal complaint. I sat at the kitchen table and felt like a college student, sure in the knowledge that I was the only person on the planet writing a term paper on a weekend. Everyone else, absolutely everyone, was having fun. That was how I felt about writing the complaint. I did not relish any of it. I wanted to lie on Sofa Loren and figure out how to get along with the porcupine. Unfortunately, we were past that.

I ruminated, constipated, and nauseated, while considering various approaches and strategies. I spoke to the people I needed to, to let them know of my intention to file. I struggled with writer's block and missed the Monday morning deadline. The woman in charge at HR was clearly frustrated with me. I explained that the porcupine intimidated me because I knew her fighting style, and I was feeling mighty wimpy. The HR department believed in their process, but I knew that no matter what I wrote, the words would be disputed and discredited. The truth does come out eventually; I reminded myself that the process can take centuries—just look at the Brontosaurus. I knew the porcupine would fight me to the end.

My Only Friend Karl came to the house in the evenings and held me. I would sit on his lap on Sofa Loren, my knees curled up like a child, resting my head against his face. We sat like that, staring out the window. Karl knows what not to say when people are stretched thin. He rocked me in hushed moves, leaning in, setting the beat.

I cried on the phone to Christie who was surprisingly direct. "Diana, you popped the zit—there is no turning back. What she is doing is bullshit. Open up that laptop and start writing." I knew this was serious. The Queen of Avoidance had told me to shut up and speak up.

Then I called Kathi, who had been telling me since the first month that the porcupine's behavior was out of line. Kathi would have complained sooner, and my hat is off to her, but I am usually less than enthusiastic about confrontation. As we spoke, I sat outside on my front steps, squinting at the harsh eight p.m. sun. I relied on the light to stay up with me all night, because the next morning I had to submit the written complaint that was yet to be written.

Whatever Kathi said to inspire me deserves to be recorded on top of the soundtrack to *Chariots of Fire*. I have no recollection of what she said when loading me up with a form of mental and emotional caffeine that charged me into the battle. I imagined spending the rest of my life feeling victimized by people like The Guy and the porcupine. And then I donned my writing hat at nine o'clock on Monday night.

I opened my bag, pulled out the Porcupine Papers, unhooked a calendar from the wall, and pressed the power button on my laptop. Fuming and frightened at the same time, I prayed for strength. I opened a Word document, knowing I had the element of surprise in my favor because the porcupine assumed that I would not fight back. The folder of the Porcupine Papers was not neat; however it was in chronological order, which kept me on track. I worked hard to stick to the facts, even though I wanted to vent. I tried not to whine. I showed examples of INCORRECT! slashed in ink across my Excel spreadsheets, when its figures missed her ten-key calculations by a penny. By midnight I was in a froth, pounding away on page twelve.

At three in the morning, I stood outside on the porch, stretching my back. After a few minutes, I lowered my stiff body to the top step. The July light was a high in itself. A reddish ring of glowing gold circled the sun, which almost hid behind wispy, overcast space. A raven landed at the tip of the big dead tree in front of the cabin, his grouchy squawk a recrimination of sorts: get back in there and finish your work. Raven, the purveyor of magic, perched high, gave me his piercing sideways glare, and urged me back to the laptop.

CHAPTER FIFTY-FIVE

FIRST THING ON TUESDAY MORNING, I DOWNED A CUP OF COFFEE on the way to deliver my twenty-five-page complaint to the Human Resources office. The woman who reviewed the letter called several hours later to let me know the company had begun a formal investigation. I was placed on administrative leave.

I was not exactly sure what that meant, yet certain I would find out. My financial security and my professional reputation were on the line. I knew that I would lose face with the people siding with the porcupine. This type of complaint always creates division, which is rarely my intention. I was in deep by then, embedded in another battle.

The summer weather and time to recharge helped strengthen my resolve. I heard myself laughing more, and I began to rest. I still didn't feel like celebrating, but the load was lighter. I had several days off before they moved me into a temporary position in a different department. The time off served as a revival before it was time to go to work and prove that I was not a dunderhead. In my lowest hours, I had my doubts. I was so acclimated to a critique on everything from where to staple the form and where to place the period in a sentence that I waited, on edge, for someone to complain about my work at the new office.

I ended up working with a fun, inclusive group of people who did not seem to think I was anything worth complaining about. I never spoke directly of the other office I worked in, and never mentioned the porcupine's name. I kept quiet and enjoyed the new, lighter-hearted environment.

Work was enjoyable, but the wait was gripping. My future rocked in the hold of a wayward ship, the high seas too rough for me to control or predict. It was another exercise in letting go, much like handing over responsibility to Judge Sage. I had no idea what the company would decide.

The investigation took about six weeks. I knew of people they interviewed; however, none of us talked about it. I functioned with my nose down, wondering what would happen next. Every cloud must have a silver lining because during that time I formed a permanent bond with my office mate, Jessica. She took the My Only Friend title away from Karl; I had two comrades by the time I left my temp job.

After the investigation, the principal investigator stopped in, asking me to join her in her office. I told Jessica I was working as a temp because I had a problem in my last position, and did not share any other details. When I gathered my purse and myself for the walk down the hall to HR, Jessica wished me luck, even though neither of us knew what that might mean.

I sat across from the investigator and tried to still my heart. The woman was straightforward and clear. "The company made a determination based on their investigation. You filed a complaint regarding bullying in a hostile environment."

"Yes, I did." There was nothing more to say.

She proceeded. "The information has been reviewed, and the company feels that the behavior you describe falls just below the borderline of bullying." She held her hands up as though to demonstrate the distinction on a thermometer of sorts, like a television meteorologist, determining the degree of derision involved. She smiled and dipped her head to the right before continuing. "We have determined that the problem is the result of a distinct difference in styles between the two of you."

Just below the borderline of bullying. I repeated those words in my mind to give my throat a few seconds to swallow that horse pill. Resisting a compelling urge to make fun of the measurements, I managed something intelligent like, "I see."

The wheels inside my mind were turning at an uncomfortably swift pace. I worked for an organization that defined bullying as a *style*. Therefore, to be mean was a fashion statement, not an act of aggression. I bit my lips together to resist speaking. I needed to keep working more than I needed to be right. And I wanted to know what was going to happen next.

I concentrated on the HR woman's lips, because doing so had worked with Mary. We agreed that going back to work in the same department was not a viable solution. I exhaled, waiting for more details.

My focus returned to the HR lips. "There are no openings for paralegals at this time, and frankly, we do not hire many. However, we do have a departmental director who is looking for an assistant. He would like to speak with you."

I walked to the Suburban, reorganizing my mental files. I had escaped the sharp clutches of the porcupine. At the same time, I thought the determination was pretty lame. It was time to hit the hold button on analysis. I had ten minutes to gather myself for an interview. I parked close to a building on a different part of the campus and called Don to tell him what transpired. He urged me forward toward the important upcoming conversation; we could talk about the past later. I said goodbye and silenced the phone's ringer. I cried for a minute then forced myself to stop. I found a bottle of Visine in the glove box and squeezed some into each eye. I combed my hair and checked my nails, which were not looking all that great, so I decided to keep my hands in my lap. Dabbing a final Kleenex below my mascara, I gave myself another pep talk: I can do this, I can do this. I am the little engine that could.

As it turned out, I was acquainted with the department director, having met him on several occasions, and I liked him. He remembered me, so we were off to a good start. He offered me the position, and I accepted, so I would begin a new work chapter right after the long Labor Day weekend.

CHAPTER FIFTY-SIX

THE NEW POSITION WAS IN A BUSY DEPARTMENT, SO TIME MOVED quickly. In another way, my life finally began to slow down. Learning aspects of the new role presented challenges, requiring an assimilation of information for four different departments. It required effort, but if that was my biggest problem, life was easy.

Late September days reflected the same light of my arrival in Fairbanks, two years earlier. Yellow birch leaves clapped against a periwinkle sky on the last day of chaise lounge season. It would snow in a few days. It had been quite the two years. I reminded myself for the hundredth time that my entanglements with The Guy and the porcupine were over. It seemed too good to be true.

Drops of ease, welcome guests, seeped slowly into my cells. Freedom was the best, albeit inadequate, word for my experience. Daily life normalized. I did not feel driven by adrenalin, and sleep often arrived on time.

I began to let down my guard. On darkening evenings at home, I licked my wounds, still shaking off life's stress. I'd been getting adjustments from a chiropractor for about six months, enjoying small successes along the way, until one of my regular appointments, about a month after the new and improved job. All of the planets and stars must have aligned perfectly with my spinal fluids, resulting in the mother of all back adjustments. Dr. E. cracked the code on the broken zipper and slipped it back into place. Finally, my back began to heal.

In October, after a fierce wind, the leaves drifted in wet piles on chilled ground. As the morning sun stirred lazy and low above the wintered earth, I sat with my steaming cup of coffee, enjoying the serene early view. The phone rang. It was my landlord, calling to say a couple of tree cutters were on their way over to the cabin. Minutes later, a diesel truck rumbled up the driveway. In less than half an hour, the two largest trees in the yard disappeared. A pair of lumberjacks, wearing cleats and harnesses, walked straight up the trees bearing chainsaws. As fast as they arrived, the two men removed their gear and drove away, leaving a path of sharp branches and devastation behind. Returning to my tepid mug of coffee, I noticed that I suddenly had a radically different view.

The dead spruce that divided the vantage point from my meditation cushion was gone. I could see above all the trees, with an unobstructed view of the mountains to the south. It was the same old tree I almost hit each time I backed up the Suburban. I remembered the squawking raven that landed on the peak of the now-chopped-down tree, the night I had decided to stand up for myself.

The tree was no longer there, and in its place an entirely new view opened up to a gentle meadow, a cleared space offering increased light. The decayed and crusted spruce was ready for compost and renewal, making room for wild raspberry bushes that sprouted with vigor over the next few summers.

They cut down a birch tree too, which grew less than two feet away from the porch. The large, white trunk betrayed a rotten core inside, which caused the tree to sag and lean toward the roof. As weeks passed, they hauled all of the dead trunks and branches off the land, so the war-zone look dissipated, leaving behind fresh, unobstructed sights. Two dead trees with crumbled, mean, decaying cores had been chainsawed into pieces and removed. I was not blind to the metaphor.

My view and life continued to expand. Still, anger festered in my heart, taunting the fresh ease. The anger was familiar, nothing new. More black charcoal dust ground through my veins and digestion, scouring my membranes. My heart felt as though the last remaining brittle outer shell, thin as the hard coating on an M&M, crackled with spider-like lines. I was still fragile.

I also see that anger has wisdom, power, and force. I should be angry about violence, oppression, crime, and injustice. They are poisons within our network of society, worth abhorring. If it takes anger for me to fight back against abusers, I honor fury and listen to her voice.

Compound wounds grow like compound interest. I was learning that it takes some time to get over that. The people who knew how to love me let me be, hugging my shadow side as I wallowed through recovering from a maze of obstacles.

Karl knows how to do that. He dedicates his life to helping people. He dashes off to help a friend who is on the side of the road with a flat tire or a dead battery. To name a few, Karl helped me through a failed starter, a frozen gas cap that refused to budge, brake fluid leaks, water tank woes, cat sitting, not to mention my employment blues. Karl does not say much. He shows up and takes care of the problem, sharing plenty of hugs and wit to go around before charging off to the next task. He doesn't take time to talk about being supportive; he just supports.

CHAPTER FIFTY-SEVEN

THE DAY PRECEDING THANKSGIVING DAY 2011 WAS A SEA OF BRU-
tal cold, where the outside air sucked my breath away. Spartacus and
Pierre woke me up early; they needed food. I opened my eyes to face two
sets of hazel cat eyes staring me down. Even though it was turned off,
Pierre had been sleeping on my heating pad. We shared a greeting of "I
adore you" from me and a "where is my food?" from them. I felt cheerful
and full of life. After feeding the cats, I pulled the front window curtains
aside to the joy of smooth, white ground and a glacier-blue sky. My heart
swelled with a gust of unabashed wonder for the natural world, and the
thrill of a life free from fierce anxiety.

A simmering sense of safety roiled from my belly to my steady heart.
I was one of the lucky people who was working. There were, and continue to be, countless people who barely scrape by. I still woke often
during the night, soothing my habitually frail nerves by reminding my
reptilian brain that, this month, I had enough money for the rent.

We had stepped over the threshold into winter. By then I had learned that a perfect winter day in Fairbanks meant a productive trip to the outhouse and a car that started. The entire day could get a perfect rating by seven forty-five a.m. when all went well. I wrapped a wool blanket around my shoulders and slipped on my heavy boots for the morning walk to the outhouse. I loved to stand in the driveway and gaze at the stars, smell the crispy air, and touch the snow with my gloves. I turned toward the cabin, the container of my physical and domestic life.

On the right side of the house, a two-hundred-gallon tank held one hundred and four gallons of heating fuel. After a year of work, I had two hundred dollars in savings, a substitute for Marilyn, an operating vehicle, running water, and a string of cheerful white Christmas lights to decorate the front door. I felt like a Financial Wonder Woman, which goes to show, everything is relative.

A sense of abundance flushed my cheeks. I truly felt like the wealthiest woman in the world. Optimism, perseverance, and elbow grease go a long way. I had been reading books and watching films about the great recession because I was still trying to figure out what happened.

I wanted and needed details. How did the one-percenters weave their way to the top through greed, derivatives, bailouts, billion-dollar bonuses, hedges, swaps, CDOs, strategic deregulation, and smarmy political influence? It looked like a band of brilliant, overpaid thieves, working within the loops and knots of our laws and regulations, got away with robbing America.

What happened in 2008 was not a housing crisis—it was a Wall Street banking crisis. The banks wagered against us. They bet we would fail, and they placed big bets.

I stopped my speculating and returned to stargazing. After several minutes, I continued my walk to the outhouse. As I scuffed through small mica slices of sheer powder snow, I thought of the events that had led to the recession and Wall Street's clever way of ripping us off.

Mid-trudge, I paused, transfixed by the outhouse. An outhouse does not let us flush things away. It reminds us about something none of us want to deal with, our own poop. My tall and humble outhouse leans extravagantly to the right, a result of sinking summer ground. In the winter months, our eliminations freeze one upon another, forming a frozen stalagmite of excrement inside that dark opening.

Suddenly, my leaning outhouse looked beautiful in its simplicity— a basic, sturdy cover for a seat, a hole, and a tall tower of frozen poop. There was no pretense. Even with all the crap, it seemed far more functional, honest, and valuable than anything I ever saw from Wall Street.

Later on in the pale, powder-blue day, I dressed and motivated myself to go out for a short and chilly ski. I bowed to the snow in gratitude, my thoughts awash with appreciation for the details, the small things, which add up quickly. By the time I finished skiing, it was four p.m. I stood still on my cross-country skis, surveying the unlit sky behind and above the cabin, and treasured my life from the vantage point of tranquil satisfaction.

Back inside, I removed layers of clothing and made myself a cup of tea. I turned on the lamp and sat on a wooden stool at the kitchen table. I opened a book from the library called *Among Wild Horses: A Portrait of the Pryor Mountain Mustangs*, by Lynne Pomeranz. Hungrily, I thumbed through the first few pages, eternally a sucker for animals, especially horses. I have never owned one—though I did spend several unsuccessful years on my father's lap begging and groveling for a horse—and still find it mysterious how the rugged power of a horse magnetizes me.

My fingertip stuck to a certain page. I opened the book further to smooth the image out flat. A wild, blond mare looked me right in the eye from large, open pages. I felt an instant gasp and adrenalin rush, almost a spontaneous jolt. The horse in the photograph was magnificent—deeply feminine, muscular, terrifying in her strength, wearing chunky pits and bumps of scar tissue on her dappled coat.

A red-pink dot of sunburned flesh hung like a pendant at the end of a thin white blaze down the center of her nose. Her alert nostrils spread wide to inhale the fresh wind, which made her face deeply alive and engaged. Her mane was frosted, shaggy, perfectly coifed by nature, with one long, sexy strand of blond hanging down further than the rest of her mane. She was a pure reflection of Mother Nature's beauty, no hair or tooth bleach required.

She was tough, exquisitely beautiful, majestic, and composed. Though I admired her beauty, I would not want to mess with the power of that mare. I searched for her name on the following page. Blanca, White Lady. I studied her face again, marveling at the reflection of her quiet, self-assured presence.

I realized that as I moved through the sorrows and high peaks of life, I wanted to be more like Blanca, not a woman pretending to wear a barrel around her chest and acting like an armadillo. Blanca was scarred, imperfect, powerful, and courageously awake. She grazed through sunny, temperate days and faced overbearing cold and adversity at other times in her life.

I read more about the exquisite horse whose photograph captivated me. The photographer described watching Blanca stand up against frigid, wind-whipping Montana winters and shake off infections, injuries, and battles with other horses. Many of her foals lived, while over twenty of them died.

I imagined Blanca running wild in her world, accepting it all with no expectation that "things will get better" or "I deserve happiness." Taking life one full nostril of air at a time is a lifelong practice. If wild, beautiful Blanca can stand tall, content with the organic unfolding of her fate, then I would like to do that too.

I left the open book on the table and walked outside to the porch. I jumped up and down in my clogs, shaking ten stinging fingers in tight circles to keep the blood circulating. Daylight moved down a notch; a slight beam of light hovered over the flat southern valley, while an unmistakable Maxfield Parrish sky glowed to the north.

Three stars popped through the blue-gray sky in front of the cabin. Iridescent light from an inside lamp streamed out the south-facing window onto the shadowed snow. Every sound seemed to be hiding in the dark, muffled by the snow. My fingers reminded me they were fully alive, prickly cold, urging me to go inside.

I took my last look at the outdoor night as I picked up my skis to take inside. The front door was stuck. Frost and ice were on the bottom, even inside, and all around the key strike, so it stuck to the ice on the door lock. I managed to push the door hard enough to get back in. I found my hair dryer and applied a blast of high heat to the frozen lock. I followed this with the now ritualistic tap-tap-tap of a hammer to dislodge the offending ice. The process had become part of my routine. Icing doors and windows were common, nothing about which to complain. I think we are all capable of winning the battle, whether over ice or crime.

CHAPTER FIFTY-EIGHT

THE NEXT DAY, ON THANKSGIVING, I HAD PLENTY TO BE GRATEFUL for: freedom from want, from harm, and from confusion. The day filled with jovial conversations, tasting the buoyancy of love over long-distance phone calls. Before dinner, I skied in the dark with my headlamp on until I was too cold to go on. Once again, I carried my skis into the cabin.

The kitchen table was set; the inside smelled of roasting squash, yams, turkey, stuffing. I was alone, not lonely, and happy to be alive. I knew other people felt unhappy to think of me spending a holiday alone, so I told my family I "was having dinner with two friends," and looked over at Pierre and Spartacus with my fingers crossed.

I licked those same fingers after pumpkin pie and coffee, and looked around at a terribly quiet existence. There is a time and place for everything, I told myself, wondering what to do with a winter's worth of alone time. I remembered Blanca, her beauty and her strength, again wishing I could be wild and free, like her.

I am wild and free, I reminded myself as my eyes rested on the laptop. I slid the computer toward me as I pushed an empty pie plate away
and realized I had two things Blanca did not—a laptop and the ability
to put a story into words. I turned on the laptop, adjusted my head and
shoulders, and began writing this book.

CHAPTER FIFTY-NINE

A FANTASTIC BLAST OF FROZEN AIR MARKED THE DAY AFTER Thanksgiving. The temperature dropped fast, to minus thirty degrees. The early morning air startled me with the sharp shock of dry ice, as I opened the door to Karl's hasty and frozen squeak, squeak, squeak steps across the loud Styrofoam snow.

As I swiftly shut the door behind him, Karl was grinning.

"Hey, I saw the greatest bumper sticker yesterday."

I playfully stuffed a bite of pumpkin pie in his mouth, trying to avoid his frosty beard. Karl wiggled his eyebrows the way he does and mumbled gratitude.

"So, what did it say?"

He swallowed and took a breath, pointing his finger to the sky. "I'm not afraid of the Rapture! Santa will save me!"

We doubled over in unison, cackling like kids. Pierre and Spartacus usually made a fuss over Karl; but they remained curled up like two sunken treasures in a blanket on Sofa Loren. Each cat opened one sleepy eye and perhaps wondered why humans would go outside on such a frigid day. After we recovered from the Santa drollery, Karl snatched my backpack and tossed it into the backseat while I locked up the cabin. We were off to our favorite place.

Opening the truck door, I smelled his cup of Scandinavian blend coffee, balanced securely on the console between us. Our seat belts clicked in unison, and I felt a flash of joy. Reversing the truck, Karl eyed my truck, parked and plugged into a steady stream of expensive electricity.

He winked at me, boldly predicting another fifty thousand miles of superior Suburban service. We huddled close to each other, our jacket sleeves hissing softly, fellow conspirators in this catastrophe called being human. We both understood that the inconveniences of existence would always manage to be a surprise—because life is a shrewd, scheming friend who likes to keep us on our toes.

I unzipped my down jacket as the truck turned north onto the bumpy road I had once dreamed about in Texas. From there, Karl steered his truck to the right onto smoother, shiny pavement as we drove toward the store with the sign that says: We Don't Call 911.

ACKNOWLEDGEMENTS

I OWE THIS STORY TO EVERY CHARACTER IN THE MANUSCRIPT. WHETHER an adversary or ally, each provided invaluable life lessons and better-than-fiction material. Understanding the fully subjective nature of this account, I know that several people will have a very different point of view regarding our interactions. The rest of the people in this story continue to back me in every way.

Loving thanks to my ever-present supporters: Christie Parker, Kathi Wineman, Karl Bergman, Russell Heath, Don, Sue, Brad, Jess, Jeff, and Lauren Martin, Kara Foley, Allison Johnson, Diana and Juan Valera, Greg Solether, Jackie Gaer, Giggy and Matt Thanheiser, Chase Powers, Tim and Stella Fullam, Milton Fried, Lara Boyle, BJ Solomon, Teresa Williams, Shulamit Krakauer, Toby Wheeler, and my cherished friends in Fairbanks—you know who you are.

I want to thank the Austin Police Department, U.S. Marshals, and the many law enforcement officers who displayed an impressive level of concern and professional enthusiasm. To Camille Haberman, Anastasia Barber, and Liza House-Friend, social workers-extraordinaire who always knew the right thing to do. To Mary Farrington and her support staff in the Travis County DA's office, your protection proved to be life changing. To the Honorable Judge Karen Sage of the 299th Travis County Criminal District Court, for listening and hearing.

Thank you to my first readers: Bob Engelbrecht and Susan Doak. Despite split infinitives, misspelled words, and jumbled story lines, you got the gist and encouraged me to push on through draft after draft.

Thank you to my editors and consultants at TED who helped turn this into the real thing: Marcia Ford, Amanda Bauch, Morgana Gallaway,

Pete Garceau, Liz Felix, Julie Miller, and Jane Ryder (particularly for her consistently upbeat emails.)

My love and gratitude to Dr. Ana Aspras Steele, who dragged me through every last comma and gerund when I was too bleary-eyed to make those decisions. Thanks to Russell Heath for stepping up to the jacket copy emergency.

A loving salute to my parents, Frederick and Dorothy Martin. Thank you to my family for standing tall when everything felt so dark and there was nothing to do or say. This story is living proof that things do get better over time.

A T-Rex-sized thank you to the ever-optimistic and loving Peter Delli Colli for fully participating in The Great Experiment, as well as providing the space and support to finish this book. I also want to thank Peter's beautiful family for swiftly wrapping their arms around me. Mama Sue, we all miss you.

Finally, Donna Blood-Ahern, we owe you big time. Persistence is a virtue, indeed.

ABOUT THE AUTHOR

DIANA MARTIN is a writer and artist, which she says translates into having worked a long series of second and third jobs.
After more than twenty-five adventurous years in Alaska, and a
few in Austin, Texas, Diana now lives with her sweetheart and
two cats in Massachusetts.

CPSIA information can be obtained at www.ICGtesting.com
Printed in the USA
BVOW08s1436090616

450598BV00005B/7/P

9 780996 110303